CIVIL WAR SISTERHOOD

Alfred Blair 65
Schuyler
Blackwell
WCAR Challenge - overcome local preferences

USSC Seal from frontispiece of Charles Stillé's History of the United States Sanitary Commission: Being the General Report of Its Work during the War of the Rebellion *(Philadelphia: J. B. Lippincott, 1866).*

CIVIL WAR SISTERHOOD

The U.S. Sanitary Commission
and Women's Politics in Transition

JUDITH ANN GIESBERG

Northeastern University Press
Boston

NORTHEASTERN UNIVERSITY PRESS 2000

Library of Congress Cataloging-in-Publication Data

Giesberg, Judith Ann, 1966–
    Civil War sisterhood : the U.S. Sanitary Commission and women's politics in transition / Judith Ann Giesberg.
        p. cm.
    Includes bibliographical references and index.
    ISBN 1-55553-434-1 (alk. paper)
    1. United States—History—Civil War, 1861–1865—Women. 2. United States Sanitary Commission. 3. United States—History—Civil War, 1861–1865—War work. 4. Women in politics—United States—History—19th century. 5. Women political activists—United States—History—19th century. 6. Women social reformers—United States—History—19th century. I. Title.
E628.G54 2000
973.7'082—dc21   99-057961

Designed by Janis Owens

Composed in Stempel Garamond by Graphic Composition, Inc., in Athens, Georgia. Printed and bound by The Maple Press Company in York, Pennsylvania. The paper is Sebago Antique, an acid-free sheet.

MANUFACTURED IN THE UNITED STATES OF AMERICA
04   03   02   01   00   5   4   3   2   1

Contents

Preface

The frontispiece of Charles Janeway Stillé's *The History of the United States Sanitary Commission* is an enormous angel descending on a battlefield to minister to the wounded.[1] The angel appears to be holding a cup in her left hand and her right hand is extended outward in a Christlike gesture of mercy. A cross adorns her chest as an indication that she will dispense aid to Union and Confederate soldiers alike.[2] Behind the angel are the rays of light that signaled her arrival to the soldiers and that seem to be propelling her toward earth. The battlefield is abandoned except for two prostrate Union soldiers with their faces turned toward the heavens expectantly. On either end of the field is an American flag, and opposite the injured soldiers is a downturned cannon.

Though there is no record of who designed the seal or how it was selected, it was an interesting choice with which to begin the officially sanctioned history of the commission.[3] The date on the seal is June 9, 1861, the day President Lincoln signed the order creating the United States Sanitary Commission (USSC), a civilian relief operation that coordinated local supply efforts, provided battlefield relief, and offered medical advice to the U.S. Army during the Civil War. Though the USSC was one of many such organizations that competed for popular support, it was the only one to receive official government sanction.

Published in 1866, the *History* was a cooperative effort by Stillé,

Henry Whitney Bellows, and George Templeton Strong, historian, president, and treasurer of the commission, respectively. Like most authors writing about the war in the years following Appomattox, Stillé, Bellows, and Strong wrote the *History* with the goal of "teaching future generations" about the commission—"to place on record for its example and guidance an account of the practical working of the most successful method of mitigating the horrors of war known to history."[4] The boldness of the seal is in no small measure an indication of how much the authors believed the organization's various efforts had contributed to the Union victory.[5] Despite the obvious comparisons that readers would make to Florence Nightingale, who was often portrayed as an angel, and the British Sanitary Commission she helped create, Stillé assured his readers that the USSC was entirely original, bearing "no resemblance whatever except in name to the body which was sent by the British Government in April 1855."[6]

Without the benefit of the commissioners' own thoughts about the choice of the seal, we can only speculate about what message it was meant to convey. Knowing what we do about the meticulous men who served on the organization's executive board, however, we can assume that they chose the image of the angel with care. Certainly the angel was a common representation of mid-nineteenth-century domesticity; her image plays a special role in the iconography of war. If we consider these uses within the context of the American Civil War, we can begin to make some preliminary assumptions about what it meant to have the United States Sanitary Commission represented as a ministering angel. I propose that the angel served three very particular purposes for the commission.

First, it is best to begin a consideration of the commission's seal in terms of what it does *not* include. There is no actual fighting represented in the scene, only the aftermath of a battle in which Union soldiers were wounded. The focus of the seal is the distinction between the heavens and the battlefield, and as such, the descending angel serves as a stark contrast to the civil unrest represented below. She seems to have come as much to save the ailing country as she has the wounded soldiers.

Throughout the war, the country was plagued by the mixed loyalties of Americans. Because most Americans at midcentury were wedded to small town values and laissez-faire government, nationalism was weak.[7] Most northerners were torn between a commitment to the idea of protecting the geographical integrity of the country and strong convictions about local sovereignty, between a vague distaste for slavery and an inability to see beyond it, between a belief that the U.S. government should respond with strength and all the force at its disposal and nagging fears of the powerful centralized state that would result from such a response. These competing sentiments were aggravated by ambiguous signals sent by the government about its commitment to fight the war to its end.

Commission men such as Bellows, Strong, and Stillé were bitter critics of the weak public spirit and government inaction. The angel's neutrality, her compassion, and her timing allowed the commission to capitalize on these ambivalent popular sentiments about the war and on the general perception that the U.S. government had failed to respond adequately to the crisis. Through the image of a mighty, ministering angel, the commission offered its agenda as a solution to government irresolution and as an alternative to the impotent nationalism that they believed had crippled the North.[8] The seal suggests that the commission gave the people of the North the chance to come together to care for the wounded and invalid soldiers, even if they could no longer work to preserve the Union. And when they did rally, they looked to the angel who came to care for the men, not the government who had left them behind.[9] As a mighty ministering angel, the commission emerges as the real heroine in the war, saving the people not only from their lackadaisical leaders but also from their own weak loyalties.

Second, the seal allowed Bellows, Strong, Stillé, and their fellow commissioners to hide behind the anonymity of its heavenly messenger. Because all members of the commission executive board were educated members of the urban middle and upper classes, their social situation put them at some distance from the largely rural middle- and sometimes working-class soldiers they served.[10] As we shall see, commission men saw in the war the opportunity to regain the social and political status they had lost due to the broadening of the franchise and the beginning of machine politics.[11] Through the commission, Bellows and his colleagues hoped to once again be in a position to influence the class of men they saw represented in the volunteer army. The classist intentions of the commission were disguised as disinterested benevolence in the image of the barefoot angel. And class also served as a measure of the angel's sacrifice for the common soldier. The fact that men of the stature of Bellows, Strong, and Stillé would concern themselves with the condition of the soldier on the battlefield served as a measure of their own self-sacrifice and of the soldier's worth.[12]

The third purpose the image of the angel served for the commission is the most ingenious and the most significant for this study. As a heavenly incarnation of an idealized, eternal femininity, the image of the mighty ministering angel effaces the work of real women. Angel imagery was very common in the nineteenth century, but angels were associated with an eternal, ideal Woman, not with actual women or nurses. The ideology of separate spheres dictated that all women were virtual ministering angels—women traditionally nursed the ill and cared for the poor. Choosing feminine imagery to represent the commission allowed Stillé and his colleagues to tap into the powerful popular association of women with the selfless care of others without recognizing the contributions of real women to the commission. The angel appeared magically out of the heavens and, presumably, disappeared again just as magically. Because she only came forth when she was needed on the battlefield, the angel reinforced the self-proclaimed subordination of the nurse. The power she wielded over men was not threatening, because it was ultimately controlled by her male superiors.[13] Because to nurse was in their natures, recognizing the contributions of individual women to commission relief efforts would belabor the obvious. More important, such recognition would undermine the authority of male commission leaders such as Stillé.

But the commission's use of natural imagery went far beyond the angel on the seal. Commission publications compared women's war relief to spontaneous acts of nature: When women met to support the soldiers it was like "the universal springing of the grass"; their associations multiplied "like rings in the water, over the face of the whole country."[14] Henry Bellows referred to the commission's work with women's war relief organizations as a struggle to stem a "rising tide of popular sympathy."[15] One of his commission colleagues described women's relief efforts as "the motherly love which kept swelling up night and day . . . in such a stream as threatened to overrun all bounds."[16] Because women's nurturing instinct knew no bounds, getting control of this force—harnessing the power of women's natural benevolence—made commission men heroes; they acted as effective intermediaries between women and the army. Although commission men portrayed their efforts as an attempt to control nature, an element of this natural imagery is intimidating—"a rising tide," "a threatening stream." Likewise, a woman's "motherly love," her very domesticity, was at times aggressive.[17] The soldiers in the commission seal are rendered childlike in comparison to the mighty angel descending upon them. Though we assume she will nurse the prostrate sufferers, it seems equally possible that she will crush them. Indeed, the down-turned cannon suggests that, though they attempted to neutralize women's power over men by representing her as an angel, commission men remained conscious of that power.

Though Stillé, and historians of the commission that have followed him, was content to leave the experiences of real women out of his account, women were the initiators, the main financial supporters, and a significant part of the workforce of the United States Sanitary Commission. They ran local relief efforts, coordinated regional supply networks, participated in the commission's decision-making processes, and volunteered on an equal basis with men to go to the battlefield to carry out the relief work. From this perspective, it seems fitting that the image of this great relief organization is a woman. But it remains to be seen how these multiple messages played out in the day-to-day business of relief. This study will explore the history of the commission from the perspective of the women who made it possible. Their story is not that of ministering angels or of women driven instinctively to nurse but of real women whose experiences belie the attempt by commission men to erase them.

Acknowledgments

Over the years I have worked on this project, I have received much kind assistance from librarians all over New England and New York. In particular, I want to thank Valerie Wingfield and Angelita Sierra of the New York Public Library, Robert at the New York Historical Society, and Virginia at the Massachusetts Historical Society. All the librarians and student workers at Boston College's excellent Interlibrary Loan Office deserve my thanks as well.

Several of my colleagues at Boston College have been consistently supportive and interested in the progress of this project, though they have been pursuing their own busy publishing schedules at the same time. Without the guidance of Lynn Lyerly, the thesis that forms the basis of this project would have never been completed. Tom O'Connor kindly guided me through the publishing process. Alan Lawson provided me with insightful comments on the project and pushed me to try to answer some of the bigger questions the manuscript addressed only indirectly. Dora Dumont went way beyond what any friend might have expected of another in helping with this project. She went patiently through this manuscript several times, always with a careful eye and good humor. Dora is my colleague here at Boston College, but more important, she is my best friend.

This project would not have been possible without the advice, criticism, and encouragement of a close community of women scholars who have taught me as much about the writing process as they have about professionalism and collegiality. Margaret Lee provided electronic advice and support from abroad, and I benefited not only from her extensive knowledge of the Civil War but also from her friendship and encouragement. Elizabeth Leonard's close reading of and advice on the entire manuscript before it underwent revisions were very helpful. Elizabeth's own work continues to inspire me, as does her remarkable ability to balance her career with her commitment to her family. Nancy Woloch encouraged me to complete the dissertation and then provided her insight on some of the elements of the current manuscript. I owe an enormous debt of gratitude to Maureen Flanagan for pushing me to think harder about the larger significance of internecine Sanitary Commission battles. Maureen's own research on women's relief work after the Chicago fire of 1871 served as a very useful model. Although friends and colleagues are largely responsible for the strengths of this project, I am solely responsible for its weaknesses.

I want to thank my family for their love and support. My parents deserve thanks for instilling in me a love of books and learning. My sisters-in-law Kathy and Karen always asked good questions about this project and they provided my husband and me with extra work time by taking care of our son Diego. Although there is very little you can count on a two-and-one-half-year-old for, Diego provided consistent impatience and much-needed distraction—both of which proved to be important to the completion of this project. As for my son Pablo, who was born while I was completing my revisions, thank you for your uncanny sense of timing. My husband Ed has been my friend and strongest supporter for fourteen years. His help on this project has taken many forms. These past few years he has patiently listened to my rambling thoughts, read drafts, provided computer assistance, and graciously taken time away from his thesis to help me finish this project. This book is dedicated to Ed. Without him and our two wonderful sons this project would not have seemed possible or worthwhile.

CIVIL WAR SISTERHOOD

Introduction

THE UNITED STATES SANITARY COMMISSION AS THE MISSING LINK

Historians generally agree that women's public activism peaked twice in the nineteenth century: first during the Second Great Awakening, when women took the evangelical call to action literally and initiated a variety of local reform efforts, and then again in the 1870s when they burst into activity in the temperance crusade, culminating in the creation of the Woman's Christian Temperance Union (WCTU). The intense activity that characterized these periods is reflected in the terms used to describe them. The revivals of the 1820s and 1830s were centered in upstate New York, a region referred to as the "burned-over district" because the fires of evangelicalism burned hottest there; Frances Willard, longtime president of the Woman's Christian Temperance Union, likened the 1870s temperance crusade to a "western prairie fire" because of the speed with which it spread throughout the midwestern states.[1] In a way, these two periods serve as convenient landmarks, helping students of the history of nineteenth-century women to ascertain where they are by how far they are from one or the other conflagration. Yet if we take into consideration that it took several decades for the energy of the Second Great Awakening to build to a climax in the 1830s and that the 1870s temperance crusade marked only the beginning of the long and varied activities of the WCTU, the period in between seems oddly quiet and bereft of organized women's activity. Women put the war ahead of any hopes for attaining the ballot, but the war-

time silencing of suffrage activism alone cannot explain why historians have so long neglected or dismissed the war period as having had
no independent female institutions and hence no connection to either
the localized moral reform that preceded it or the highly politicized
women's activism that followed.[2]

Yet women were everywhere during the American Civil War.[3] They
were nurses, spies, civil servants, and soldiers. Women were on the
battlefield, behind the lines, at home, and in Washington and Richmond. They collected much-needed money and supplies from their
neighbors, took care of wounded soldiers at the front and their families back home, and were vocal advocates for the humane treatment
of the war's many victims. Women searched for men who were missing
in action, filed for the pensions of their husbands or sons, sought
financial support and jobs for invalid veterans, and volunteered to
teach former slaves after the war. Southern white women defended
their homes and property from invading forces and slaveholding
women took over the management of plantations and slaves. Black
women uprooted and risked their lives to bring their families to freedom in the North and then struggled to keep them together in the
massive dislocation of the postwar years. During the war, black
women worked as nurses, laundresses, and cooks for both armies.
Thanks to recent research, we know the Civil War affected women as
much as it did men and we are beginning to appreciate how much
they contributed to its outcome.[4]

With all that we now know about individual women's participation
in the war, we are still unsatisfied that not one independent women's
wartime organization stood out as a reminder of all that women had
accomplished in their antebellum reform initiatives and advocated for
a broad spectrum of women's issues, such as the postwar temperance
crusade. In the antebellum period, suffrage activists were a distinct
minority and had as yet failed to attract widespread support. Once
the war began, Elizabeth Cady Stanton, Susan B. Anthony, and Lucretia Mott agreed to place abolition ahead of women's rights. Yet after
the war middle-class and elite women who were too young to have
participated actively in evangelical moral reform nonetheless exhibited distinct organizational and political skills, planning and executing
a multitude of reform initiatives affecting women, children, and workers and challenging the hegemony of machine politics. Was the intense

activism of the postwar years indeed as spontaneous as Frances Willard liked to remember it? Or was there an organization that engaged young women during the war, one that gave them the opportunity to hone skills they had learned from their mothers and fathers but that still allowed them to begin to develop their own distinct agendas?

Historians estimate that some 7,000 soldiers aid societies in towns and villages throughout the North and West supported the United States Sanitary Commission during the Civil War.[5] Twelve major regional branches administered this vast network of local organizations, or affiliates, and the branches were run by women with a variety of backgrounds and skills.[6] There were commission branches in New York, Boston, Philadelphia, Cleveland, Cincinnati, Chicago, Louisville, Pittsburgh, Buffalo, New Albany, Detroit, and Columbus. New York, Boston, and Chicago boasted the largest number of soldiers aid society affiliates and the most effective organization; they informally (and sometimes formally) set the pace for the other branches. Though the branches were technically expected to defer to the commission's all-male executive board, branches maintained independent command structures and agendas and in practice the reverse was often the case— the executive board often deferred to the branches in matters of day-to-day operation. New York branch chair Louisa Lee Schuyler and Boston branch chair Abigail Williams May participated actively in commission decision making. Through their efforts, in conjunction with those of other branch women and their commission colleagues, millions of dollars worth of food, medicine, and clothing were sent to the soldiers at the front. Branch women's wartime achievements were surpassed only by their successful postwar careers. After the war Schuyler lobbied for improved conditions in New York state asylums, and May and Mary Livermore of the Chicago branch were suffrage leaders in Massachusetts and later advocated for improved working and living conditions for women and children.

With such accomplished women leaders and such an extensive reach, one would think the United States Sanitary Commission (USSC) would have attracted the intense interest of women's historians. Indeed, the commission's 7,000 affiliated soldiers aid societies are comparable to the American Female Moral Reform Society's (AFMRS) 445 auxiliaries in 1839 and the National American Woman's Suffrage Association's (NAWSA) 13,000 members in 1893, though they are still dwarfed by the Woman's Christian Temperance Union's (WCTU) "150,000 dues-paying members" in 1892.[7] The network of women-run commission branches is comparable to women's organizations before and after the war in other ways. Like the AFMRS and the WCTU, the strength of the commission came from its local affiliates, and, although the regional branches and the commission provided guidance and institutional support for local affiliates, local women's agendas were respected and often encouraged. Like the WCTU, the women-run branches of the commission envisioned turning a grassroots network of local reformers into a cohesive operation and sought a political voice for women's interests. Yet the AFMRS, NAWSA, and the WCTU are the subjects of numerous studies and, until very recently, the commission was not.

In fact, until recently the commission received very little attention at all. Because women operated branches of an organization run by men, no women's historian has attempted to link it to the nineteenth-century continuum of women's independent reform activism. Women's branch status is dismissed as a capitulation to men and male values, and the war generation is left with individual heroines but no organized women's movement. In these recent works, commission women largely remain pawns of middle-class men—they have neither a separate agenda nor a public life after the war. These assessments of the USSC have not gone beyond the official male rhetoric of the organization nor have they done anything to lift the war period out of its obscurity. Although it is true that during the war many women focused their energies on supporting their families and fulfilling the immediate needs of their communities, some women sought a larger meaning for their individual sacrifices and a connection to other women.

No one appreciated women's sacrifices or their need for connection better than Louisa Lee Schuyler. In her wartime travels Schuyler encountered towns throughout the North where people were just barely getting by. As the war dragged on, average Americans of modest incomes were finding it increasingly difficult to support their families in the context of wartime inflation and rising prices. Growing government demand forced staples such as beef, coffee, sugar, eggs, and bread to double in price from 1861 to 1863. During the same period, coal and wood prices went up significantly and the price of clothing went up even more.[8] The absence of male wage earners left many women to support their families on substantially diminished resources. Yet despite the hardships, Schuyler met women everywhere who found the time and resources to contribute food and clothing to the soldiers. Coming from comfortable urban middle-class surroundings herself, Schuyler was struck by the sacrifices made in towns in rural New York, for instance, where members of local soldiers aid societies went "from house to house begging money and materials" and where "even the window-curtains had been made into hospital clothing." In Schuyler's eyes, these women were "the truest patriots."[9] What follows is the story of how women of privilege, such as Schuyler, and women of more modest means, such as those in the towns she visited, came together to create an effective network of supply that provided critical support to the U.S. Army throughout the war and how, in doing so, these women of the war generation created a model organizational structure for women's organizations in the postwar era.

Within the ranks of the United States Sanitary Commission, a vanguard of talented women leaders such as Schuyler, Abby May, and Mary Livermore emerged who were eager to undertake reform initiatives that differed in significant ways from those of their fathers, brothers, and mothers. Commission women were committed to preserving the vitality and autonomy of women's local relief work for the soldiers but they understood that the unprecedented political and economic circumstances of the Civil War required more heroic measures. Under the auspices of the commission, a group of women leaders worked to transform local women's benevolence into a national force. These young women drew on common traditions of women's culture and preserved the sex-segregated autonomy of women's local grassroots activism. At the same time, however, they imagined themselves and their interests as part of an extended women's community that transcended local interests and the borders of towns and states and that spoke with a unified political voice. Abby May believed the war provided the ultimate opportunity for women to begin to come together in a larger movement, to create a "sisterhood of states," as she called the network of local relief organizations.[10]

In addition to broadening the impact of their local benevolence work, the commission sisterhood offered wartime leaders the opportunity to participate in politics. Because the commission attempted to remedy some of the unique problems created by a nation at war, the organization allowed women leaders to engage in the highly politicized debate over the expansion of the state during wartime. In the process of encouraging the government to support soldiers' families and other victims of the war, commission women hoped to influence the shape of the postwar state. This wartime work, then, was political in nature and required more of wartime women leaders than a simple expansion of their local moral reform work. It required that young women leaders begin to see that the problems of poverty, disease, and injustices done to women and children demanded political solutions rather than moral reform.

The young women of the commission combined grassroots women's activism with centralized access to political authority and created a new political culture for women. During the war, these women began to elaborate a distinct women's agenda in a national organizational structure while experimenting with new political skills, testing the power of their coordinated efforts against the limits placed on them by their male colleagues, and raising local women's consciousness about the power of a national coalition of women. Women of the war generation experimented with a form of coalition politics to further their interests, offering women's grassroots support in return for access to political decision making. After the war, women leaders such as Schuyler and May began to introduce concerns expressed by their extended female constituency directly into debates over public policy instead of enlisting the support of politically active men. And by the Progressive Era, the new women's political culture launched by the war generation had come of age; women formed nationwide grassroots lobbies and their work captured the imagination and the legislative support of politicians everywhere.[11]

THE first full-length scholarly history of the commission was William Quentin Maxwell's *Lincoln's Fifth Wheel: The Political History of the United States Sanitary Commission*. Maxwell's is a sympathetic account of the commission's work during the war. The author accepts the image of Bellows and his colleagues as humanitarians and does not attempt to go beyond the carefully disguised intentions of the commissioners of using the commission as a vehicle for the resurrection of their class.[12] Maxwell similarly falls victim to commission rhetoric when he concludes that "[t]he commission often found women difficult to direct."[13] *Lincoln's Fifth Wheel* recognizes that although "most women contributors lived in comparative poverty," the value of their contributions in food and clothing exceeded contributions of money made by wealthy men. Maxwell adopts the nineteenth-century language of domesticity, however, when he generalizes about women's selflessness and the female "zeal [that] sometimes outran good sense." As such, *Lincoln's Fifth Wheel* greatly understates the work of commission women and accepts that as relief workers women were unruly and often difficult to work with.[14]

In *The Inner Civil War: Northern Intellectuals and the Crisis of the Union*, George Fredrickson considers the commission record much more critically. Fredrickson finds that middle-class and elite northerners who had been avid humanitarians, abolitionists—anti-institutionalists, even—abandoned these antebellum sentiments in response to the war. According to Fredrickson, the success of the commission in attracting the support of such a broad cross section of the American public is an indication of how northerners lost faith during the war in individual humanitarianism and embraced an impersonal bureaucratic ethos instead. Fredrickson exposes the elitist, anti-democratic tendencies of the commission "intelligentsia" and argues that, in the final analysis, the commission's legacy is the way in which it changed the field of philanthropy, aligning it with the conservative desire for social control and, in all, encouraging a new callous attitude toward suffering among middle-class and elite northerners.[15]

Although Fredrickson's analysis remains the most thorough treatment of the commission as a product of a social class, he does not deal with issues of gender. That is not to say that Fredrickson did not recognize that women made critical contributions to the commission, for he implicates commission women and men equally in the elitism and callousness of the organization. For their role in turning idealistic antebellum philanthropy into postwar social control, however, he condemns the war generation of women more harshly because they are women. Fredrickson estimates that "being women, they were not so likely to feel the need for a 'manly' suppression of feelings," implying that women who became indifferent bureaucrats in the USSC were particularly reproachable.[16]

recent works have taken up where Fredrickson left off and have begun to look closer at how women and men worked together in the commission. In her dissertation "'A Swindling Concern': The United States Sanitary Commission and the Northern Female Public, 1861–1865," Rejean Attie argues that the women working as local volunteers to collect supplies for the commission were aware of the value of their supply work and used it as a means of asserting their own vision of nationalism.[17] The women who directed the local supply efforts that were essential to the survival of the commission contributed their labor to the organization as long as the commission respected the value of their charitable efforts and did not pose a threat to their concept of local autonomy. When it became apparent that the commission executives had a vision of nationalism—based on centralization, discipline, and professionalism—that conflicted with theirs, women at the local level found other ways to get their supplies to the front. Although her work suggests that there was grassroots resistance to the commission, Attie does not directly challenge Fredrickson's conclusion that middle-class and elite women and men colluded in the creation of an organization that was a conservative attempt to impose a class-specific agenda on the working classes.

In *Women and the Work of Benevolence*, Lori Ginzberg confronts Fredrickson's argument more directly.[18] Ginzberg argues that during the 1850s women's benevolence work underwent a significant transformation to meet the demands of organization and professionalization. According to Ginzberg, in the 1830s women of the elite, middle, and working classes alike used the Victorian attribute of a unique "women's sphere" as a basis for the claim that the work of benevolence required distinctively feminine virtues and, in so doing, fostered a novel cross-class sisterhood that through such work as temperance activism sought to change men.[19] However, Ginzberg contends that during the war and its aftermath a new generation of elite women reformers gave up the sisterhood they stood to inherit from their predecessors for a more conservative, class-based approach to benevolence—represented by organized, centralized bureaucracies such as the commission—and, in so doing, contributed not only to a masculinization of the work of benevolence but also to a marginalization of women's traditional leadership.[20]

Ginzberg's argument is consistent with other accounts of women's reform in the nineteenth century that highlight two peak periods of women's activism and characterize the period in between as the age of consolidation, when women's voluntary associations were institutionalized and taken over by men. The new corporate institutions, these accounts continue, were notable not only for their lack of female leadership but also for their unapologetic allegiance to the urban middle class. Although such accounts allow for the emergence of the Woman's Christian Temperance Union, an effective national organization run by middle-class women that seized the public's attention by closing down saloons throughout the country in the 1870s, these accounts focus on the "rituals of deference" that were resurrected between men and women and between the bourgeoisie and the lower classes.[21] In all, the mid-nineteenth century appears as a dark period that is remarkable for its contrast to the Progressive Era of settlement houses, middle-class women's support for labor activism, and the renaissance of a united suffrage movement that followed.

In this study, I recommend a more rigorous consideration of this awkward "in-between" period and a reconsideration of Fredrickson's conclusions about women's hapless collusion in commission men's class designs. Attie's findings advise a closer examination of the relations of power within the commission, for it appears that middle-class women and men might have at times had different agendas. Transitional reform organizations such as the commission cannot simply be written off as examples of men co-opting women's grassroots benevolence work in the interests of their class, as Ginzberg has argued. This argument fails to recognize the continuities between antebellum, wartime, and postwar relief strategies and cannot account for the appearance of the WCTU in 1874. This highly successful popular crusade appears as an odd exception to the rule. The Sanitary Commission served as an interim structure—the missing link, if you will—between the localized female activism of the first half of the century and the mass women's movements of the late nineteenth and early twentieth centuries. Within the confines of this wartime bureaucracy, middle-class white women expanded the reach of their reform work to include working-class and rural women, men, a geographically dispersed constituency, and a long-term agenda. Commission women experimented with extensive administrative authority and studied the intricacies of a corporate strategy. Young women who came of age

during the war generation came to think of themselves as professionals and political actors and asserted themselves as such. But instead of
blindly enlisting these new strategies to the self-serving agenda of the
men of their class, as Fredrickson has concluded, commission women
took their experience into the progressive reform of the postwar era.
Women's work for the United States Sanitary Commission set the
groundwork for the sweeping reform efforts and the emergence of
mass women's politics that characterized the rest of the nineteenth and
most of the twentieth century.

WITH the goal of rethinking how the war generation was part of a
transitional political culture in mind, then, five of the seven chapters
that follow focus on how the women of the commission built a widely
cast relief network that supported the commission and how they created relationships between women that would lead to postwar reform
efforts and political activism. But first, chapter 1 considers the inspiration behind the formation of the two organizations that form the basis
of this study: the Woman's Central Association of Relief (WCAR),
Dr. Elizabeth Blackwell's relief organization that predated the commission and that brought the commission into existence, and the
United States Sanitary Commission. This first chapter introduces Dr.
Elizabeth Blackwell, Dorothea Lynde Dix, and Henry Whitney Bellows, three people who played critical leadership roles. Chapter 2 considers Blackwell's rationale for affiliating the WCAR with men, the
benefits that she believed would come from making wartime relief a
collaborative endeavor, and the results of Blackwell's decision to bring
women and men together under the aegis of coordinated wartime
relief.
    Chapter 3 introduces Louisa Lee Schuyler and Abigail Williams
May, the two women who, together with other young women such as
themselves in cities throughout the North, built an effective network
of information and supply that provided critical support for soldiers
at the front and their families at home. This chapter argues that the
policies adopted by Schuyler and May recognized local sympathies
as resources to be exploited—rather than stubborn prejudices to be
conquered—in the attempt to create a national network of relief.
Chapter 4 looks at how women such as Schuyler and May, and Mary
Livermore of Chicago, maneuvered within the confines of the male-

run commission bureaucracy and how they adopted distinct political behaviors in order to directly challenge commission men. Chapter 5 explores the one commission effort to employ women as nurses on the battlefield. The commission's hospital transport campaign in the summer of 1862 serves as the most explicit measure of how well the USSC lived up to its own rhetoric that promised to discipline and control women's natural benevolence and turn it into a resource that could be packaged and made available to men on the battlefield. Chapter 6 considers how the male and female commission leaders greeted the end of the war and the closing of their relief work, and chapter 7 is a brief look at the postwar careers of Schuyler, May, and Livermore that suggests ways we might begin to relink the war generation to the larger continuum of an evolving women's political culture.

I

"You will probably not see our names"

THE LEGACIES OF ELIZABETH BLACKWELL AND DOROTHEA DIX

Throughout the northern states, news of the Confederate attack on Fort Sumter in April 1861 and President Lincoln's call for 75,000 volunteers to put down the rebellion was greeted with outbursts of patriotic enthusiasm. Everywhere, men rushed to volunteer and women gathered to collect supplies for the soldiers to take with them. Mary Livermore, a Chicago journalist visiting her ailing father in Boston, noted the speed with which men left their civilian pursuits:

> The plough was left in the furrow; the carpenter turned from the bench; the student closed his books; the clerk abandoned the counting-room; the lawyer forsook his clients; and even the clergyman exchanged his pulpit for the camp and the tented field, preaching no longer the gospel of peace, but the duty of war.[1]

Women greeted volunteers gathering in Boston with equal enthusiasm. As the soldiers began arriving in Faneuil Hall, they were cheered on their way from the train station as "windows [were] flung up; and women leaned out into the rain, waving flags and handkerchiefs."[2] Women turned their homes into supply depots where they collected food, clothing, and medical supplies for the volunteers to bring with them, and in every town a soldiers aid society met and pledged to continue sending soldiers supplies from home.[3] The rapid proliferation of local societies intent on supporting the soldiers at the front and their families back home was matched by a rush of women volunteering to serve the Union as nurses. American women had closely followed Florence Nightingale's work in the Crimea and believed that the war was their opportunity to follow in her footsteps.

For northern women accustomed to local reform work fighting intemperance and immorality, the attack on Fort Sumter was a moral outrage of national consequence. Women inspired by the evangelical message of fighting male vice and providing relief to its hapless victims believed the war was to be fought against the immoral institution of slavery and the intransigent southern slave owners who sought to protect it. For years women had worked in their own homes and communities to save men from themselves, and now the war offered them the chance to carry on that work into a different theater. Whether they collected supplies in their own communities or nursed wounded soldiers at the front, women regarded the war as an extension of their local moral reform work.

The patriotic fever was infectious, causing northerners to act in uncharacteristic ways. It compelled otherwise reserved Jane Stuart Woolsey, daughter of a wealthy New York family, for instance, to indulge in patriotic whimsy when she gave the small American flag she was carrying a "little twirl" as a large carriage of gentlemen passed her on the street, "not daring to look right or left—and instantly the whole load of men broke out into vociferous cheers."[4] Even George Templeton Strong, Wall Street lawyer and aloof observer of human behavior, was moved by patriotism in the spring of 1861. Watching a Massachusetts regiment march through New York City on its way to Washington, Strong was uncharacteristically expressive when he recorded "My eyes filled with tears, and I was half choked in sympathy with the contagious excitement."[5] In an attempt to capture the intense interest of the North for a friend in Europe, Woolsey explained that "[w]e all have views now, men, women, and little boys."[6]

Despite the unanimity of feeling, however, not all northerners waving the troops on saw clearly what their individual role would be in the war. Some men wrestled with the idea of becoming soldiers but worried about their own abilities. George Strong entertained the idea of becoming a soldier when he added his name to a list for a projected Rifle Corps, despite fears that "my near-sightedness is a grave objec-

tion to my adopting that arm."[7] Describing himself in his diary as
the "feeble, myopic, flaccid, effeminate G. T. S," Strong later explained
why he decided to hire a substitute instead.[8] Frederick Law Olmsted,
a landscape architect and superintendent of the Central Park project
in New York City, was almost forty years old and permanently disabled from a serious carriage accident, yet he wondered what part he
would play in the war as it was developing. Though he thought briefly
of joining the navy, he also entertained the idea of taking charge of
the freed slaves in the South, writing to a friend, "I think, in fact, that
I should find here my 'mission' which is really something I am pining
to find, in this war."[9] For men who did not or could not enlist, watching the rush of volunteers forced them to confront their own limita-
tions and fears. They wanted to take an active role in the war but they
did not know how.

For women, too, the headiness of the first days of the war was more
complicated than their expressions of support for the departing soldiers might suggest. "It is easy to understand how men catch the con-
tagion of war," Livermore explained, "[b]ut for women to send forth
their husbands, sons, brothers, and lovers to the fearful chances of
the battle-field . . . involves another kind of heroism."[10] Many women
registered their reservations about the war in their resistance to their
men leaving.[11] The war did not present women with the uncomfortable decision whether to enlist or not, but it did leave some wonder-
ing about where they fit in. Although some women were attracted by
the opportunity to contribute to the war effort in traditionally feminine ways—cheerfully sending off the men, rolling bandages, sending packages of homemade specialties, and nursing the sick and
wounded—not all women were satisfied with these roles. For women
as well as men, the war raised difficult questions about their individual
service to the cause. Some women dreamed about becoming soldiers
instead of bravely seeing the men off to battle.[12] More often women
joined departing regiments as nurses or traveled to Washington to volunteer. Dr. Elizabeth Blackwell, a physician in New York City, could
not understand how women with no experience or training rushed to
volunteer as nurses. As a physician in charge of her own practice,
nursing did not capture Blackwell's imagination as it did for so many
other women.

Unlike women who rushed to volunteer because they identified the war as a moral outrage, Elizabeth Blackwell greeted the war as a challenge to practitioners of medicine, sanitation, and hygiene. Blackwell traced her decision to pursue a career in medicine back to her liberal education in the charged intellectual environment of Cincinnati. Because medical schools and hospitals did not allow women to practice medicine, Blackwell was compelled to travel back and forth between Europe and the United States during the 1850s in search of medical training. After receiving a medical degree and practicing for a time in hospitals in Europe, Blackwell returned to New York to begin her own practice. The New York–based American Female Moral Reform Society published an account of Blackwell's pathbreaking efforts in the society's widely circulated journal, *The Advocate*.[13] Blackwell delivered popular lectures on infant and maternal health in New York and enlisted the aid of middle-class women and men in several institutions that were devoted to urban sanitation and hygiene. In 1853, Blackwell opened the New York Dispensary for Poor Women and Children "to give poor women, an opportunity of consulting physicians of their own sex," and in 1857, with the help of her sister, Dr. Emily Blackwell, she expanded this effort into the New York Infirmary for Women and Children.[14] Though most mid-nineteenth-century hospitals were, in fact, charities, aspiring women doctors who managed to gain access to medical school found their entrance to the hospital blocked by male doctors' notions of the impropriety of women practicing medicine. Faced with this intransigence, Blackwell's infirmary offered trained women doctors the opportunity to practice medicine.[15] In 1859, Blackwell extended the operations of her hospital when she sent a doctor into the streets of lower Manhattan as a "sanitary visitor," employed to "give simple, practical instruction to poor mothers on the management of infants and the preservation of the health of their families."[16] On the eve of the war, then, Blackwell had established herself as an advocate for women medical professionals and as an urban reformer interested in the plight of poor women and children.

In 1861, Blackwell was just forty years old. Yet her work had begun to capture the imagination of influential reformers and attract the attention of the medical establishment. Convinced of the superiority of scientific knowledge, Blackwell was one of a number of reformers who wanted to make information about hygiene and sexuality readily available to all men and women. Bourgeois health reformers believed that ignorance about science and the processes of the body, rather than any lapse in faith, was the cause of disease and disorder.[17] Understanding the body as an organic system integrated with its environment, health reformers argued that disease was preventable and that good health relied on maintaining a careful balance of the elements— air and light, work and rest, discipline and indulgence.[18] In arguing that health (rather than faith) was the way to salvation, health reformers promised to secularize women's reform. To Blackwell, the war opened the door for women to pursue training in science and medicine and to begin to make significant contributions to the health and well-being of their families and their communities.

Whereas the health reform work of Elizabeth Blackwell was just becoming familiar to middle-class New Yorkers when the Civil War began, in 1861 Dorothea Lynde Dix was already a household name. In a highly publicized campaign beginning in 1841, Dix successfully appealed to state legislatures throughout the country to build appropriate facilities to house the mentally ill.[19] Driven by her evangelical upbringing in rural New England, Dix pursued her ends with the single-mindedness of a religious crusader. Dix visited prisons where the insane were held and exposed the horrible conditions there in a series of memorials to state legislatures. By the time the war began, the fifty-nine-year-old Dix had established herself as a formidable political lobbyist. While Blackwell watched in amusement as women inspired by an evangelical urge similar to Dix's rushed to volunteer, Dix arrived in Washington on the same day of the Fort Sumter attack and went directly to the White House to offer her services.[20]

Historians have often noted that the Civil War marked the end of the type of moral reform that Dix represented and the beginning of the ascension of a new faith and commitment to science and scientific reform. Though bourgeois health reformers such as Elizabeth Blackwell did not advocate a departure from the essential humanitarianism of mid-nineteenth-century reform, they directly challenged the religious inspiration that motivated women reformers such as Dix. The intense emotionalism of the Second Great Awakening in the 1820s had attracted female converts by appealing to women's particularly moral "nature" and to women as custodians of their children's salvation.[21] Millennial religion inspired legions of women to assert their moral authority over a society that had become perilously immoral and to engage in social reform outside the home. Women's reform movements evolving out of midcentury evangelicalism often provided a direct challenge to men and male values, as was the case in temperance and anti-prostitution campaigns.[22] With an eye toward their children's future, evangelical reformers confronted men who drank and provided inappropriate role models for their sons and those who threatened to lure their daughters into prostitution. On a local level, women formed temperance and moral reform societies to fight vices and to provide refuge and support for the women and children who were most often the victims. True to this tradition, Dix exploited her "feminine" outrage at the deplorable conditions in the nation's asylums and forced the male political establishment to accept moral responsibility for their charges—in this case, the indigent insane.[23]

Beginning in the 1840s, health reformers likened a healthy society to a happy marriage: Both required a delicate balance of the masculine and feminine elements. Grounded in the nineteenth-century recognition of separate spheres, health reformers recognized distinct male and female values, corresponding to those associated with the capitalist marketplace and the middle-class home, respectively. Bourgeois health reformers' critique of mid-nineteenth-century society concluded that social ills such as prostitution and intemperance were indicative of a larger disorder—excessive male individualism and competitiveness. Whereas the revivals had appealed to the emotions of largely female congregations and inspired them to take the moral high ground against immoral men, health reformers advised women to rely on reason, facts, and science to help men exercise more self-control. During the revivals, women had converted en masse and had brought their children into the church with them. In the end, this shared religious experience accentuated the differences between the spheres of husband and wife, men and women.[24] In the hope of reaching something closer to sexual symmetry, health reformers sought rather to decrease the social distance between women and men. Reformers advocated a healthy cooperation between women and men, wives and husbands, to combat social ills and to establish the kind of sexual balance that was in their mutual best interest.

Blackwell, for instance, devoted her life to "an absorbing occupation," as she recalled it in her autobiography, because she had "become impatient of the disturbing influence exercised by the other sex" in relationships of love.[25] For Blackwell, escaping the imperfect institution of marriage allowed her to work actively for sexual equity in other venues. While she worked at making the male medical establishment rethink their prejudices against women in medicine, Blackwell took to the lecture circuit where her practical ideas about the need to educate both girls and boys about physiology and hygiene began to be well received. In the meantime, she continued to work quietly and persistently to open medical schools to women and advised women looking for a medical education to seek the assistance of "influential men" rather than invest their energies in "an anti-man movement," as Blackwell described contemporary women's rights campaigns.[26] During a period of study in Europe, for instance, Blackwell described her commitment to the parallel development of the sexes when she wrote home about a women's rights convention: "[T]he true end of freedom may be gained better in another way. . . . [T]he great object of education has nothing to do with woman's rights, or man's rights, but with the development of the human soul and body."[27] In the end, Blackwell's moderation, high professional standards, and measured perseverance began to wear down the resistance of male medical professionals. By 1861 she had enlisted the support of several prominent New York physicians and had convinced middle-class New York reformers of the legitimacy of her strategies to promote hygiene and sanitation among the urban population.[28]

Yet in focusing exclusively on the differences between the two women, the types of reform they represented, and their individual responses to the war, we not only run the risk of overlooking any similarities but we also make it difficult to see how the two came together under the auspices of the two wartime relief organizations that form the focus of this study: the Woman's Central Association of Relief (WCAR) and the United States Sanitary Commission (USSC). As the revivals spread through the burned-over district of upstate New York and elsewhere earlier in the century, they left behind widely cast, sophisticated networks of women adept at organizing, raising funds, and building charitable institutions. Reform movements that emerged out of evangelical values in the North and West encouraged women to plan and pursue courses of action independent of men and empowered women to publicly criticize male society. In 1834, for instance, the American Female Moral Reform Society was formed in New York City, and the organization soon boasted 445 very active, mostly rural auxiliaries and an assortment of popular publications.[29] The American Female Moral Reform Society launched a highly effective public campaign against prostitution by exposing the men who seduced unsuspecting young women into accepting money for sex.

If we understand the revivals as, in part, a response to the unchecked ascension of the commercial economy, the reign of party politics, and the marginalization of women and the home, then bourgeois health reform offered a secular and "culturally cosmopolitan" way of regaining a more favorable balance.[30] Within the context of promoting the health of their families and, in turn, their society, health reformers asserted domestic values as a check to the excessive individualism and greed of the marketplace. If the secular-scientific means of middle-class health reform made women raised on a diet of revivalist religion skeptical, surely they could identify with goals that were informed by domestic values.

With some success, Elizabeth Blackwell enlisted complex communities of women left in place after the revivals for a wartime scheme based on her ideas about science and health reform—the Woman's Central Association of Relief. Even Dorothea Dix briefly lent her name to the United States Sanitary Commission, an organization run by the kind of "influential men" Blackwell was in the habit of enlisting to her projects and that would serve as the Washington link for the Woman's Central. Nonetheless, though their influence and vision served as the impetus for and the driving force behind this novel cooperative experiment, the effort quickly outgrew both Blackwell and Dix. In a letter to a friend in June 1861, Blackwell described her work selecting and interviewing nurse candidates for the WCAR and predicted that "you will probably not see our names."[31] And she was right, for it would ultimately fall to a younger generation of women reformers to lead the legions of women rushing to volunteer in the early days of the war.

With established careers in public activism, either Dix or Blackwell might have led either the United States Sanitary Commission or the Woman's Central Association of Relief. Dix's experience in a traditional type of women's moral reform could have allowed her to create grassroots public outrage at the condition of the military camps and hospitals. The public's reaction would have licensed her to bring in women nurses to "clean house," much like the temperance and anti-prostitution campaigns had allowed women into the streets to expose men's immorality. Blackwell's commitment to professionalism, on the other hand, was much more rational and modern. Had Blackwell led the Sanitary Commission, and hence overseen its cooperation with the Woman's Central, the commission might have focused on the development of female medical professionals. Such an agency would have had potentially radical consequences for the medical profession, the military, and the middle class, and would have met with significant official and unofficial resistance. Although Dix and Blackwell each provided a model for how a civilian relief operation might have evolved, the Woman's Central Association of Relief took elements from both of these models, and in the end was run by young women, who, although they were not satisfied with Dix's model of a provincial moral reformer, were not ready to wholly embrace the independence of professional women such as Blackwell. And although the United States Sanitary Commission was run ultimately by middle-class men with a different set of concerns than the women who originated the project, the commission provided the opportunity for Blackwell, Dix, and the young women who emerged as leaders during the war to have a collective influence in wartime Washington.

Elizabeth Blackwell and the Idea for the Woman's Central Association of Relief

From her downtown New York Infirmary, Elizabeth Blackwell watched as the entire city joined the war effort. On April 23, 1861, Blackwell described the mobilization to a British friend: "[R]ebellion threatens the subversion of the government and invasion of our very houses."[32] In response to the attack by rebel sympathizers on Union troops in Baltimore on April 19, people with no formal training or experience volunteered for service as nurses. Blackwell noted "every man is drilling—and we are compelled to direct the women who in a frantic state of excitement are committing absurdities in nursing talk."[33] The consummate medical professional, Blackwell viewed the initial rush of untrained women volunteers with skepticism. "There has been a perfect mania amongst the women to 'act Florence Nightingale,'" Blackwell protested.[34]

But Blackwell's initial dismissal of the spontaneous rush of volunteer nurses also came in part from her inability to relate to the impulse. Blackwell and Florence Nightingale were close friends and had for years discussed building a hospital to train women in medicine.[35] Blackwell and Nightingale agreed on many things, such as the need for women to have access to formal medical training and the importance of sanitation and hygiene, and both women were critical of traditional medical practices such as heroic medicine that involved purgative treatments that produced dramatic, and often violent, reactions.[36] Like Blackwell, Nightingale considered disease a preventable evil and encouraged women to trust observable phenomena and to practice the science of sanitation, to "know the facts" rather than to rely on intuition.[37] Yet in *Notes on Nursing*, the well-known English heroine encouraged her female readership to identify with her work in the Crimea by beginning with the declaration that "every woman is a nurse."[38] On this point, the two "old friends" disagreed fundamentally.

Though Blackwell and Nightingale agreed on the need to provide formal medical training for women, Nightingale often portrayed nursing as a calling rather than a profession. Indeed, the popular image of Nightingale emphasized her feminine self-sacrifice and contributed to the impression that nursing came naturally to women. After reading Nightingale's book, which she predicted would be "very useful," Blackwell remarked on the difference of opinion: "I see also how impossible it would have been for me to do her work. The character of our minds is so different that minute attention to and interest in details would be impossible to me for the end proposed—nursing. . . . I have no vocation for nursing."[39] And in a letter to John Stuart Mill, Nightingale defended Blackwell's intentions but questioned the condition of the entire medical profession, when she wrote that "instead of wishing to see more Doctors made by women joining what there are, I wish to see as few Doctors, either male or female, as possible."[40] Whereas Nightingale was convinced that women could do more for their patients as nurses than they could if they became doctors, Blackwell felt that embracing nursing as women's natural vocation was antithetical to the goal of women gaining access to medical schools on equal footing with men.

As the opening shots were fired, women turned their energies toward caring for the casualties of the conflict—wounded soldiers and women and children on the home front. Traditionally entrusted with the care of women, children, and the ill in their own homes and with providing material assistance to the needy in their communities, women volunteered to extend these services to take into account the wider military and political conflict. In the idea that would soon take shape as the Woman's Central Association of Relief, Elizabeth Blackwell planned an organized system of relief based on the responsibilities northern women were already taking and on systematizing these spontaneous offers of service and supplies. Despite her personal determination to have women enter the male domain of medical professionalism, Blackwell, like other health reformers, drew on the gender-specific experiences of nineteenth-century America, in which women and men were thought to reside in separate spheres—one private and one public. Within the private sphere of the home, middle-class women were expected to live up to the expectations of what Barbara Welter called "the cult of true womanhood"; that is, they were expected to care for the family and to devote themselves to upholding the timeless values of Christian morality in a rapidly changing political and economic environment. They achieved this feat by staying out of the public sphere and by remaining carefully ignorant of the competitiveness of party politics and aloof from the materialism of the marketplace.[41] But Nancy Cott has shown that domesticity did not merely act to exclude women from the public sphere; it also provided the opportunity for women to begin to develop a collective consciousness and the sense of sisterhood.[42] In fact, as Paula Baker has argued, it was in the domestic sphere that middle-class women developed a distinct women's politics as they fought injustices toward all women and children through temperance activism and related activities.[43] Women began moral reform societies and local benevolent organizations in the 1820s and 1830s and through this network of female institutions began to articulate an original political language that allowed them to expand women's sphere into the public world while not directly challenging the separation of spheres. When the war came, women extended the focus of their local reform work even further. In seeking to direct a centralized women's relief organization, Blackwell intended to bring local women's political culture to work at Washington.

As Blackwell saw it, fighting a war of this magnitude required more than individual sacrifice or traditional approaches. By enlisting men to a venture based on women's political culture, Blackwell endorsed the ideology of separate spheres even as she intended to overlap the spheres further.

Henry Whitney Bellows and the Idea for the United States Sanitary Commission

Rev. Henry Whitney Bellows was a good candidate for Blackwell's vision of a wartime relief organization that would bring women and men into closer working relations. In his own antebellum reform work, the Unitarian minister had recommended integration between men and women's spheres in lectures and sermons encouraging middle-class audiences in New York to become involved in social reform. Bellows recommended treatment for the social ills of mid-century America that was very similar to the advice bourgeois health reformers offered about individual and social health. Not unlike popular domestic advice manuals recommending a combination of water, fresh air, rest, and exercise for individual health, Bellows compared a healthy society to a healthy body that required the right combination of elements and a careful integration of all its component parts.[44] By adopting the language of domestic health advice that sought a balance between men and women, Bellows tapped a rich heritage of middle-class women's resistance to the individualism and self-interest of the marketplace and party politics and established himself as a leading critic of the social ills of American society.

But there was more to Bellows's prescription than overlapping the male and female spheres, for Bellows believed that ultimately the ills of society derived from the separation of the classes as much as from the separation of the spheres. In fact, the day before Lincoln's call went out for volunteers, his wife recorded that Bellows had delivered "to-day a sermon on the best modes of doing Charity, which undoubtedly is to come more in contact with the Poor than most of us do."[45] In the earliest days of the war, Henry Bellows's own thoughts continued to be about the social health of the urban Northeast and about bringing the bourgeoisie into closer contact with the city's working classes. Years later, Bellows recalled that it was his interest in preventing "the existence of poverty" that led him to become involved in the Sanitary Commission, for through it he believed poverty might be prevented "by encouraging self-respect & self-reliance, & by withholding careless Relief."[46]

Although his advice to his parishioners often borrowed from the language of family and family relations, Bellows's approach to urban reform—as it was later to wartime relief—clearly reflected his concerns for social order and security. Like Blackwell's Woman's Central, Bellows's idea for a United States Sanitary Commission drew from nineteenth-century gender-role expectations and from experience in male institutions. Individual men greeted the war as an affront to the nation's political and economic interests and often perceived it as a personal challenge.[47] For those men who did not volunteer to fight— either because they were apprehensive about their inadequacies or because their class status offered them an alternative—the war still left them with a sense of urgency.[48] In nineteenth-century America, the separate spheres ideology entrusted men with the care of the economic integrity of their families and the political integrity of their nation. Accordingly, men came together in unions and civic improvement associations to look after their economic interests and participated avidly in party politics as Whigs or Democrats. As much as they were expected to be masters of party politics, however, because of the expansion of the franchise, middle-class men now shared this arena with white men of all classes, and by midcentury, many increasingly felt they were losing their traditional political leadership. The Sanitary Commission offered men such as Bellows, Olmsted, and Strong a chance to regain a sense of public purpose by advising the United States government that seemed to be overwhelmed by the war.

The men who came to support the commission proposal were all members of an urban middle class who welcomed the war as an opportunity to regain social status they had lost in the years before the war.[49] In the antebellum era, cities in the North had undergone rapid changes as immigrants moved in and industry expanded. Wealth became highly concentrated in America's eastern cities, and as a result, class divisions became more pronounced and relations more contentious.[50] The elite responded to the mounting class tensions by moving to exclusive neighborhoods that would spare them the daily inconvenience of mingling with the working classes and by building grand urban institutions that provided entertainment and distraction.[51]

Whenever possible, the middle class followed them into their neighborhoods and their theaters. Nonetheless, working-class activism in the decades leading up to the war mounted, erupting into battles such as the the Astor Place Theatre riot in New York in 1849, when frightened middle-class and elite theater patrons called on soldiers to fire on a crowd of working-class protestors.[52] In addition to increasing working-class activism, cities experienced rising incidents of ethnic, racial, and gang violence and crime, leading one historian to refer to the 1850s as "a decade of disorder."[53] Working-class New Yorkers, for instance, vented their economic frustrations on free blacks in the anti-abolitionist riots of 1834 and again during the Irish dockworkers' strike in 1854. In Boston, in 1836, a clash between Yankee firemen and Irish mourners produced the Broad Street riot, and in 1854, abolitionist-initiated popular resistance to the Fugitive Slave Act turned violent as urban crowds descended upon the Boston Courthouse.[54]

These conflicts amounted to a serious fight for control over the public space of the city. In the antebellum years, the social status of middle-class northerners was threatened from above and below.[55] To make matters worse for men such as Bellows, Strong, and Olmsted, whose Whig ancestors had enjoyed more exclusive political power, a new class of upstart industrialists who had aligned themselves with the Democratic party was slowly taking over the city government in New York and Boston and squeezing them out. Middle-class men's fears of social rebellion were compounded by the realization that they were becoming politically impotent. George Strong filled his diary with fears of social unrest and frustration with the industrialists he thought were to blame. As he watched tenements and factories burn down and working-class people lose their lives, Strong mused: "[I]f a few owners or builders of factories and tenement houses could be hanged tomorrow, life would become less insecure."[56] Bellows shared Strong's sentiments and worried that the secession of the southern states during the winter of 1860–1861 would wreak havoc in the city, "driving our populace into panic for bread and violence toward capital and order."[57] In the years before the war, Frederick Law Olmsted had spent considerable time thinking about how to ameliorate the class tensions Strong and Bellows described by building urban institutions that would "force into contact the good and bad, the gentlemanly and rowdy."[58]

Though Bellows initially feared that the war would aggravate social tensions, when it came it seemed to offer men like him a new opportunity. When Bellows visited the capital in the midst of a mass mobilization of men who had descended upon a government still reeling from the first wave of hostilities, he began to see more clearly the potential for the work at hand. On the evening he arrived, Bellows described his first impression of the city to his wife Eliza: "Washington has a curious camp-appearance."[59] Olmsted came to Washington a few weeks after Bellows and described the experience in the following terms:

There seemed to be no effective military control of the city, and the streets were full of fugitives, groups of men wearing parts of uniforms, some without coats, some without caps, others without shoes. All alike were dirty, unkempt and dank with dew; they were around fires made in the streets of boards wrenched from citizens' fences. Some were asleep on doorsteps, or sitting on curbstones resting their heads against lamp posts, others were begging at house doors. Some were ferocious, some only sick and dejected; all were hungry, weak, and selfish. No officers were among them. There was no apparent organization.[60]

The men Bellows approached with his idea for a Sanitary Commission were interested in finding ways of extending their influence over a populace that lived in a world remote from their own bourgeois social relations, one that was, in their eyes, often more like the disorderly streets of wartime Washington. An institution such as the commission would answer the immediate needs of soldiers and would also offer middle-class men the opportunity to educate the men they served.

When Bellows and his associates came up with the idea for the United States Sanitary Commission, they were promoting an entire sanitary package. Their program of sanitary reform in army camps and hospitals, on the one hand, was in part loosely based on Florence Nightingale's ideas about the importance of rest, proper food, and fresh air to the health and efficiency of the army.[61] The more original aspect of the bourgeois sanitary agenda, on the other hand, included instruction in the polite relations with and the benevolence of the genteel class, a message that they hoped the soldiers would take home with them.

By looking after the proper discipline of the soldiers, providing for their comfort, and keeping up their morale, the middle-class men of the commission were making an investment in the future health of the body politic, or as Olmsted expressed it in the official commission literature:

> If five hundred of our young men could be made to acquire something of the characteristic habits of soldiers in respect to the care of their habitations, their persons, and their clothing, by the training of this war, the good which they would afterwards do as unconscious missionaries of a healthful reform throughout the country, would be by no means valueless to the nation.[62]

Within the context of urban uplift and wartime patriotism, middle-class men who did not or could not enlist saw the commission as a means of reclaiming their social status. If they could regain the respect of soldiers on the battlefield, perhaps their success might facilitate efforts in the urban theater, where upstart industrialists and scheming Democrats were winning the allegiance of the working classes. Though Union soldiers were mostly middle-class, commission men believed they had an opportunity to exercise a benign influence over the soldiers that would reach beyond the battlefield and, more important, beyond their own exclusive neighborhoods. Bellows and his colleagues believed that the war offered them the chance to combat "social evils" such as poverty and crime that were making the streets of their cities unsafe and middle-class urban inhabitants uncomfortable.[63] Barred by their own insecurities from the kind of active participation in the war that they thought might help to reinvigorate their class and salvage their social prominence, Bellows, Strong, Olmsted, and men like them sought an acceptable alternative. If they could not lead soldiers into the good fight, they could direct "[t]he Army, whose bayonets were glittering needles."[64]

Despite commission rhetoric revealing middle-class men's class aspirations and referring to women's wartime work in very traditional terms, the circumstances that brought these two ideas for wartime relief—Elizabeth Blackwell's plan for a system of organized home-front relief and Henry Bellows's vision of winning the class struggle by serving the Union soldiers—together did not create one uniform agenda of wartime relief. The two wartime relief organizations allowed men and women to collaborate within their separate institutional structures while maintaining distinct visions and command structures. But the collaboration also offered women and men the opportunity to begin to find ways to work in a more integrated manner.

"In the background"

THE WOMAN'S CENTRAL ASSOCIATION OF RELIEF AND THE UNITED STATES SANITARY COMMISSION

*F*lorence Nightingale's exhortations to all women contributed to the popularity of her advice manual and to the "perfect mania" that overwhelmed Dr. Elizabeth Blackwell and her small staff at the New York Infirmary for Women and Children in the early days of the Civil War. *Notes on Nursing* was published in the United States in 1860 and was quickly consumed by middle-class women who had followed Nightingale's stellar career in the newspapers. Nightingale reassured her readers that an informed nurse (her nurses were always women and patients were always men) "will be able to arrive at a much truer guess as to the probable duration of life of [patients] than the most scientific physician to whom the same persons are brought to have their pulse felt."[1] Directing her manual to a popular audience, Nightingale put the "science" of nursing into simple maxims that were easily mastered, such as "[w]indows are made to open; doors are made to shut."[2] Middle-class women who had read this dynamic book of nursing truisms came to Blackwell looking for a way to pursue their calling when the war began.

Impressed by two manifestations of female patriotism—the collection and donation of supplies for soldiers and the numbers of women volunteering to serve as nurses—Blackwell recognized the potential of developing an organized system of female voluntarism. Blackwell felt that if she could direct women's contributions of supplies and service she could provide a valuable service to the Union war effort and at the same time continue to promote medical training for women.

Blackwell was in a good position when she launched an initiative in April 1861 to "organize the whole benevolence of the women of the country into a general and central association," the results of which would be the Woman's Central Association of Relief (WCAR).[3] As the established head of a medical institution in New York City, Blackwell had at her disposal the infrastructure and public support for such an organization. Recalling the difficulties she had faced finding work, Blackwell believed that individual women were best supported by an institutional structure and the collective strength of their combined efforts. The New York Infirmary offered women graduating from medical school the opportunity to acquire experience treating patients in an environment that was both demanding and supportive. It was a separate female institution that allowed women to extend the sphere of their antebellum work for women, children, and the poor—work that was accepted as properly belonging to women—by providing them with emotional and financial support.[4] But Blackwell's own experience also convinced her that in addition to the strength of a female institution women medical pioneers often needed the endorsement of influential men. With this practical need in mind, her infirmary was advised by a board of consulting physicians, men prominent in the medical establishment in New York.[5] Blackwell's Woman's Central initiative promised to bring the benefits of this endorsement to groups of women collecting supplies and to individual women looking for work as nurses.

This was an ambitious proposal that promised to put Blackwell and her infirmary associates in a strategic position to direct an impressive force of women's "labor, skill and money" and to link it directly to the national conflict.[6] The venture that Blackwell was undertaking also promised to put to the test the ideas of Blackwell and other mid-century health reformers about creating an environment in which men and women could work on more equitable terms. If her plan succeeded it would indicate that the war had indeed offered the opportunity to overlap the separate institutions and the unique political experiences of women and men. If the cooperative venture failed, on the other hand, it would reveal the limits of enlisting the support of men in a woman's initiative.

DESPITE her initial reluctance to encourage overzealous nurse volunteers, on April 25, 1861, Blackwell called "an informal meeting of the lady managers . . . at the [New York] [I]nfirmary to see what could be done towards supplying the want of trained nurses so widely felt after the first battles."[7] The meeting was well attended by women who were prominent in many facets of urban reform and had significant experience in community-based reform work. As Blackwell recalled it later, the excitement in the city turned the informal meeting into a much larger event when "a notice . . . accidentally found its way in the *New York Times*" and "the parlours of the infirmary were crowded with ladies, to the surprise of the little group of managers."[8] Despite the overwhelming turnout, the two Blackwell sisters and their infirmary associates managed to lay out the objectives of their plan. As Blackwell and her associates saw it, the Woman's Central Association of Relief had three objectives. First, the WCAR would manage the relief efforts of existing charities and encourage others into existence. Second, the organization intended to communicate directly with the United States Army's Medical Department regarding the changing needs of the rapidly growing army. Finally, the group would create a board for the selection, registration, and training of women nurses.[9] As a result of this initial meeting, Blackwell invited all interested women to a meeting at the Cooper Institute four days later, a meeting at which the Rev. Henry Whitney Bellows would preside. Blackwell published a formal appeal "To the Women of New York, and especially those already engaged in preparing against the time of wounds and sickness in the Army," which appeared in the New York newspapers the day before the important Cooper Institute meeting.[10]

The hall was packed for the second meeting of the Woman's Central on April 29.[11] Judging by the number of times he was interrupted by applause, Bellows's speech was well received. Bellows spoke of women who rushed to the hospitals of the Crimea and those who "carefully concealing their sex, rushed to arms," admitting their identities only on their deathbeds. Then Bellows described the great outpouring of offers from women to serve Union troops that convinced the "ladies of the city that all such societies should have an appropriate head." With this conclusion in mind the women of New York created the Woman's Central Association of Relief, Bellows explained, "to give explicit answers to the ten thousand questions everywhere rising."[12]

Bellows's rousing speech was followed by one by Vice President Hannibal Hamlin and then the women laid out the specifics of the WCAR plan. The WCAR created a board of managers composed of twelve men and twelve women, and this board in turn elected Dr. Valentine Mott as president and Bellows as vice-president.

From the beginning Blackwell's WCAR proposal was an attempt to combine conventional types of women's and men's midcentury relief work. Recognizing the grassroots female momentum that was bringing new soldiers aid societies into existence every day throughout the North, the Woman's Central intended to keep that momentum going. But Blackwell's plan also accepted the Victorian reality that without male endorsement and spokesmen, access to military decision makers would hardly be possible. Inviting men such as Mott and Bellows to join their initiative offered Blackwell and her colleagues their best chance to reach central political power structures and to find a wider arena for women's local relief work. As a woman and a political outsider, Blackwell anticipated government resistance to the plan and hoped that male endorsement would help to mitigate it.

The next order of business was establishing a direct link to the military so that the Woman's Central could keep informed of the changing needs of soldiers. With this in mind, in mid-May the WCAR authorized Bellows to lead "a committee to Washington to confer with the Medical Department in order to learn more definitely in what way . . . the women could serve the volunteers."[13] Bellows was not familiar with Washington nor did he have personal contacts who could lead him to the right government officials. It made sense for Bellows and the other WCAR representatives to meet with someone who was a Washington insider and who might provide them an entree. The morning after he arrived, and several more times in his first few days in Washington, Bellows met with Dorothea Dix who had come to Washington to seek approval for organizing a corps of nurses.[14]

When news of the attack on Union troops in Baltimore reached Dix in New Jersey, she responded quickly: "I followed in the Train three hours after the tumult in Baltimore. . . . It was not easy getting across the city—but I did not choose to turn back. I reached my place of destination."[15] This swift move would have made little sense for any woman other than Dix. By this time, though, Dix was a seasoned traveler with free passes on most railroad lines and an office in Wash-

ington. More important, Dix knew Washington well and was p
to address the necessary people to find the proper venue for her
Indeed, though she arrived in Washington late on April 19, the same
day as the attack, Dix went straight to the White House.[16] As she
explained to her friend: "I have reported myself and some nurses for
free service at the war department and to the surgeon-general wherever we may be needed."[17]

Like Blackwell at her New York Infirmary, Dix's Washington office
was inundated with nursing inquiries. Dix was so overwhelmed that
a month after she reached Washington she published the following
appeal in the newspapers: "All persons are respectfully and earnestly
requested not to send to army headquarters, or moving station,
women of any age in search of employment, unless the need is announced ... there being no provision made by the government or
otherwise for such persons."[18] Despite her request, local aid societies
familiar with Dix's Washington office began sending supplies to Dix
as well as directing any nursing applicants to her.[19]

Despite the flood of applicants and supplies, Dix welcomed the
opportunity to direct women nurses like her idol Florence Nightingale did. In fact, during a tour of asylums in Europe in 1855–1856,
Dix had made a special trip to Scutari to meet Nightingale in person.[20]
Dix tried again but never succeeded in meeting Nightingale. She was
impressed by Nightingale's *"great work,"* though, and read *Notes on
Nursing* with interest.[21] While other middle-class American women
made do with reading about Nightingale in the newspapers and in
her nursing manuals, Dix visited Europe at the peak of Nightingale's
popularity and befriended some of Nightingale's prominent English
benefactors. Returning to the United States on the brink of civil war,
Dix surely had thought about the possibility of leading a corps of
women nurses after Nightingale's model. In deciding to go directly to
President Lincoln with her proposition, Dix followed Nightingale's
example of circumventing regular military protocol to appeal to the
highest authority. Dix subsequently discussed her nursing plans with
Secretary of War Simon Cameron.[22]

Dix, then, was the logical person for Bellows to contact immediately upon arriving at the capital. In Washington, Bellows explained
the WCAR plan to Dix, discussed his delegation's efforts to get official
government sanction and surely benefited from Dix's knowledge

of Washington politics.[23] Establishing a connection to the WCAR through Bellows appealed to Dix, for it would put her in a position to direct the nurses selected and prepared by Blackwell.[24]

With the help of Dix, who had the authority to tour military camps and hospitals, Bellows got his first glimpse of the inadequate government accommodations made for the troops arriving in Washington every day.[25] Matters at home were pressing Bellows to return, but he wrote his wife Eliza that "the amount of sickness and suffering among the troops forbids my neglecting anything I can possibly do to bring the matter home to the Government."[26] In a letter to Secretary of War Cameron on May 18, Bellows presented the intention of the WCAR to "methodize the spontaneous benevolence" of the women of the country, a popular enthusiasm that would otherwise overwhelm the army with the "incessant and irresistible motions of this zeal, in the offer of medical aid, the applications of nurses, and the contributions of supplies."[27] This initial proposal clearly reflected WCAR intentions; it focused in particular on the selection, training, and placement of women nurses; asked "that the War Department consent to receive, on wages, [women nurses] in such numbers as the exigencies of the campaign may require"; and asked for official recognition.[28] The proposal Bellows brought to the Secretary of War in May reflected Blackwell's vision that women's traditional community relief work be sanctioned and supported by the United States government.

Little seemed to come of Bellows's initial modest appeal for "some positive recognition of their existence and efforts," though, and the WCAR representatives in Washington became discouraged.[29] Though Bellows and Dix had both been warmly received when they initially came to Washington, their appeals for government recognition made no headway. Bellows was reluctant to return home, however, without establishing a Washington link for the WCAR and asked his wife to reassure the "Central Association . . . that their agents are most laboriously and successfully laboring at their mission, and that they did not know until they came here how profoundly important it was. They must be patient with us."[30] Influenced by his conversations with Dix and the poor conditions of the military camps in Washington, Bellows was more convinced than ever of the need for civilian support for the war.[31] The United States Army's Medical Department was in some flux at the time, and Bellows and Dix hoped that they might be able to press for the creation of "a sanitary commission, to keep the whole question of Army health constantly stirred up here at headquarters" [underscored in original].[32] After meeting with Dix in Washington and touring the camps and military hospitals there, Bellows recommended an expansion of the original WCAR idea "to include a resident organization in Washington."[33] Such an affiliation would not only permit representatives to process WCAR supplies but would also allow Bellows and others to be in constant contact with the troops coming through the capital and would put them in a position to be privy to military decision making.

During Bellows's early days in Washington, however, the WCAR request for formal recognition and for access to information about the troops and their needs underwent a significant metamorphosis. The beginnings of this change were already evident in Bellows's correspondence with his wife less than a week after his arrival in the capital and, after having had a series of discussions with Dix, correspondence in which he began mentioning the need for a resident organization.[34] When he returned to New York, Bellows explained to the WCAR that he had altered the proposal because the army turned a deaf ear to his initial advances. Although it is difficult to determine exactly how the proposal evolved from a request for formal recognition of the WCAR's tripartite plan—managing local relief, communicating with the army about their needs, and selecting and training women nurses—to a proposal for a commission modeled after Florence Nightingale's Sanitary Commission in the Crimea, several points seem clear.

First, Dorothea Dix influenced Bellows's decision to pursue a more ambitious proposal for the creation of a sanitary commission. Second, touring the camps and hospitals in and around Washington convinced the delegates that inadequate government accommodations provided a novel opportunity for them to become actively involved in the war, not simply as the mouthpiece for women's organized homefront relief but as special advisors to the national government.

The benefit of creating an intervening body—a sanitary commission—was that it allowed the delegation to present itself as the solution to a problem that the army had not yet considered—the potentially disruptive power of women's spontaneous relief efforts. Not satisfied with their initial reception, early in June Bellows and the delegation of doctors addressed themselves to the Secretary of War in a formal letter on behalf of "the enthusiasm and zeal of the women of the Nation." In their informed opinion, the delegates believed, the "War Department will hereafter inevitably experience in all its bureaus the incessant and irrepressible motions of this zeal, in the offer of medical aid, the applications of nurses, and the contributions of supplies."[35] Offering their services as members of a newly conceived United States Sanitary Commission (USSC), as Bellows recalled it later, the men asked "[H]ow shall this rising tide of popular sympathy, expressed in the form of sanitary supplies, and offers of personal service and advice, be rendered least hurtful to the army system?"[36] The delegation's portrayal of the potential ill effects of women's relief work successfully appealed to Victorian notions of women's natural benevolence, whether or not this was a strategic approach or a genuine concern of Bellows and his colleagues. On June 9, the Secretary of War approved the creation of "A Commission of Inquiry and Advice in respect of the Sanitary Interests of the United States Forces."[37]

The recognition that a commission of inquiry provided was more ambitious than the original Woman's Central proposal, but, at the same time, much of its original intent was lost. The approved commission proposal reflected the ambitions of middle-class men who were interested in finding an appropriate outlet for their philanthropy. Through the Sanitary Commission, middle-class men such as Henry Bellows were in a strategic position to market their services to the Republican government as experts in organization and urban sanitation. The proposal signed by Secretary of War Cameron outlined farsighted plans to improve the health, discipline, morale, and care of the troops; to oversee the organization of military hospitals and camps; and to recommend appropriate means for transporting the wounded. This plan had evolved during the month Bellows and the delegation had spent in Washington. The ambitious design of the new commission, however, came at the expense of initial Woman's Central intentions. The approved proposal made no mention of the impressive WCAR reserves of "labor, skill and money" that sent the delegates to Washington in the first place, and the provision of women nurses was relegated to the margins. Under the general heading of "Relief," the commission planned to "inquire into . . . the precise regulations and

Woman's Central Association of Relief officers inside Cooper Union office. From left to right: Mrs. William B. Rice, Louisa Lee Schuyler, Mrs. Griffith, Mrs. T. d'Oremieulx, and Ellen Collins. Museum of the City of New York.

routine through which the services of the patriotic women of the country may be available as nurses."[38]

Meanwhile, the WCAR had been given office space at the Cooper Union in New York City, and the women began work. Louisa Lee Schuyler, a young parishioner at Henry Bellows's church, oversaw the organization of the WCAR offices and later recalled the humble circumstances: "We began life in a little room which contained two tables, one desk, half a dozen chairs, and a map on the wall. . . . We sent out circulars, wrote letters, looked out of the windows at the passing regiments, and talked about our work, sometimes hopefully, sometimes despairingly."[39]

Schuyler began writing to women in charge of local aid societies

The exterior of the WCAR offices. Museum of the City of New York.

from the WCAR office even though communication with Washington
had not yet been restored following rebel activities in Maryland.
Though the women were not aware of the status of the WCAR proposal, Elizabeth Blackwell nevertheless began sorting through the
flood of nursing applications. She reported to a friend toward the end
of the month that "we are oppressed with work, but we stand by the

country to the last." Emily Blackwell was at first skeptical about the plan but she was soon won over to the idea of training women nurses. As her sister Elizabeth explained it, they were not trying "to make men out of women, but to educate women in benevolence, intelligence and activity so as to find their own place and work."[40]

Despite their differences, Dix and Blackwell had combined their resources to select and train qualified women nurses while they awaited formal approval.[41] In May, Blackwell seconded Dix's plea to women "who now go on to Washington with the idea of nursing" to rethink their decision by reminding potential applicants that "nursing in the military hospitals is a very different thing from . . . private nursing."[42] After receiving instructions from Dix, the WCAR issued a list of nursing qualifications. Blackwell had originally intended to consider all qualified candidates regardless of their social class or age, but Dix's preferences were more bourgeois. Her request for "persons of the highest respectability" who could afford to support themselves prevailed in the end.[43] Accordingly, nurse candidates had to "be between the ages of thirty and forty-five years," had to be "women of strong constitutions," and were expected to "present a written testimonial" of their moral character.[44] Women who met Dix's qualifications, who were prepared to wear the "regulation dress," and who would agree to adhere to the authority of "the general superintendent" and military and medical authorities were invited to come to the WCAR offices in the Cooper Union where Blackwell and the registration committee interviewed applicants each afternoon.[45]

Despite the slow progress in Washington, work at the Woman's Central Association of Relief proceeded undisturbed by Bellows's predicament. As chairman of the registration committee, Blackwell worked continuously through the summer and fall to select and examine appropriate nurse candidates from the flood of willing applicants. Blackwell hesitated to send women nurses to Dix in Washington until they could be guaranteed a respectable wage and official army standing. Military necessities, however, sent Blackwell's nurses into the field without these guarantees.[46] Between April and October, the registration committee selected, trained, and dispatched thirty-two nurses to Dix for assignment in hospitals in and around the capital.[47]

Once Blackwell and Dix began to cooperate to train and place nurses, the Woman's Central became an experiment in combining the resources of two noted women reformers and two different strains of women's public activism. The registration committee's approach to nursing represented elements of Dix's experience with a type of reform that relied on a middle-class, middle-aged woman's moral reputation, yet it also reflected Blackwell's commitment to medical science. Blackwell's plan to place women in hospitals for training as nurses was consistent with her dedication to developing a medical curriculum for women that included practical experience. Dix's successful use of her own reputation as a selfless reformer convinced her to narrowly define the age requirements and to discourage applicants who were looking for remunerative employment. The registration committee's nursing protocol combined benevolence and science. The broader Woman's Central agenda was similarly inclusive, attracting reformers committed to local agendas and those interested in a centralized movement, women with experience in grassroots campaigns and others who were interested in an administrative strategy.

After the commission received formal recognition, the precise nature of the USSC–WCAR relationship was for a time unclear. Blackwell anticipated serving on the commission's advisory board, where she could make use of her experience working in urban sanitation and hygiene to consult the army on how to reorganize hospitals.[48] When news of the commission's official standing reached New York, the WCAR recommended that the commission recognize the WCAR as auxiliary. Addressing herself to Bellows, Eliza Schuyler, a member of the WCAR correspondence committee, explained that this arrangement would offer WCAR women "a means of widening our sphere of usefulness." With the commission established in Washington, she explained, the women could "feel assured that our supplies would be more efficiently and satisfactorily disposed of by it than in any other way."[49] Frederick Law Olmsted responded to say that the commission was convinced "of the mutual advantages of a close connexion between" the USSC and the WCAR. In September, the commission passed a resolution formally recognizing the Woman's Central Association of Relief as an auxiliary branch of the United States Sanitary Commission, with the WCAR "retaining full power to conduct its own affairs in all respects independently of the Commission."[50]

In June 1861, however, relations between Blackwell and the commission soured, and without this institutional affiliation, the differences between Dix and Blackwell were aggravated. On June 9, the Secretary of War recognized the United States Sanitary Commission, making virtually no mention of Blackwell's original plan for selecting, training, and employing women as nurses in military camps and hospitals. Though not able to identify personally with women who wanted to be nurses, Blackwell surely greeted this news as a defeat. By the time the new United States Sanitary Commission had received formal recognition, however, Bellows had more in mind than simply securing a Washington link for the WCAR or appropriate placement and compensation for Blackwell's nurses. By then, an impressive group of men had gathered in Washington to support the commission appeal. Included among those who had come to support Bellows and his efforts were Elisha Harris, a New York doctor experienced in sanitation and a member of the advisory board of Blackwell's New York Infirmary; Samuel Gridley Howe, a Boston doctor and well-known reformer; and George Templeton Strong. Bellows was unanimously elected United States Sanitary Commission president, Strong was appointed commission treasurer, and Olmsted accepted Bellows's offer to join the commission as general secretary, to remain resident in Washington.[51] Here Olmsted found the "mission" he had been hoping for and fussy George Strong, too, was now part of the war effort. The USSC that was taking form reflected the wartime intentions of the male board members rather than those of the women they had been sent to represent.

As if the men's abandonment of Blackwell's nursing protocol was not bad enough, on June 10 Secretary of War Cameron appointed Dorothea Dix Superintendent of Women Nurses, giving her the responsibility "to select and assign women nurses to general or permanent military hospitals."[52] News of Dix's appointment surely suggested to Blackwell that the men she had entrusted to go to Washington to seek approval for her WCAR plan had simply sacrificed her nursing initiative for an endorsement from Dix for their USSC plan. Perhaps expediency convinced Bellows and the other delegates not to push for approval of Blackwell's nursing plan. Or the men in Washington had strategically sided with Dix because she seemed most likely to receive recognition from the Secretary of War. Next to Blackwell, Dix was less of a threat to military and medical authorities. After all, according to the Nightingale model that Dix adhered to, nursing was merely an extension of the domestic ideal and nurses were proudly subordinate to male doctors. In contrast, Blackwell's professionalism meant that she was committed to creating a corps of trained nurses whose work was recognized by an appropriate contract and salary. Unlike Dix, Blackwell had no intentions of allowing a woman's moral reputation and her experience in the middle-class home to stand in for rigorous training in science and sanitation. As a doctor, Blackwell represented a direct threat to male medical hegemony. In suggesting that women be paid for work that was considered to be within their sphere, moreover, Blackwell's plan threatened to upset the balance of domestic power that shielded the middle-class home from the self-interest of the marketplace and that prevented women from seeking economic independence. In comparison, Dix's nursing intentions must have appeared selfless and innocuous to medical (and military) professionals willing to go to great lengths to keep women out and to bourgeois commission men who were not willing to promote Blackwell's radicalism. Although both the June 9 and June 10 resolutions mentioned nurses, the army did not officially sanction the use of women nurses in military hospitals for some time, and the propriety of allowing women into the camps and hospitals continued to be debated.[53]

Although the status of women nurses was still unclear, Blackwell still hoped to be appointed to the commission's advisory board, where she could best use her experience in urban sanitation and hygiene to advise the army on how to reorganize hospitals. The committee of New York doctors who had come to Washington to support Bellows, however, balked. "We would have accepted a place on the health commission which our association is endeavoring to establish," Blackwell explained to a friend, "but the Doctors would not permit us to come forward."[54] To make matters worse, though Blackwell had "selected a good amount of excellent [nursing] material," the commission doctors intended to assume responsibility for training women nurses in New York hospitals. In an abrupt move that revealed nineteenth-century medical prejudices against women physicians, the doctors Blackwell had consulted with for her original WCAR plans "refused to have anything to do with the nurse education plan if 'the Miss Blackwells were going to engineer the matter.'" With Dix ultimately in charge of the final selection and placement of nurses and commission doctors prepared to train the nurses, Blackwell was left with only the responsibility of selecting appropriate candidates from the applications submitted to the WCAR's registration committee. Blackwell noted Dix's appointment as Superintendent of Women Nurses with disgust, describing Dix as the army's "medler general [sic]." Dix's appointment and the vague recognition lent to women nurses in the commission agreement convinced Blackwell to stay "in the background." Nonetheless, Blackwell and her sister Emily continued to work for the commission in the coming months and even cooperated with Dix, though they were convinced she was "without a particle of system."[55]

As a close friend and confidante of Nightingale, Blackwell appreciated the importance of selecting and training women nurses for service to the military. But as an accomplished doctor experienced in implementing the latest in sanitary science, Blackwell resented being denied the semi-official recognition extended to Dix and the commission men by the military. Dix was not a professional and had no medical training or experience. In Blackwell's eyes, Dix, like so many of the women who rushed to volunteer, was compelled by some vague sense of a higher calling. More important, Blackwell understood that Dix's superintendency did not indicate a new willingness to accept women as medical professionals. Appointing Dix did not require the army or the commission doctors to rethink their gender prejudices. Because she claimed divine inspiration and offered her voluntary services as a nurse, Dix's personal ambitions were disguised by her more traditional approach.

But the June 9 approval for the USSC had also left out the question of how local women's labor, skill, and money would be administered. Without explicit recognition of the relief efforts of local women and of the WCAR women who would administer them, Blackwell was left with little to work with.

Despite her title and the stringency of her qualifications for women nurses, Dix's authority was compromised by similar professional prejudice among army doctors. The first of Blackwell's carefully selected nurses were handled roughly by military doctors who did not approve of female medical practitioners. Dix went to Olmsted at the commission offices in Washington in September and complained that there was not "a woman in all the hospitals of Washington . . . who is not constantly watched for evidences of favor to individuals and for grounds of scandalous suspicion and ... talked to with a double meaning."[56] In October the WCAR registration committee noted that women nurses in the military hospitals were the "objects of continual evil speaking among coarse subordinates, are looked at with a doubtful eye by all but the most enlightened surgeons, and have a very uncertain, semi-legal position, with poor wages and little sympathy."[57] Dix had become accustomed to the respect and success she enjoyed in her earlier asylum campaigns and was ill-prepared to handle organized resistance. Perhaps the entry of women into military hospitals under the auspices of the superintendent made those doctors nervous who remembered Dix's willingness to sacrifice physicians' careers in her asylum campaign. Though he empathized with Dix's plight, Olmsted could do little to help.

While she continued to push for official recognition of women nurses through the Sanitary Commission, Dix's patience ran thin. In her asylum campaign, Dix had not had to deal with an entrenched bureaucracy like the military. In the fall of 1861, Bellows and the Sanitary Commission began to lobby for a complete restructuring of the United States Army's Medical Department and recommended a comprehensive program of medical reform that they would administer and that would establish the commissioners as experts in institutional reform.[58] Realizing that they were in for a protracted fight, Bellows's men in Washington began to realize that Dix's impetuous style would do little to further their interests in long-term bureaucratic change. With this in mind, commission representatives began distancing themselves from Dix in September.

Though it was perhaps her reputation for intrepid moral reform that had convinced Bellows to align himself with Dix over Blackwell when he presented his case before the U.S. Army, Dix's notorious impatience and ill temper strained the working relationship between Dix and the USSC men. In appealing to politicians and the media for support for her asylum reform efforts during the 1850s, Dix had used her reputation and moral outrage to produce prompt results. This tactic did not make her work in the military hospitals easier, nor did it impress the bourgeois men of the commission. Early in August, George Templeton Strong described Dix as "energetic, benevolent, unselfish, and [suffering from] a mild case of monomania" and seconded Blackwell's opinion of Dix when he noted she had "no system whatever."[59] By September, Strong's opinion of Dix had not improved. Dix "is disgusted with us," he wrote, "because we do not leave everything else and rush off the instant she tells us of something that needs attention."[60] Strong recalled Dix interrupting a commission meeting "in a breathless excitement to say that a cow in the Smithsonian grounds was dying of sunstroke."[61]

Dix's association with the commission was strained further by her indifference to WCAR–USSC intentions. Despite WCAR efforts to direct supply efforts, Dix insisted on circumventing the WCAR and collecting and distributing her own supplies, but she also expected to have commission supplies at her disposal. At their offices in New York, Louisa Lee Schuyler and her associates were beginning to handle daily supply shipments from all over the North and, in the interest of the greatest military efficiency, were attempting to direct the supplies where they were needed most. At Schuyler's request, Olmsted prepared a circular instructing local relief organizations on the preferred methods of forwarding supplies and explained the WCAR–USSC policy of sending supplies to areas of need rather than to individuals or to particular state regiments.[62] Dix took offense at Olmsted's circular and read it as an attempt by the commission to undercut her authority. Olmsted wrote an apologetic letter in which he explained: "I was not aware, nor do I think that any of the Commissioners were aware, that the collection and distribution of supplies for the sick independently of the Commission was desired by you."[63] Olmsted reassured Dix that "the employees of the Commission had been strictly and repeatedly instructed to regard requests from you as orders from me."[64] As obliging as he was, however, Olmsted's reassurances to Dix appear disingenuous. Surely these remarks were intended to remind Dix that it was the commission, and not Dix, that had the ultimate authority to collect and dispense supplies. And, in fact, Dix had to complain to Olmsted that commission representatives were not honoring her supply requisitions once again just two months later; it appears that the commission was indeed intent on obstructing her. This time Olmsted did not even bother to reply to Dix. Alfred Bloor, Olmsted's assistant, responded instead, and again the reply did more to remind Dix of the commission's power than it did to reassure the superintendent of improved relations. Bloor assured Dix "that any requisitions which . . . you may consider it your duty to make on the stores which the Commission have in trust for the patriotic women of America, will be cheerfully and promptly honored."[65]

As much as this exchange reveals about the commission's relationship with Dix just six months after she had helped Bellows get government approval, it also serves as a measure of the growing confidence among commission men about the kind of power they wielded. Clearly by December 1861 commission men were convinced that they had exclusive rights to command the labor of the northern female home front and to distribute the money and supplies that resulted from that labor as they saw fit. Contrary to an earlier understanding that the Superintendent of Women Nurses and the USSC would work cooperatively, the commission now implied that any decisions or requests that Dix made would not be honored unless they came with explicit approval by a commission executive such as Olmsted or Bloor. The marginalization of Dix—and the kind of moral reform she represented—was almost complete.

Dix further insulted the fledgling USSC when her name was associated with a splinter organization in St. Louis. From the beginning Bellows had established a Western Department of the USSC and had appointed Dr. John Newberry to head commission efforts there. In September 1861, when General John Frémont, commander of the Army of the West, announced the creation of a Western Sanitary Commission, "to act under the direction of Miss Dix," Bellows, Strong, and Olmsted believed that Dix was behind the move.[66] In fact, Dix had been in St. Louis working with Frémont in response to a telegram she received from him in August asking her to "come here and organize these hospitals."[67] Perceiving Dix's move as a direct challenge to the USSC, Bellows addressed the Secretary of War asking "that [Frémont's] order may either by rescinded by your authority, or the Commission at St. Louis be, through him, instructed to work under our instructions."[68]

By October 1861, Dix's relationship with the USSC was in shambles. Commission men in Washington continued to fulfill Dix's requests for supplies, but they circumvented her authority over women nurses. Olmsted and Bellows no longer looked to Dix before assigning nurses, and nursing inquiries were directed to Blackwell and the WCAR registration committee.[69] In April 1862, Congress passed the USSC–sponsored bill to reorganize the Army Medical Department, including the resolution "[t]hat in general or permanent hospitals, female nurses may be substituted for soldiers, when, in the opinion of the surgeon-general or medical officer in charge, it is expedient to do so."[70] Here at last was some official military recognition of women nurses, but it had come too late for either Dix or Blackwell to greet it as a victory. Indeed, by the time the U.S. military officially sanctioned the use of women nurses, Blackwell and Dix had both been outmaneuvered by commission men. And although at first the USSC's hand-picked Surgeon General, William Hammond, reaffirmed Dix's position as Superintendent of Women Nurses, a year later Hammond and Stanton issued Army General Order #351 that essentially stripped Dix of authority.[71] In the summer of 1863, Olmsted likened Dix to General George McClellan, at a time when the general had fallen from public favor. "Both are popular heroes," explained Olmsted, "both are great at beginnings and in promises and hopes."[72]

Like Blackwell, Dix continued her work despite her estrangement from the USSC and the series of blows to her authority. Blackwell and Dix stayed "in the background" because they were convinced of the importance of getting women into military hospitals. Both watched as the USSC reorganized military hospitals along the lines outlined by Florence Nightingale, though they knew that, unlike Nightingale, their names would never be associated with the work.[73] A year into the war, the commission was a national relief organization with the sanction of the U.S. government, a formal connection to the army, and broad popular support. Though Dr. Elizabeth Blackwell and Dorothea Dix provided critical support—inspiration, even—for the project in its formative stages, their influence was all but forgotten by the commission's second year. The USSC executive board was composed of "medical men" and "professional gentlemen" who were self-described "civilians distinguished for their philanthropic experience and acquaintance with sanitary matters."[74] Young women who were undistinguished in leadership or in large-scale organization ran the WCAR. And, as branches of the WCAR developed throughout the North, women who were little known outside of their families and immediate communities and unaffiliated with any national movement assumed administrative control.

If the account of the work of these two relief organizations ended here, this study would simply be a confirmation of the phenomenon

identified by historians who have written about the commission from
the perspective of the class struggle of middle-class urban men against
new immigrants and the working class. With prominent women removed from positions of influence, these accounts conclude, men assumed leadership and control over local women's benevolence work
and turned it into a tool for the resurrection of their class. In a series
of abrupt maneuvers, commission men had strategically positioned
themselves to have the ear of the U.S. government while commanding
the financial and material support of the northern female home front.
As long as they did not squander these resources, commission men
were well positioned to realize their agenda of regaining the political
and social status they had lost by administering an organization that
dispensed humanitarian relief. Surely the young women who replaced
the prominent women would be easily manipulated and would not be
so bold as to develop and follow independent agendas, like Blackwell
and Dix, that would compromise commission men's plans.

From this perspective, the rise of the commission marked the unsat-
isfactory end to Dix's and Blackwell's efforts to lead the patriotic
women of the North into military hospitals and camps and to command the labor of women producing supplies on the home front. In
the Woman's Central Association of Relief, Elizabeth Blackwell had
envisioned an organization that would capitalize on the grassroots energy of the women of the nation to make a measurable contribution
to the war effort and that would provide institutional support and a
political voice for women's individual relief efforts. In her identification with Florence Nightingale, Dorothea Dix had imagined that she
would lead like-minded women crusaders onto the battlefield where
together they would save lives and expose the inhumanities of the
treatment of soldiers by medical men and the U.S. Army. Because of
the deliberate actions of ambitious middle-class commission men,
these women's initiatives had indeed been sabotaged.

But although Dix and Blackwell were undercut by USSC men, the
initiative they had launched would yield long-term benefits for a
younger generation of women leaders. Though the formation of the
United States Sanitary Commission was a strategic decision made by
men such as Bellows, Strong, and Olmsted, the success of the experiment still depended on the support of the Woman's Central Association of Relief and the good will of middle-class women who would

work directly for the commission at home and at the front. From the perspective of the war generation of women, the government's recognition of the Sanitary Commission and the decision of the Woman's Central to become an independent auxiliary suggested the beginnings of a fruitful relationship. The commission, the WCAR, and the other women-run branches that opened later across the North combined their efforts to save the lives of many soldiers and to provide critical support for their wives and families. This collaboration proved to be beneficial for both the men of the commission and the women of the branches, and it exhibited the possibilities of combining the grassroots strength of women's independent antebellum reform initiatives with men's access to centralized political power.

The young women in Blackwell's circle had been active in the community in the antebellum years, and their involvement in Blackwell's infirmary reflected their ongoing effort to find ways to meet the needs of a diverse urban population. Because they were politically disfranchised, middle-class women reformers were not directly affected by changing political power structures in the city as more immigrants moved in and gravitated toward Democratic political demagogues; and their traditional community leadership was not challenged by the changing urban environment. The war, then, did not present itself as a chance to regain something women had lost, as it did for the male commission leaders. In the end, however, it proved to be an important opportunity to experiment with collaborative institutional structures and new political power.

The integral contributions of Blackwell and Dix to the joint WCAR–USSC effort are too often overlooked. In terms of hospital reform, the promotion of sanitary science, and the introduction of women nurses into military hospitals—the interests that the two reformers shared and that inspired each to begin her individual campaign in the early days of the war—the joint effort was a success. The WCAR and the other regional branches that it helped create effectively appealed to an evangelicalism that championed women's social reform outside the home. Much as Dix had done in her asylum campaign, the women-run commission branches forced the male political establishment to begin to extend public services to care for those who became dependents of the state during the war. The joint effort offered women the opportunity to widen the sphere of their work without requiring them to give up the essential humanitarianism that informed local moral reform in the antebellum period. Many young women would launch entire careers based on their commission experiences. Louisa Lee Schuyler was one such woman. Schuyler was twenty-four when she took over the WCAR offices in Manhattan; at seventy-seven, at the end of an impressive career, she recalled "the work of the Sanitary Commission was a great educator to the women of that day."[75]

Indeed, these women would go further than either Dix or Blackwell to successfully bring the concerns of their female constituency to the attention of the state. For a younger generation of women, participation in the commission would be a formative experience. In this context, it seems almost incidental that Dix and Blackwell's initiatives came together under the aegis of a group of bourgeois men searching for an effective outlet for their philanthropy, but that is not the case. Although certainly in the beginning bourgeois commission men were in a strategic position to command the support of an impressive force of organized women recruits, in the end, the resulting USSC–WCAR affiliation reflected Blackwell's vision of closer, more equitable relationships between women and men, as we shall see in the following chapters. Indeed, young women who had gravitated toward Blackwell or Dix in the opening days of the war with little direction other than a vague desire to become involved would by the end of the war stage a serious challenge to commission men's claims to represent the best interests of the benevolent female public and threaten to disrupt the progress of commission men's social resurrection. By the end of 1861, for instance, commission men believed they held the authority to determine how the fruits of home-front labor were dispensed based on the deference they enjoyed from women of their class; two years later, however, branch leaders had made it clear that they did not. Commission success, then, relied on a reordering of relations between women and men. And, in the end, the WCAR's affiliation with the USSC men allowed young women such as Schuyler to take the first steps toward transforming localized grassroots women's political culture into a national lobbying force.

III

Coming of Age

THE WAR GENERATION
AND A NEW POLITICAL
CULTURE FOR WOMEN

*I*n the spring and summer of 1861, women throughout the northern states came together in towns and villages to provide uniforms and supplies for local volunteers leaving for Washington. In many towns, women formed themselves into soldiers aid societies and agreed to meet regularly to collect and forward supplies until the local soldiers returned.[1] Women's public and private expressions of patriotism encouraged men to volunteer, and through well-established networks of community welfare women prepared uniforms for soldiers and looked out for families with absent male members. Few women had experience outfitting soldiers, but, as tradition dictated, they made sure that men did not leave empty-handed. Northerners on the home front seemed confident that once the soldiers reached Washington, their needs would be looked after. Despite care taken by local women to provide for the soldiers, reports circulated in the first few months of the war of neglected soldiers at the front who suffered "bare feet, tattered and unchanged shirts, blanketless limbs, and untold destitution."[2] Other rumors told of ruthless army regulars and opportunists who duped naive recruits and intercepted care packages sent by concerned mothers and wives. The northern public was shocked to hear that some regiments were well fed and clothed with supplies from the army and from home, while others had to scavenge for provisions. The government in Washington

seemed ill-prepared to care adequately for its soldier volunteers, and
community efforts only went so far to provide the additional support.

In a few larger cities, young women were convinced they could do
better. Initial contacts with women at home convinced Louisa Lee
Schuyler and her colleagues at the Woman's Central Association of
Relief (WCAR) in New York City, for instance, that with guidance,
local soldiers aid societies had the ability to provide for the troops
what the government could not. As chair of the WCAR, the primary
branch of the United States Sanitary Commission (USSC), Schuyler
directed an extensive effort to establish communication with local soldiers aid societies in order to make the most efficient use of their relief
efforts. According to its founder, Dr. Elizabeth Blackwell, the goal of
the Woman's Central was to systematize women's relief work by keeping informed of the changing needs of the army and soliciting the
necessary supplies from its affiliated soldiers aid societies. As affiliates, local aid societies agreed to send supplies to the WCAR and to
other branches located in major cities such as Boston, Chicago, and
Philadelphia, where they were sorted, labeled, and forwarded to the
Washington offices of the USSC for disbursement. In return, the
Woman's Central and its sister branches guaranteed contributors that
supplies would be distributed "without distinction of State or Regiment, giving first to those who *need it most,* and *wherever the need
is greatest.*"[3]

Accordingly, the Woman's Central's first order of business was to
recommend that the United States Sanitary Commission issue a notice
"as soon as possible, respecting the necessary outfit for volunteers,
their underclothing & c.—which is *not* supplied by the State," with
the hope that home-front women might better prepare soldiers for the
front.[4] In mid-fall, the commission issued a circular addressed "To the
Loyal Women of America" that described the need for a system of
organized relief and outlined the relationship between the commission and the Woman's Central.[5] Schuyler and her Woman's Central
co-workers took this opportunity to clear up any misunderstandings
about how WCAR money and supplies were to be collected and
used.[6] They did not intend to have the WCAR simply act as a voice
for the interests of local relief societies, much less a supply depot
whose stores were subject to the whim of local prejudices. The
WCAR and the other regional branches meant to transform women's

temperamental individual benevolence, determined by local conditions and personal connections, into a united home front committed to consistent, long-term national interests and to the power of women's coordinated, collective efforts. Theirs was to be a corporate benevolence, with resources committed to shared principles and immune to individual caprice.

In their effort to convince women to overcome their preference for personalized local relief, the Woman's Central faced formidable challenges. The WCAR agenda represented a significant departure from antebellum approaches to reform, work that had always relied on the moral reputation of local leaders and a personal connection to the recipients of aid. Typically, women's soldiers aid societies preferred to send supplies gathered in towns and villages directly to individual soldiers or local regiments rather than hand them over to a central organization to be disbursed anonymously. Such impersonal benevolence made women accustomed to the older approach suspicious and has led contemporary historians to dismiss the war generation of women because they allowed such a change, and in so doing, expedited the process by which men took over women's grassroots reform work. With the effective dismissal of the two prominent women leaders who were integral to the creation of both the Woman's Central and the Sanitary Commission—Elizabeth Blackwell and Dorothea Dix—the way might well have been cleared for an easy male takeover of women's local wartime relief and the imposition of male values of efficiency and regulation.

Yet, as this chapter will argue, although they were willing to engage in a cooperative venture with middle-class commission men with access to centralized political power, young branch chairs drew on common traditions of women's culture and preserved the sex-segregated autonomy of women's grassroots activism. Women such as Louisa Schuyler and Abby May, at the Boston branch, were committed to a system that respected women's responsibilities to their families and their communities and that made the most of existing female reform strategies, such as those used by soldiers aid societies. But branch women—those women who ran regional commission branches in major northern cities—understood that the particular circumstances of the war demanded more than local women living in small towns throughout the North and their local relief networks were equipped to offer. Branch women imagined themselves and their interests as part of an extended women's community that transcended local interests and the borders of towns and states—a sisterhood of states. Convinced that the work of this female community could play a critical role in the Union war effort, branch women were eager to represent women's interests to the army and the government through the commission. Despite their commitment to a centralized system of uniform relief, however, Schuyler and May were flexible in dealing with diverse women on the northern home front and often shaped branch policies according to local aid initiatives. The young women of the Woman's Central Association of Relief and the other women-run commission branches combined grassroots women's activism with centralized access to political authority to offer a model of women's political culture that best served the needs of a new generation of women.

THE contemporary tendency to overlook women's wartime benevolence is bolstered by the fact that the WCAR and the other branches that followed it were just that—branches. Their branch status suggests that they were strictly subordinate to the male-run USSC, an assumption that has enabled historians of the period to focus almost exclusively on how the middle-class men of the commission stood to benefit from this arrangement. Historians argue that middle-class men who were spared military service found an alternative in working for the commission, which allowed them to simultaneously serve the Union and further their professional aspirations.[7] In cooperating with the commission, historians conclude, these women played into the hands of a middle class interested primarily in self-preservation. Women's traditional, independent, sex-segregated, cross-class benevolence work was sacrificed by young women who had stronger allegiances to middle-class men than they had to other women.[8]

To make this point, historians focus on how the Woman's Central agenda differed from antebellum approaches to reform and how women on the home front continued to prefer the intimacy of local soldiers aid societies over giving to the commission branches. In particular, Lori Ginzberg argues that midcentury reform bureaucracies such as the USSC indicate the encroachment of middle-class male values on women's reform work. According to Ginzberg, men appropriated relief in the 1850s and 1860s by taking over women's successful evangelical reform campaigns, exiling women to auxiliaries, and making charity organizations conform to masculine notions of anonymity, efficiency, and consistency. In the end, Ginzberg writes, the new mixed organizations denied women of the war generation not only the opportunity to identify with other women in meaningful work outside the home but also the chance to feel invested in women's collective moral vision.

With women's leadership skirted, Ginzberg argues, members of mixed organizations no longer identified with each other primarily as women but as members of a newly invigorated middle class. The language of benevolence was purged of references to a shared female morality that had made antebellum reform potentially radical for women. With evangelical fervor, middle- and upper-class women activists had reached out to working-class and poor women to fight male vices such as intemperance and prostitution that threatened the domestic sphere that all women inhabited. The new mixed organizations characteristic of wartime benevolence, in contrast, were run by men, and, as such, they became the tools of a defensive middle class trying to make sense of a rapidly industrializing competitive economy and aggressively partisan politics. Faced with the choice between emulating a traditional, gender-defined activism that was openly critical of the emergent male economic and political culture or creating a new model of women's reform that embraced politics and industrial discipline, middle-class women chose the latter. In the end, Ginzberg concludes, this decision required that the war generation trade cross-class women's benevolence for an allegiance to middle-class men and male values.[9]

Yet the agreement struck between the Woman's Central Association of Relief and the United States Sanitary Commission does not fit this construction. The two organizations came together because they believed the alliance would be mutually beneficial. The male-run commission, for its part, had much to gain from collaborating with a group of well-connected ambitious young women who were poised to tap the rich resources of widely cast networks of women's evangelical reform throughout the northern states. Presented with the opportunity to call on this resource and to reach a government apparatus grown unreceptive to their interests, commission men did not refuse.[10] Because it was the older organization, however, the Woman's Central

"full power to conduct its own affairs independently of the
Commission."[11] Schuyler and her colleagues were convinced that the
merger would give the women an official voice in Washington and "a
means of widening [their] sphere of usefulness."[12] Through its connection to the USSC, WCAR women were convinced, women's local
relief work could be put to much better use. Now local women could
fill boxes with supplies that soldiers at the front desperately needed
and soldiers could look forward to enjoying the fruits of home-front
labor.

In proposing to centralize and streamline the work of war relief and
seeking the cooperation of politically influential men, WCAR women
consciously broke with a type of traditional women's reform, one that
had served women well in efforts to relieve local needs and that had
been based on personal connections between contributors and recipients. Yet, although their attempt to regulate the work of local relief
societies and their interest in political influence shared some of the
values of the industrial workplace and male party politics, such
changes were not simply an indication of a younger generation's rejection of the values of an older female community. For years, benevolent
women had defied gender stereotypes and proved their business acumen and political savvy by raising and managing impressive sums of
money to fund their favorite ministers and grassroots reform efforts.[13]
Organizations such as the American Female Moral Reform Society
(AFMRS) offered the revival generation the opportunity to strengthen
women's moral influence through collective social action. In its heyday, the New York City–based AFMRS was supported by 445 auxiliaries and lobbied the New York state legislature for more stringent
prosecution of sexual crimes. The success of the AFMRS did not rely
on either a consistent rejection of traditional male power structures
or a singular commitment to decentralized reform initiatives. Women
were drawn to the AFMRS because they sought "a feminine-sororial
community," but the organization's success relied in part on its administrative efficiency and the favorable attention it received from politicians.[14]

For the war generation of women, the Woman's Central Association
of Relief served very similar purposes. In joining forces with the
United States Sanitary Commission, the WCAR identified with a potent Washington lobby that promised to open the doors of an en-

trenched government bureaucracy to their collective influence and to bring public recognition to women's private supply efforts. Despite this alliance—or perhaps in part because of it—the women who ran the branches were committed to the creation and maintenance of an extended community of women and the autonomy of women's local activism. Establishing connections with a diverse constituency and proving themselves capable of sustaining the work over an extended period of time, branch women built a women's network that was national in scope but that drew strength from local initiatives. The resulting WCAR–USSC alliance marked a shift in women's political culture rather than a clean break from the past. Whereas evangelicalism had led to the episodic grassroots women's politics of the antebellum years, the war ushered in a new era in women's political activity. In war relief, as in abolitionism, young women learned about political organization and public speaking and found a secular contemporary alternative to evangelical Protestantism.[15] The young women who ran the commission branches learned to work with men and the male political process in ways that would further their own interests and that prepared many of them for careers as professional reformers and agitators in the politically charged environment of the postwar years.[16] But young women were not simply studying the male political process during this period; they were also learning how to elaborate a distinct women's agenda and how to introduce women's concerns collectively into the political debate. This experience would serve them well in the postwar era when powerful women's organizations, such as the Woman's Christian Temperance Union, made a clean break from male domination yet sought progressive political alliances with male leaders of labor unions and other organizations whose agendas complemented theirs.[17] At the end of the war, Schuyler, May, and many of their women colleagues were at the beginning of very long careers in political activism, during which their paths would cross again in temperance, industrial reform, and women's rights.

AT twenty-four, Louisa Lee Schuyler was much younger than many of the local leaders of soldiers aid societies. As the daughter of a well-to-do New York family, Schuyler was expected to follow her mother's example and devote time to charitable causes. But when Schuyler's pastor, Henry Whitney Bellows, encouraged her to take charge of the work of the Woman's Central Association of Relief, even her mother worried about her daughter taking on so much responsibility.[18] Some years later, when she looked back on a long career of activism, Schuyler admitted that her work for the commission had "opened my eyes to the great value and the great power of organization—of which I had known nothing."[19] The many triumphs of her distinguished career as a hospital reformer and an advocate for the improvement of conditions in prisons, poorhouses, sanitoriums, and schools, Schuyler believed, could be traced back to her work in the WCAR. "The work of the Sanitary Commission," Schuyler remembered, "was a great educator to the women of the day."[20] The work made a similar impression on Schuyler's close colleagues Ellen Collins, who was thirty-three years old when she became Chair of the WCAR's supplies committee, and Angelina Post, who was probably in her early twenties when she co-chaired the correspondence committee with Schuyler.[21]

When Abigail Williams May took control of the New England Women's Auxiliary Association (NEWAA), the Boston branch of the United States Sanitary Commission, she was following Schuyler's example. Like Schuyler's, May's parents had distinguished themselves in local reform and had introduced their daughter to the work early in her life.[22] Inspired by her activist family and the preaching of Theodore Parker, May participated in a number of reform ventures in Boston at a young age. For two years, May worked with Dr. Marie Zakrzewska, a veteran of Elizabeth Blackwell's New York Infirmary for Women and Children, at the New England Female Medical College in Boston.[23] May was only thirty-two in February 1862, when she assumed the responsibilities of coordinating war relief for the New England region and, like Schuyler, she enjoyed a postwar career of some local prominence, founding the New England Women's Club to lobby for women's right to vote for school board members, working for the Association for the Advancement of Women for several years, and serving as the vice-president of the Massachusetts Suffrage Association. May's career illustrates—perhaps more explicitly than some others—how the war generation of women took part in a transitional political culture that provided a link between earlier forms of women's grassroots evangelical reform and the collective demand for a political voice that began to gain momentum in the postwar years.[24]

Branch women's public activism was made possible by their mem-

Portrait of Louisa Lee Schuyler, by Leon Bonnat, 1879. New York Historical Society.

bership in a strong female support network. Though for most mid-nineteenth-century women marriage and a career were considered incompatible, the support of other women meant that career-minded women did not have to give up family for careers in public activism.[25] Like their predecessors in the work, Blackwell and Dix, Schuyler and May never married, choosing instead to pursue public careers and to

Portrait of a mature Abigail Williams May, c. 1888. Framingham State College, Framingham, Massachusetts.

surround themselves with like-minded supportive women.[26] They were fortunate enough to be able to draw on the financial resources of their families when they needed to, but they also relied on the support—both financial and emotional—of their women friends.[27] Though Schuyler, May, and their many women associates came to the work with varying degrees of knowledge, skill, and support, they all had experience in what Carroll Smith-Rosenberg calls "the female world of love and ritual."[28] In nineteenth-century America, white middle-class women formed enduring intimate relations with women, particularly within their peer group before marriage. After marriage, women sustained their female friendships through regular correspondence and, when possible, by frequent visits.

Louisa Lee Schuyler and Abigail Williams May were very much a part of this female world and considered their relationships with women invaluable. Abby May was part of a close female network and, as one of her friends remembered, "had many friends very closely attached to her,—younger friends, who idolized her, and waited upon her, and saved her time and strength by their service; new friends, to whom she was like a draught of the elixer [*sic*] of life,—but she was never disloyal to an old friend."[29] In addition to her many close women friends, "Lou" Schuyler, as she preferred, drew on the support of her sister, Georgina, with whom she lived for more than eighty years. "Miss Georgina," one of her associates recalled, "who adored her sister, was always Aaron to her Moses, holding up her hands and helping her to climb those Sinais on the summits of which she came face to face with the Infinite."[30] Many of these close relationships emerged because war women were united in a common mission, though they were separated by geography. The letters Schuyler and May shared were very warm, and each often spoke of how much they thought of and about the other.[31] More than affection, though, the young women at the branches respected each other as colleagues. Schuyler described her friend May as "*the* woman of the Commission . . . for ability and comprehensiveness of its work, *anywhere*."[32] The war generation looked for competent associates with whom they could share affection and respect. Their female world extended beyond their neighborhood and valued organizational skills and professionalism as much as familiarity.

To turn war relief into work, young women of the war generation came to see their intimate female connections as professional assets that could be extended far beyond their immediate circles of friends. Membership in this world of female affection was exclusive and dependent on a woman's race, class, and education. Unmarried white women of May and Schuyler's social standing, living in the more thickly settled Northeast, were ideally situated to participate in dense overlapping circles of female activity. In appealing to diverse women throughout the North, however, branch representatives imagined a broader community of women, one that included their many correspondents, often women in remote rural areas and of clearly more modest means. Using the language and many of the conventions of intimate female connections, Schuyler and May created and largely sustained tributaries all over the Northeast—in poor, sparsely populated farming towns, such as those in Maine, and in more industrial urban areas, such as the cities in upstate New York along the Erie Canal.[33] And although some seasoned leaders of local aid societies no doubt balked at the pretension with which the young women addressed them, Schuyler, May, and their many associates were not easily discouraged. Using a variety of approaches, the leaders of commission branches brought together a scattered female constituency around their vision of a progressive female community and a centralized system of relief.

Imagined communities and sisterhoods aside, however, it was not easy work. When Bellows, Olmsted, and Strong approached potential commission colleagues, they contacted the men directly, often choosing men with whom they had had prior business dealings, those who shared political ideals, or those with whom they had family connections. Appealing to men based on these established connections was acceptable and did not challenge middle-class standards of propriety. Branch women, on the other hand, had to be more creative in reaching out to women with whom they were not related. Though many of their female contacts had distinguished careers in their communities, these initiatives had been launched under the auspices of their local church and usually with the explicit approval and guidance of their minister. Approaching local reformers directly to enlist their communities in the commission effort might appear improper because it circumvented the authority of the church and assumed that communities invested women with the power of representation. But as Schuyler and May quickly learned, the nature of the work required that they go well beyond their circles of friends and associates—testing middle-class tolerance of women's public activities as they went—and that they convince local women of the potential of doing the same.

In the first year of the war, though, all branch women could do was plead with local soldiers aid societies for supplies in order to keep up with the pressing needs of an army extended well beyond its means. Little time was spent debating the propriety or the benefits of local versus nationalized relief. Until February 1862, when the WCAR was joined by the second branch, May's NEWAA, Schuyler and her new staff could barely keep up with the frenzied requests of Alfred Bloor, the commission's liaison to the branches, who reported serious government shortages in winter clothing, bedding, and hospital supplies.[34] Preliminary branch initiatives had attracted the financial support of prominent New York and Boston businessmen, and these initial contributions had provided branches a modicum of security through their first year. Renewed claims on branch stores in the summer of 1862, when eastern fighting moved south along the Potomac River in the bloody peninsula campaign, however, reminded branch women of the need to secure the consistent support of local women and, particularly, of women outside the major cities and in more remote rural areas. Ships filled with wounded and sick soldiers began arriving in northern ports in May and June; city hospitals filled quickly, and hasty preparations were made to care for the excess. For commission branches in Boston and New York the situation was critical because many middle-class families vacated the cities during the warm summer months, leaving Schuyler and May to provide for soldiers from substantially diminished stores and with little hope of finding additional resources within their own social circles.[35] The predicament they faced encouraged branch women to establish more consistent relief relationships with local affiliates, allowing the branches some independence from the urban bourgeoisie.

By the end of 1862, the two main women-run commission branches had galvanized the support of more than 1,600 local relief societies throughout the North—a community of women that was perhaps more extended than any individual branch leader had imagined. To command the consistent support of these scattered societies and to meet the needs of a diverse constituency, young branch women such as May and Schuyler developed a mode of organization that was both uniquely female and unusually political.[36] In November 1862, branch women from New York, Boston, Philadelphia, and Chicago met with Dorothea Dix and commission representatives in Washington, where they visited commission rooms, shared ideas, and discussed strategies that had worked for them in their respective fields. When the meeting adjourned, branch women had a better idea of where their individual strengths lay and began canvassing their respective fields with renewed determination.

As chair of the largest branch, Schuyler was particularly adept at convincing women that though they lived in diverse environments and circumstances, the home-front experience erased their differences. Schuyler's letters to local agents were highly personalized missives in which she made references to common friends and shared experiences. Before moving on to the business of organized relief, Schuyler reminded her correspondents of a pleasant visit: "I shall always remember the morning spent with you at Norwich with the greatest pleasure and wish we could have another long talk." Other times, Schuyler established familiarity by referring to a mutual friend or relative: "Miss May of Boston, your niece I believe, was with me in Washington. . . . Your name is not unfamiliar to me. I have often heard my father speak of you." If she could not invoke a personal connection with her correspondent, however, Schuyler could still communicate an intimacy with her many female correspondents by more indirect but no less convincing means: "I hear your house was illuminated in honor of the President's [Emancipation] Proclamation. It is delightful to find some public expression of sympathy with what should have been hailed as the new birth of liberty in our land."[37] Although it is difficult to measure the effect of these personalized appeals on supplies, the letters allowed Schuyler and May to create an extended yet intimate community of women, even with women they had never met.

Making the broadest possible use of their many female friends and associates, Schuyler and her various branch colleagues approached each town through a woman distinguished in local leadership. Some women accustomed to participating in church-centered reform expressed surprise that branch women contacted them directly to solicit information about local societies and community sentiment instead

of going through the loc
church continued to be th
and ministers played an ac
ticipate. Though local wor
their societies, the commit
nized rational system of r
work of the affiliate societie
ing their supplies—if it mea
minister. As a general rule, h
cal clergymen only when a co
so or when a correspondent c
name of another woman with a
community organizer. Althoug _____ ., the intention
of commission women to thwar _____ gymen who might have been critical of the commission's connections to Unitarianism, their decision
to appeal directly to local women as companions in a common cause
acknowledged women's leadership in their communities.[38] Branch
contact with leaders of soldiers aid societies offered local women a
direct connection to a national network of women associates and correspondents and, indirectly, a way to address their personal concerns
in a national agenda. Accepting the offer to become a branch affiliate
put a local woman in the position to represent the concerns of her
community.

The directness of Schuyler's approach paid off as more and more
women responded to branch inquiries. Schuyler came to value these
extensive communications with the home front and launched an ambitious effort to elicit the sentiments of her vast northern female public in a survey conducted by the WCAR in January 1863.[39] Schuyler
sent out more than 1,500 surveys to women asking different questions
about community knowledge of the USSC and local sentiment toward
its program of providing centralized relief for Union soldiers.[40] Despite the limited nature of its scope, this survey was an unprecedented
solicitation of the sentiments of northern women. Certainly the nov-
elty of the request contributed to the impressive returns and the care
that women took in preparing lengthy and revealing answers to the
questions. The women Schuyler reached with her survey had never
been asked to express their opinions outside their own homes or communities and, in the context of wartime, women took the responsibil-

huyler and her colleagues, the survey and its
mportant tool in building consensus among
ping branch policy. The responses helped branch
tand that the work they were conducting had impor-
uences not only for the soldiers for whom they supplied
othing, and medical supplies but also for their families at
e. Each soldier, they came to realize, was part of a family and
a community that faced challenges of their own during wartime—
challenges that the WCAR might help to alleviate. The survey helped
legitimize the work WCAR women were already conducting, and it
helped them to shape branch policy to respond to the needs of their
broad constituency. The survey suggested to local women that branch
women were not only sympathetic to the female experience on the
home front but that they were also interested in the needs and the
expectations of women and their communities. This canvassing of
public opinion allowed women leaders to secure the support of their
constituency—a political skill that would continue to serve them well
in more overtly political endeavors branch women would undertake
in the future. The WCAR survey and other broad solicitations like it
convinced Schuyler and her branch colleagues to look at the work
they were conducting in terms of long-term consensus building. For
the rest of the war, branch women took very seriously their responsibility to communicate regularly and sincerely with local women, and
it was this commitment that ensured that branch women built relationships with women that continued into the postwar years.

For many local women, contact with the women-run commission
branches was the only connection they had to the government, perhaps the only communication they had outside their own community.
In towns far removed from centers of economic and political power,
local women believed commission women were representatives of the
federal government and considered their responses to branch inquiries carefully. Although not all local aid societies sent their supplies to
commission branches, hundreds of women responded to letters from
Schuyler and May.[41] From this correspondence, women with more
modest means who were often isolated in remote areas of the countryside heard about the progress of the war, learned what other communities were doing for the soldiers, and inquired about relatives. Branch
women heard of the many hardships faced by their correspondents

and began to see how they could develop a system of organized relief that was responsive to the varied needs of a diverse constituency.

Empowered by this direct solicitation from women with the ear of the government, local women expressed concerns about how the war was affecting their families and communities. In response to inquiries about supplies for the army, women all over the North wrote about how hard it was to find money enough to feed their families with rising prices and scarce resources. Although the cost of items such as bread, rent, and fuel increased dramatically during the war, wages did not increase proportionately.[42] Wartime taxes, profiteering, and the absence of male wage earners aggravated home-front hardships, making it even more difficult for many women and men to support their families. High prices and heavy taxes hit middle- and working-class families hard. From Bangor, Maine, Abby May learned that "the towns in Maine are generally very poor. It is a new State and a hard state to live in. In the farming districts it is comparatively so recent that it was a wilderness that there is but little wealth and much poverty."[43] Schuyler received similar explanations from women in response to the WCAR questionnaire.[44] Mrs. L. Seymour, from Jamestown, New York, wrote "[t]his winter our citizens are feeling the 'hard times' more than usual."[45]

In their letters to commission branches women described farming communities and manufacturing centers where families with modest incomes were having trouble getting by. "This is a country place," Cornelia Huntington wrote of the town of East Hampton, New York, where "none are wealthy, none are verry poor generaly in comfortable circumstances."[46] Hattie Bennett, secretary of the Ladies' Relief Society of Georgetown, Connecticut, characterized her community as "a manufacturing place," where "the people are mostly of moderate means."[47] Regardless of the local economic base, however, women complained about inflation and scarcities that put an unanticipated strain on meager family resources. L. B. Fitch from Paulet, Vermont, explained to Schuyler, "It is true that there is scarcely a *rich* man in our village," and, she added, due to the taxes, "the wives feel as poor as their husbands."[48]

· Often the more immediate needs of the family and the community consumed women's time and scarce resources. Local women reminded May and Schuyler that mobility and freedom from domestic responsibilities were luxuries that many women did not enjoy. When asked about soldiers aid societies in their towns, local women wished for more time away from domestic duties to attend to the business of war relief. A. J. Groves of New Hartford declared, "it seems to me if I had not a family of 5 small children and health very poor, that I would spend my whole time for a few weeks at least, in trying to mitigate such suffering."[49] Often meetings were canceled or postponed due to "family cares," ill health, and poor weather.[50] From East Varick, New York, B. B. Williams explained that she had been unable to send supplies because "we have had much sickness in our family and since Sept[ember] sever[e] and dangerous cases, which have confined me verry closely at home."[51] Therese Seabrook, a woman of more comfortable means, apologized in a similar manner for her inability to get up a society tributary to the WCAR in Keyport, New Jersey. "The day appointed was stormy," Seabrook reported, "and as my family were sick with measles including one of my servants I could not do anything during the past week."[52] In rural areas some women had to travel great distances to reach their neighbors and even farther to reach a railroad station, making it difficult for local agents to hold meetings and gather supplies in their communities. Mrs. L. S. Clement explained that the town of Canadea was "a country place and the ladies, some of them have some distance to come to attend our meetings. Many times this winter it has been so stormy on our day for meeting that only one, two, or three attended."[53] Despite the hardships of raising families alone, often on the frontier, women expressed a desire to join the effort or to contribute more often. And if the WCAR did not immediately convince correspondents to contribute, the WCAR leadership at least established critical contact with communities to whom they might apply for help later.

In other towns, Schuyler and her colleagues found well-established women's organizations that moved easily into the business of war relief. The women of the Ava Female Sewing Society had been meeting for ten years, and the Ladies Benevolent Society of New Marlboro had been at work for twelve years when they began preparing hospital clothing for the WCAR.[54] The women of Colchester, Connecticut, had met for years, explained Mrs. E. C. Curtis, "[s]o as we have a room for meetings we naturally kept on in the old way rather than organize anew."[55] Other societies were newer, but they had already established a protocol when they were contacted by a commission branch. The Salem Social Circle was established in 1860 in South Hadley Falls, and in 1861, Emily Knight and the other women of the society had "resolved into a *working* circle."[56] In other towns women began meeting only after the war began, but they had already developed effective systems for rotating officers and collecting weekly dues from their members.[57] Some women, on the other hand, held out little hope for any organization in their neighborhoods, such as Mrs. William Grave of Florence, New York, who explained to Schuyler, "there hasent ben one Society ever formed here and idont see as they are Agoin' to."[58]

In towns where May and Schuyler found societies, women reminded them that "charity begins at home."[59] Correspondents indicated that local women's organizations intended to provide relief for members of their own communities before committing scarce time and resources to the commission. In many communities, women's organizations were busy supporting families left destitute by absent male members. Though the "leading ladies" of Newport, New York, for instance, intended to send supplies to the commission, Mary Carlisle explained, "we have just been making contributions to releave our Soldiers families. They were *suffering*, but we will do for you as soon as we can."[60] Many women had their hands full looking after returning soldiers, like the women from Chatham Valley, Pennsylvania, who had to care for soldiers returning with "the small-pox," which discouraged the women from attending meetings, "on account of its spreadding as you know it is a contagious disease."[61] Libby Pratt described the priorities of the soldiers aid society in Danby, Vermont, in the following manner: "[I]n reguard to our society of this place . . . we have ben adoing and still are adoing for the comforts of sick and wounded Soldiers. . . . There is a call from our Govoner for suplies for our sick and wounded Soldiers of this state which are being brought to Brattleboro. Which will take some little time to suply them with what they need for theirs comfort."[62] Few people had prepared for an extended war, and women's work had always gone first to their families and then to their neighbors.

In the competition over the rights to women's labor and scarce resources, Schuyler and May discovered that local charities often won out over a proposed system of nationalized relief. E. B. Towner, a member of a women's group in North Hartford, for instance, kept the WCAR informed of the progress of "a warm and violent debate" over how her organization would spend the $45.89 the women had raised in a town festival. For a month the residents of North Hartford argued over whether the money should go to the commission or whether it should "be used for the benefit of the soldiers who went from this town." Several meetings were held on the matter, and in the end, "a 'compromise' was 'patched up,' and it was agreed that $23.29 should be used for the purposes of the Sanitary Commission, and the balance for the 'Hartford Boys.'" A few days later, Towner was delighted to report, the other side gave out, and decided to send the $22.60 to the commission as well. "We have not yet discovered the reasons for their sudden change," she intimated, "[w]e were happy to get the money, however, and so let the matter drop."[63] Indeed, in some communities, the issue of soldiers aid had become divisive; the United States Sanitary Commission competed with a multitude of more localized relief agencies and the United States Christian Commission, another national relief organization with ties to the Young Men's Christian Association.[64]

Despite community dissent, most women responded positively to branch solicitations and promised to send supplies when they could. Though they keenly perceived commission women's access to political power, local women spoke to May and Schuyler in terms they believed branch women would find familiar, referring often to their need to care for elderly parents and dependent children and the multitude of domestic responsibilities that continued to consume most of women's time and energy. With little to spare, rural correspondents were determined to send supplies and money where they thought they would be used most effectively and where their hard work would do the most good. For decades women had created and sustained highly effective systems of community welfare to support local families when delicate family economies proved inadequate. Before women agreed to turn the products of their benevolent labor over to the commission, they expected the commission to exhibit a similar level of efficiency and to respond to the concerns of its local constituencies. "We want to feel that the utmost economy is exercised in the use of our gift," Jennie Vosburg of Ames, New York, explained.[65] Although they sent supplies to New York, Boston, or the other branches, women also sent directly to their local regiments and saw no reason to give up one for the other. Local leaders candidly reported these decisions to the NEWAA and the WCAR and expected that branch women would understand their interest in sustaining local systems of welfare. After promising the cooperation of Connecticut's East Haddam with the WCAR, Lucretia Brainerd stipulated that "sometimes individual cases will decide our offerings, and they must be sent to *regiments*."[66] Though the aid society of East Hartford, Connecticut, had been contributing supplies to the WCAR, Lucretia Spring reported that "[w]e shall not probably, however, send more for sometime," as the women had decided to send supplies to Hartford for local distribution.[67]

Though they readily responded to branch inquiries in terms familiar to the female experience, local relief agents believed that their communication with branch women had political consequences. Local women were careful to establish that their commitment to the people in their communities—whether soldiers' families or "local boys" at the front—did not reflect poorly on their patriotism. A ladies aid society in Newport, New York, had already sent the WCAR twelve boxes when it turned its attention to the needs of "Soldiers familys," yet the women felt compelled to defend their decision to focus temporarily on local needs. Mary Carlisle explained, "our *village is for Union* ... but the people are powerless to help Just now."[68] The WCAR's imagined community offered women the chance to turn their local welfare toward a national effort, and local women understood this to be a novel opportunity to make their work count outside of their own neighborhoods.

In rural areas where access to the marketplace was limited and households depended on the productive labor of all family members, middle-class women were experts in the prudent managing of the family budget.[69] When approached about their willingness to give food and clothing to the soldiers, these women could not understand why, in the face of rising taxes, the government was not providing adequately for the troops. Local women believed their branch correspondents would appreciate their unwillingness to upset carefully balanced domestic economies to support a government that did not share their interest in prudent financial management. "[W]hile we are obliged to use the utmost care and economy to keep our households and have something left for other purposes," Mary Barstow complained to

Schuyler, the legislators in Washington were "spending millions with less consideration than we use in spending single dollars."[70]

Women suspected that the government was irresponsible with their tax money, and sometimes these suspicions rubbed off on the commission. If commission women were agents of the government, as local women believed, then they were responsible for seeing to it that the government used the resources of home-front women as wisely as would the women themselves. Women at the branches regularly received inquiries from local affiliates asking about reports that commission supplies never reached the soldiers and that agents of the commission sold supplies provided by ladies aid societies for the men.[71] "Sum say one thing and Sum say a nother and Sum Say that solgers hafto b[u]y All that we send to them," reported one of Schuyler's correspondents.[72] Women demanded to know whether "the noble men and women who lead in this movement . . . are engaged in the nefarious business of plundering the public under the guise of philanthropy," or whether "these complaints are without foundation."[73] Home-front women would send the hard-earned supplies of local aid societies to branch women to be distributed at their discretion, but they expected to be kept informed about how and where the supplies were used and reserved the right to criticize and influence commission policy. As the commission liaison to the branches, Alfred Bloor appreciated the significance of local women's demand for a strict accounting of their supplies. In a moment of frustration, Bloor complained to his commission superiors, "I do not know whether you and others recognize how hard it is to carry on this correspondence from week to week and month to month and year to year with women. . . . [T]hey all require a little, and some of them a good deal, of mere figures and facts."[74]

Schuyler and May's correspondence in the fall and winter of 1862–1863 taught them a few things about what it would take to bring northern women together to create an orderly system of war relief. Commission women reached out to their correspondents as members of an extended female community and convinced women to share intimate details about their lives and about their towns. Their scattered constituency was surprisingly candid about their concerns for their families, their preference for local relief, and their apprehensions about sending money and supplies to the commission. In fact, even Schuyler was startled by the friendly, "sympathetic, and . . . even confidential" nature of the responses she received. Though certainly local women's refusal to commit to an exclusive supply relationship with commission branches confounded branch women's vision of raising women's benevolence work out of its antebellum provincialism, Schuyler and May took pride in their successes. Schuyler noted with some gratification the progress the WCAR had made in gaining the confidence of northern women. In particular, Schuyler was pleased that one correspondent had remarked how glad she was *"to find we are not a soulless corporation!"*[75]

In order successfully to sustain a national relief network, however, the Woman's Central Association of Relief, the New England Women's Auxiliary Association, and their sister branches had to do more than overcome the popular preference for local autonomy and personal connections to aid recipients. In an effort to compensate for the seemingly impersonal nature of the relief they advocated, commission women imagined a broad but intimate community of women that connected urban bourgeois women such as themselves with middle-class rural women, women living in new factory towns, and those isolated in remote frontier villages. Close ties with commission women as supply intermediaries served as a substitute for an intimacy with the soldier-recipients of relief. Canvassing was delicate work, however, and Schuyler and May appreciated that their most loyal support came from rural and remote constituencies, where women confessed "we only know of war by hear say, and high prices, and bounties and all sorts of incidental taxes."[76] Branch representatives had to convince women who conceived of the war in these local terms that the commission was neither a spendthrift government agency nor just one more local charity. In fact, because the war was not a local problem, commission circulars argued, effective war relief could not be conducted by relying on women's local welfare networks. That did not mean, however, that local concerns and initiatives would be overlooked. Whereas responding to branch inquiries had provided a forum for women to air local concerns, committing resources to women-run commission branches could allow home-front women to carry their standards of efficiency and economy in local benevolence to a national relief agency. And, to their credit, young branch women were willing pupils of women leaders of local societies with experience in getting the most out of limited community resources.

As resourceful as the home-front women were, war made their lives more difficult. Responses to the WCAR's January 1863 survey convinced Schuyler that in the face of economic hard times branch policy had to remain flexible. Turning a multitude of local societies into a rationalized system of relief required that they make room in their national agenda for approaches proven at the local level and that they remain sensitive to the needs of their diverse constituency. Even when soldiers aid societies agreed to work with the commission, local conditions dictated the terms and the pace of the work. For instance, women whose family resources were hit hard by inflation and rising prices apologized for their inability to send money or supplies, but they repeatedly offered to work for the cause. "The Cloth is verry dear here and Scerce there isent Wool Enough raised in our town to half Cloth them," reported Mrs. William Grave of Florence, New York. "I cant do much as I would like to for iam getting Some Advanced in Years," she added, but she thought "if we had the Materials to do with we might make some Cloths."[77] Elsie Wheeler of Deposit, New York, described a similar situation: "[W]e have many more who are more willing to work than to *pay*."[78] From New Marlboro, Mrs. A. Warren lamented, "If we only had money to purchase materials, we would send you monthly."[79] And Mrs. E. A. Follett explained that North Pitcher, New York, was "not a wool growing community therefore [the ladies] are not supplied with flanells to bestow."[80] If Lucretia Brainerd and her neighbors had materials, she promised, "we would *work now*."[81] These local concerns frustrated branch women's shared vision of a corporate benevolence that had overcome provincial idiosyncracies, but Schuyler and her branch colleagues also appreciated that women operating in small and scattered communities were more experienced in such matters.

When it came to the provision of army clothing, for instance, branch women took the advice of their local correspondents. The commission resorted to buying much-needed army clothing from manufacturers of ready-made clothing when demand for such clothing exceeded the commission's supply. Newspapers reported that many of these industries were disreputable and made army clothes out of "shoddy," a cheap fabric that fell apart readily.[82] At the local level, women suggested that instead of buying clothes, the branches ought to buy material in bulk and then pass it on to women's relief societies to be made up into uniforms. This would not only ensure that the army received quality homemade garments, but it would correspond to local notions of the efficient use of money and supplies raised by women's relief societies. More important, however, if the commission provided material, local agents could hold regular meetings and keep societies together that would otherwise have disappeared for lack of work. Though removed from the war and the chains of command, home-front women understood that the commission needed their support. They believed that the central organization ought to commit to a policy of sustaining local relief societies. Mrs. E. C. Sterling wrote to Bellows explaining that it had long been the policy of her society in Bridgeport, Connecticut, to buy material to support various sewing circles, and she suggested that he was "mistaken in expecting the Commission will be supplied by Societies as heretofore, simply because very many of these Societies have ceased to exist from want of means."[83] Sterling was not the only one who pointed out that the commission had a vested interest in supporting the work of grassroots associations and in allowing local soldiers aid societies to determine how best to obtain clothing for soldiers in the field and in the hospital.[84]

But when May and Schuyler proposed buying material to be made up by local women, the commission dragged its feet.[85] Because the commission was beholden to the branches for its support, commission men were reluctant to allow the branches to use funds earmarked for the USSC to buy material for local soldiers aid societies. Commission men complained loudly about money raised at the local level that never reached the USSC treasury, attesting to a critical difference in the way the commission men and the women-run branches measured efficiency. Women at the branches recognized that local leaders needed to have access to materials in order to sustain home-front commitment and understood that purchasing material in bulk in urban centers saved the added costs country retailers charged. Taking the lead from their local affiliates, then, branch women began buying materials in 1862 and 1863 without commission approval. When the commission sent Abby May money to buy clothes from manufacturers in Boston, for instance, May explained, "I have not deemed it advisable to expend the $500 in ready made clothes. . . . We have spent $2,000 in flannel just now, which is being rapidly converted into garments."[86] In fact, May made arrangements to buy material wholesale as early as the fall of 1862 and sent it to women's organizations all over Massachusetts and Connecticut to use at their discretion.[87] To May and her branch colleagues, such cash expenditures made sense. Providing local affiliates with materials cost the branches money up front, but in the end it delivered valuable returns. Instead of lining the pockets of industrial clothing manufacturers interested in profiting from the war, branch women invested in a long-term relationship with local women and their communities. Buying material and arranging to have uniforms made at home conformed to local women's standards of efficiency and economy—and not to the standards of commission men.

But there is more here than young branch leaders simply deferring to local women's traditional measures of economy. In intercepting the flow of money from the home front to the commission, Schuyler and May were challenging commission men's claims to having the exclusive rights to money raised from the northern, largely female, public.[88] Branch women acted as brokers, mediating between home front women and commission men about how money was collected and spent. In so doing, women leaders were asserting their own right to determine how the public's money was spent—a move that had political implications.[89] In part branch women's decision to spend money on the local production of army clothing reflected their understanding of their female constituency's resentment of wartime profiteering, for letters from home front women often referred to stories circulating about corporate giants getting rich selling supplies to the U.S. Army. But this decision also suggests that wartime leaders had an emergent sense of how dispensing public funds could be used to garner public support. Decisions about how commission funds were spent were made with commission men's established business relations and political connections in mind. Though committed to wartime relief, perhaps branch women were beginning to understand the process by which middle-class men such as their commission colleagues dispensed money in return for political patronage. In this case, women asserted their right to use money collected from the female public to secure that public's more consistent support.

Not all financial questions resulted in a conflict between branch women and commission men, however, for at times commission men simply deferred to branch women's greater understanding of the female public. When Schuyler proposed a way of providing financial incentives to local soldiers aid societies, for instance, the commission followed her lead. As responses to her survey began arriving in January 1863, Schuyler reported to Bellows that she believed the high cost of materials and transportation prevented "little villages" from sending materials to New York with regularity. Schuyler solicited franking privileges for packages addressed to the New York offices and asked Bellows to help secure similar arrangements for the other branches.[90] Later, Schuyler developed a novel system of fund matching that would help women in remote areas keep their soldiers aid societies operational and that allowed women with limited means to contribute their labor to the cause. Early in 1864, Schuyler began offering that "to every contribution of $20 we will add the same amount, and send them either material to this value, or the money when they believe that they can spend it more advantageously at home."[91] Schuyler's fund-matching policy proved to be highly effective at stocking the rooms of the New York branch and at keeping marginal aid societies functioning when they would otherwise have disappeared.[92] Proving that they too were willing to be flexible, though arguably less patient with initiatives that detracted from their vision of centralization, the commission approved the program and began contributing a month later.[93] Perhaps even commission men could not continue to deny the substantial savings there was to be had in making soldiers' uniforms at home for almost half the cost of purchasing ready-made clothing.[94]

In a similar vein, enterprising urban women applied for government contracts to make clothing themselves. With the support of the Boston branch, Helen Gilson in Chelsea, Massachusetts, Anna Lowell in Boston, and Katharine Prescott Wormeley in Newport, Rhode Island, hired large numbers of needy wives and daughters of soldiers to produce army clothing for the commission.[95] Mrs. E. C. Sterling had a similar program in mind for Bridgeport, Connecticut, where society members were interested in hiring women to make up clothing, particularly townswomen from "Volunteer families, [who were] living literally hand to mouth" and who "would be doubly delighted with the opportunity of helping themselves and the Sanitary at the same time."[96] These experiments in female proprietorship proved so successful that the Boston branch began its own Industrial Department and hired women at wages that were adjusted to account for the high price of food and other staples.[97] Although the women employed in these endeavors left no records, we can assume such work was welcomed by women with families to look after and for those whose only alternative was working for manufacturers of ready-made clothing, where wages were determined by the market and not by family considerations and the price of food.

Hiring poor women on government contract and paying them a living wage for the work was truly original, and once again, it corresponded to a different notion of efficiency than buying clothes from the ready-made industry. Urban middle-class branch women used their power and position to support initiatives that helped diverse women meet the needs of their families and communities while they paid respect to women's commitment to provide quality clothing for the soldiers. These initiatives introduced a concern into the political debate that branch women were beginning to articulate in their communications with one another and with commission men—federal support of soldiers' families. In lobbying for contracts, branch women brought the plight of soldiers' families to the attention of the government and encouraged the government to assume responsibility for the welfare of these forgotten casualties of war.[98] In so doing, these women were participating in the heated wartime debate about the extension of the role of the federal government. Indeed their postwar endeavors indicate that this experience made a long-term impression on wartime leaders such as May, Schuyler, and Mary Livermore, an abolitionist journalist who became chair of the Chicago branch during the war and a prominent temperance and suffrage activist after the war. After the war, these women leaders continued to pursue initiatives to benefit veteran soldiers and wartime widows and orphans, particularly those who ended up in state asylums or who sought refuge from periodic unemployment in poorhouses.

In these initiatives and in others, Schuyler and May took cues from their local constituencies and committed branch resources to sustaining women's relief work. Although the WCAR, NEWAA, and the other branches were committed to a centralized system of relief, branch policies reflected women's traditional demands for local welfare relief and the integrity of women's grassroots benevolence work. This pragmatic approach to the work informed many of the decisions made at the women-run branches. Although early on in the work commission men and branch women had expended a great deal of energy fending off attacks and competition from the Christian Commission, for instance, branch women began to consider such efforts wasteful and inefficient. If women in some towns chose to give supplies to the commission's detractors, Schuyler explained to a Woman's Central colleague, "why not 'agree to disagree' frankly, nobly?" Why should they not foster "a generous rivalry" among the various societies, Schuyler speculated, a competition from which the soldier would ultimately benefit?[99] The challenge for branch women such as Schuyler and May was not to eliminate or discredit the competition but to attract diverse women to the women-run commission branches by appealing to them in terms they could understand and providing the means for them to contribute what they could. In the long-term work of building a community of women branch women were unwilling to allow a rivalry between two relief organizations to consume their immediate energies.

With that said, though, the strategy the women used to build a consensus among women was unique. Though branch women shared commission men's commitment to centralization, they did not allow it to so narrow their range of vision that they lost sight of their responsibility to the scattered and diverse communities of the northern home front. And although branch women allowed local concerns and initiatives to coexist with—and at times supersede—their goal of directing a coordinated central relief operation, they never lost sight of their plan for a united community of women. Branch women recognized local women as leaders and respected their ability to determine what was best for their communities, but they were also building a consensus among women about how local needs could be fulfilled through a coordinated effort. The women running the commission branches were testing their limits and were challenging local women to do the same. To illustrate the potential power of such coordination, branch women exploited the potent possibilities that their connection to the commission offered—making unilateral decisions about the proper outfitting of U.S. Army soldiers and dispensing public funds to families and communities in need, for instance. Together they were learning to work comfortably in a women's culture that was both overtly political yet skeptical of men with political aspirations and their schemes.

In developing a strategy that dealt respectfully with local variances, branch women overcame the main obstacle to their effort to centralize wartime relief—but not the only one. One of the biggest tests of branch women's practicality and organizational acumen came in dealing with the urban bourgeoisie. In her travels through the countryside in 1863, Schuyler was struck by "the noble spirit of self-sacrifice" she found in small towns such as South Windsor where poor townspeople begged house to house for contributions for the soldiers.[100] Schuyler's respect for the self-sacrifice of farmers and villagers stood in contrast to her reaction to the inconsistencies of the urban elite. In October 1863 Schuyler complained that, although they had called regular public meetings of the women in their own social circles, the Woman's Central had "utterly failed . . . in inducing our citizens to co-operate with us."[101] Though members of the urban bourgeoisie continued to provide the branches with money, because of inflation and scarcities, well-preserved food and homemade clothing were often more valuable than currency. Branch women had found it fruitful to appeal to rural women as producers. Faced with a fickle urban constituency whose loyalties were limited by whim and weather, Schuyler and her branch colleagues decided to approach urban women as consumers.

After failing to interest affluent New Yorkers in the day-to-day work of the Woman's Central, Schuyler invested her hopes in a series of "non-importation" meetings and participated in a campaign to make urban women loyal by convincing them to refrain from buying luxuries and products imported from countries sympathetic to the Confederacy.[102] Branch women hoped that urban bourgeois women might adhere to a boycott without having to rearrange their social calendars or reconsider their seasonal urban flights. Even so, some women attended these meetings for the chance to see abolition and suffrage luminaries such as Elizabeth Cady Stanton, Susan B. Anthony, and Lucretia Mott, who spoke at one such meeting held in May 1864.[103] Though Schuyler attended these meetings and expressed interest in this "non-importation business," as she described it, she was not as impressed as others were with the presence of female celebrities. "There was a good deal that was intensely amusing" at the meeting, Schuyler privately wrote her assistant Angie Post, "[d]id you see the woman who stood up on her seat, waved her h[an]dk[erchie]f and called out for 'Miss Susan B. Anthony again!'"[104]

As amusing as it was to see elite women who had been lackadaisical in their support of the war effort fawning over Anthony, Stanton, and Mott, Schuyler appreciated the need to get them involved in the work. Whereas branch leaders such as May and Mary Livermore moved easily from antebellum abolitionism to their USSC work of war relief and finally to postwar feminism, Schuyler had not committed herself (nor would she after the war) to either abolitionism or suffrage. In fact, with her conservative rural constituency and male commission colleagues in mind, she might have been apprehensive that her attendance at such a meeting would link the Woman's Central to these causes in the public's mind, but perhaps that was a risk she was willing to take.[105] On the other hand, boycotts had long been a respectable and effective way for the politically disenfranchised to express their opinion and to use economic pressure to enforce political loyalty. Once again, a flexible approach to diverse constituencies allowed branch women to make use of traditional forms of women's grassroots activism while they experimented with the collective power of a centralized body.

By experimenting with a variety of arrangements and granting ample weight to local initiatives, Schuyler, May, and their counterparts laid the foundation of a new women's political culture. These young women were committed to enlisting women in a national agenda and finding a political voice for women's coordinated war relief. This new political culture owed much to a rich history of women's work for their local communities, but the strategy that emerged was original. Recognizing Lou Schuyler, Abby May, and their colleagues as government agents, local women on the northern home front eagerly responded to branch solicitations, sometimes with supplies and money, more often with advice and criticism they were convinced would positively affect the government's war efforts. Branch communication allowed local women's diverse interests to be aired in a national context, but it also provided local women with the opportunity to identify with a dynamic and widely cast network of local women leaders and a centralized system of home-front relief with a political arm. Connections to commission branches allowed women at local societies to learn from one another. Empowered by local women's willingness to accept branch women as government agents, young branch leaders were flexible about how local women expressed their support for the work of the commission. Young branch leaders were willing to negotiate for local loyalties in order to create a coalition of women's grassroots relief operations. And in seeking an alliance with commission men branch women took an equally pragmatic approach to turning the power of this coalition into a political force. All the while, they were learning how best to elicit support and advice from their diverse constituency and to use their collective voice to influence government policy. Branch women's tact, however, had its limits, as we shall see. Schuyler, May, and their various branch counterparts were unwilling to allow their cooperation with the commission to compromise what had become a carefully nurtured women's chain of command.

Branch Women Test Their Authority

*I*n Alfred J. Bloor's mind, women's work for the United States Sanitary Commission (USSC) and their collective demand for a political voice in the postwar years were explicitly linked. Two years after his dismissal from the organization, Bloor, the commission's former liaison to the branches, wrote a personal letter to Senator Charles Sumner praising the work of the wartime relief agency.[1] In particular, Bloor wanted to make it clear "that the chief work in the practice of the Sanitary Commission was exceedingly well done by women, and comparatively ill done by men." Bloor estimated that some 15 million dollars in supplies "were almost universally collected, assorted, and despatched, and re-collected, re-assorted, and re-despatched, by women, representing with great impartiality, every grade of society in the Republic."[2] In contacting Senator Sumner, Bloor hoped to set the record straight and give women their fair share of the credit for the commission's war relief. Bloor suggested that the Senator might find this information useful in the pending "question of the enfranchisement of women." Though much had been written about the commission and its successes by 1866, Senator Sumner found Bloor's information about the amount and quality of female labor "a revelation."[3]

Yet the official histories of the commission draw a very different picture of the organization, and it is because of the male-centeredness of such accounts that most historians have missed the significance of the USSC experience for the development of women's political culture. Focusing on commission histories written by men, these accounts conclude that women's role was strictly supportive and that they contributed to men's efforts to win political and social power back from new ethnic and working-class men.[4] Certainly commission men always assumed that branch women were strictly subordinate to the commission executive board and expected that they would only mediate between women's charitable endeavors and the commission's work with the U.S. Army.

Charles Stillé's *History of the United States Sanitary Commission*, for instance, published in the same year as Bloor's letter to Sumner, details the trials and tribulations of the commission's "true founders": Henry Whitney Bellows, George Templeton Strong, Frederick Law Olmsted, and other members of the executive board.[5] Despite their many professional responsibilities, these "overworked" men pushed on bravely with their plan for a civilian relief organization, Stillé argues, facing down not only obstinate government officials but also the "State-ish spirit" that informed popular preferences for sending supplies directly to local regiments.[6] In Stillé's and other official male accounts, women everywhere responded to the war with "spontaneous and self-sacrificing efforts" to send food and supplies to the soldiers they knew. Recognizing that this "natural" feminine preference for helping local soldiers was potentially harmful to the national war effort, Bellows and his associates determined to harness and control these feminine impulses.[7] While their ideas for a fruitful marriage of women's and men's work were still "in *embryo*," Bellows and Dr. Elisha Harris fortunately stumbled into the first meeting of the Woman's Central Association of Relief (WCAR), where they "found . . . a number of ladies, full of zeal and enthusiasm in the cause" but otherwise undirected.[8] It was here, according to Stillé, that the details of the men's plan became clear to them. No mention is made of either Elizabeth Blackwell or Dorothea Dix in Stillé's version, and, in the end, the official accounts agree that without the paternal guidance of commission men, the reckless work of women's provincial war relief would have been at best ineffective, at worst, a nuisance. The commission represented the triumph of the federal (male) influence over local (female) prejudices, or as one commissioner described it:

on the one side, the motherly love which kept swelling up night and day . . . in such a stream as threatened to overrun all bounds. On the other side, the manly demand for law and system to guide and control this great moving tide. Except for that union—the masculine and this feminine element—that tremendous tide of love, and impulse, and anxious tenderness, would ere long have been met by pointed bayonets and turned back, and forbidden entrance to the camp and hospital.[9]

Stillé's account, like those written by Bellows and other commission executives, contributed to the image of the organization as a heroic effort by middle-class men.[10] Commission men flattered themselves by recording how they stepped in to help an overwhelmed government and to save women from themselves. Most commission women were unnamed in these accounts and were praised as selfless volunteers who were drawn to the work by instinct and who gladly accepted male guidance. Official accounts used natural imagery when describing women's wartime work, eliminating any possibility that women were guided by anything other than natural feminine inclination. "Little circles and associations were multiplying, like rings in the water," said one account of the commission.[11] Although commission agents received salaries for their work, in part to compensate them for absences from their professional commitments, commission literature was always careful to point out that women's work was donated.[12] Official commission accounts relied heavily on traditional middle-class images of women as ministering angels and dutiful workers. "Women," one publication argued, "are alike the world over, always the same loving, self-sacrificing creatures."[13]

By stressing the voluntary nature of women's work, spokesmen constructed a gendered account of the commission. In the middle-class ideal, men were paid for their work outside the home and women's work was simply an extension of their domestic duties and was, hence, unpaid. By characterizing women's work as selfless and instinctual and men's as professional and disciplined, the commission aligned itself with this ideal. Yet by choosing a self-sacrificing nurse-angel as the organization's official insignia, commission men's class-specific aspirations were disguised as disinterested and as natural as a mother caring for her son or a wife, her husband.[14]

But women's work in the USSC, in fact, never fit into this male notion, as even some commission men who worked closely with female colleagues recognized. Nor was women's war work a triumph of middle-class male discipline and professionalism over well-meaning but sometimes overbearing feminine impulse. Bloor was not alone in his admiration for commission women, even if he at times found communicating with the women-run branches challenging.[15] Women's work at all levels of the organization's relief operations proved to Bloor that they were efficient, thorough, and professional and were ready to accept the responsibilities of the franchise. It is more important, however, in the end, to look at what women actually did while working for the USSC than it is to draw conclusions about their working relationship with that organization based on what various men thought about the women they worked with. Securing a consistent and reliable flow of money and supplies to commission offices in Washington required women to organize and canvass their region and to secure the cooperation of leaders of local soldiers aid societies as well as the commitment of women of individual households to contribute part of their family's income. To conduct this work, women everywhere drew on more than maternal impulses or feminine sensibility, as official commission literature would have it, and those commission men who worked most closely with women understood this best.

As Bloor, Olmsted, and others who developed close working relations with women at various levels of the commission discovered, their female colleagues were often vocal, opinionated, and secure in their positions of authority; they understood the value of their work, believed that it contributed positively to the war effort, and, on occasion (contrary to the popular middle-class stereotype), asked for and accepted pay. At the local level, women were discriminating and sent their supplies when (and where) they believed their standards of efficiency were adhered to. Women at the regional branches were willing to be flexible with their rural suppliers but were often unwilling to compromise with their immediate male colleagues. In all, the experience of working together under the auspices of the commission gave mostly middle-class men and women the opportunity to experiment with various divisions of responsibility and authority outside the domestic setting.

The merger between the male-run commission and the female-run branches allowed a fruitful exchange of talents and leadership styles between women who effectively commanded the support of a dynamic grassroots constituency and men who sometimes underestimated them. The cooperative venture gave women at the commission branches a new consciousness of the power of women's combined efforts, the possibilities of enlisting the support and cooperation of men with access to political power, and the strength of a national organization. These were political skills generally attributed to men's functioning in the "public," yet women's work for the commission challenged the legitimacy of this arbitrary distinction. Young branch women did not simply pledge solitary allegiance to middle-class men and male prerogatives, as Ginzberg argues, nor did they limit themselves to making women's antebellum benevolence work more efficient in wartime. Instead of operating under the careful watch of the male members of their class, branch women developed their own distinct wartime agenda that guided their actions with their female constituency and their male colleagues. Branch women learned how to mobilize a diverse female constituency around a new concept of gender solidarity, one based on decreasing the social distance between women and men. This experience helped them rethink and reshape women's political culture, incorporating elements of the antebellum concept of difference while at the same time asserting their equal right to become involved in political decision making. Women working for the commission acted as equals with men and expected to be treated as such. Along the way, Schuyler, May, and their branch colleagues exhibited a nascent sense of themselves as professionals and an acceptance of their responsibility to speak for other women.

In 1863, Lou Schuyler and Abby May made significant changes to their operating procedures in response both to needs expressed by their constituency and to changes underway in the U.S. Army and the commission. In November 1862, the work of the WCAR registration committee had officially come to a close; the organization decided not to select, train, or appoint any more than the 125 women nurses they had already sent.[16] Although the issue of training women to be professional nurses remained on the minds of branch women and at times became a lightning-rod issue in debates about authority, branch women focused their energies on expanding and strengthening their system of centralized relief. By the end of 1862, the WCAR and the New England Women's Auxiliary Association (NEWAA) were joined by a branch in Chicago run by Mary Livermore and Jane Hoge and, early in 1863, by a branch in Philadelphia run by Maria Grier, a veteran of the USSC's hospital transport campaign, and Clara Moore.[17] Branch women met in Washington in November 1862 and decided to adopt a system of associate managers that May had developed in New England. The associate manager system gave branches the power to appoint regional liaisons in geographically significant towns (i.e., those with access to railroads and telegraphs, often corresponding to what branch women called "Centres of Collection"), allowing branch leaders to focus more on branch planning and management and less on canvassing towns and villages for support and supplies. May's associate manager system proved so effective that Olmsted asked May to draw up guidelines for the organization and operation of all commission branches and encouraged the commission itself to reorganize along similar lines. Changes within the women-run branches were paralleled by changes underway at the commission. In 1862, the USSC had successfully launched a campaign to overhaul the United States Army's Medical Department. In the fall, the commission's choice for Surgeon General, William Hammond, was appointed and commission doctors were employed as sanitary inspectors to report to Hammond about sanitary provisions at military camps and hospitals.[18]

In part, branch reorganization was a response to the growing demands of the administration of the work of hundreds of scattered soldiers aid societies. Branch women did not want to become so narrowly focused on the solicitation, processing, and distribution of supplies from their auxiliaries that they missed the opportunity to diversify the services they provided soldiers and their families. Because the women-run branches were located in major northern cities, for instance, their offices had become way stations for women visiting convalescent soldiers or searching for lost relatives. By 1863, some of the early recruits had completed their tours of duty and when sons, husbands, and brothers did not return home, family members went to look for them. Correspondence with Schuyler and May encouraged local women to come to branch women for help. Unfortunately, though an increasing number of distressed women came to the

WCAR's offices looking for missing soldiers, Schuyler regretted that "a busy day will not give us the spare half hour to cheer those who are anxious and despondent, or to listen to the story of 'how the battle was fought.'"[19] Other women, prevented by distance and limited means from visiting husbands or sons in hospitals in New York and Boston, wrote Schuyler and May asking if they would visit the men in their place. Schuyler recognized the situation as an opportunity to provide critical services to the women with whom the Woman's Central had built a relationship over the two years of war and their "soldier-relatives and friends lying sick within an hour from our doors."[20] Schuyler knew that helping women find lost relatives and visiting wounded soldiers in city hospitals required that she and her colleagues take on more work, but this did not deter her. As part of her reorganization proposal, Schuyler recommended that both the branches and the commission investigate how best to begin assisting the families of returned soldiers and those of soldiers who did not return.[21]

From the beginning, women at the branches adhered to exhausting work regimens that rivaled those of their male colleagues. For months after the commission received official recognition, commission executives met in long sessions to work out the details of the organization.[22] At the Woman's Central in New York, Lou Schuyler and her colleagues had established an arduous pace for themselves from the beginning. Schuyler worked long hours in the Woman's Central offices and always took work home with her, conducting much of her extensive correspondence in the evenings.[23] A postwar colleague once remarked that "[h]er favorite hours lay between 9 p.m. and 3 a.m.," when she had uninterrupted time at her desk to think.[24] Schuyler demanded a similar commitment from her colleagues. Writing to her assistant Angie Post during Post's vacation, Schuyler encouraged Post to rest and then added, only half in jest, "by the way (speaking of rest) did you take headed paper and envelopes with you, or shall I send them?"[25]

Schuyler's demanding schedule and high standards earned her the respect of her colleagues at the Woman's Central and at the commission. Even Strong, who was not easily impressed, remarked on Schuyler's work at the offices at the Cooper Union, where he noted that she carried "on a correspondence with some 1400 affiliated village societies, churches, clubs, and circles. The young lady works there from 10 a.m. till 3 or 4, and I should designate her as a *Brick and a half*, if it did'nt look irreverent."[26] Bloor was impressed that the Woman's Central refused to close when racial hostilities erupted in the New York City draft riots of July 1863, and he commended the women for their courage. "I would not have consented to close the office," Ellen Collins, WCAR Chair of the Committee on Supplies, dismissed his compliment, explaining that "[n]othing increases excitement so much as to have the respectable people lay aside their regular habits."[27]

At the Boston branch, Abby May held herself and her organization up to similar standards. May was particularly adept at conducting the meetings of the New England Women's Auxiliary Association and on other occasions "where gentlemen were present ... the beautiful blending of authority and courtesy with which she conducted [the meetings] impressed [the men] with wonder and respect."[28] And May inspired her colleagues with a demanding pace of work. Three months after the NEWAA offices opened, May recorded in her diary her first day of rest, "I stay away from the Sanitary today for the first time, for eleven weeks."[29] Many of the women she worked with at the auxiliary continued to recognize her authority well into the postwar years, calling her "'Chair' as long as she lived."[30]

Whereas Schuyler seemed to have an unlimited ability to take on more work for herself and her closest colleagues, May was more adept at delegating responsibility. Neither handled the rest that concerned friends and family members periodically forced on them very well, but Schuyler was at first reluctant to let others take care of many of the details of the work. The mounting responsibilities of coordinating the relief operations of the New England region convinced May to design a system of graduated responsibility early on. In the fall of 1862, May began appointing associate managers in significant towns throughout her region to carry on much of the canvassing work of the auxiliary.[31] May initially described the work of an associate manager briefly as "in a general way to stimulate workers in the immediate neighborhood of each manager, to answer the doubters, to communicate intelligence from Washington as to the needs and the working of the Commission, in short to do all that can be done to increase the amount of work done in New England."[32] In order to extend the reach of the Women's Auxiliary, May was willing to allow her associate managers to determine how best to involve their neighbors. This flexibility was consistent with May's and Schuyler's willingness to accept support from local soldiers aid societies in whatever form they were willing to give it. Over the next several months May refined this system, and even Schuyler began assigning many of the canvassing responsibilities to associate managers. The associate manager system freed May, Schuyler, and their branch colleagues to consider new venues and to devise new strategies for providing war relief, but the pace of the work at the branches did not slow.

By the end of 1862, when commission men and women had been working together for more than a year, routines at the branches and at the commission offices were beginning to take shape. Representatives from the commission branches met in Washington in November to compare notes with each other and to be briefed by various commission officers about the progress of the war and commission efforts to promote sanitation in the army. At this women's council meeting May and Schuyler met with Mary Livermore and Jane Hoge from Chicago and with women conducting similar work throughout the North and West.[33] Dorothea Dix attended the meeting, despite her increasing estrangement from the commission. This meeting represented a significant step in the process by which women's political culture was evolving from its local community focus to more large-scale organization and administration and a willingness to address national issues as women.

In Washington, the women compared the working arrangements of their respective branches, and they agreed to adopt May's system of associate managers to more effectively canvass their regions.[34] Olmsted asked May to lay out her organizational plans more explicitly so that the other branches might have a model to follow.[35] May drew up eight "Duties of an Associate Manager," detailing how she thought managers might best solicit the support of soldiers aid societies but carefully leaving many of the details to "our Associate, who can judge better than we can how best to produce the desired result in her own section."[36] With this delegation of authority, May, Schuyler, and other branch chairs invested the associate manager with vast discretionary powers to administer her region. More important, this new organizational structure allowed branch women to develop their program of relief and to plan for the future.

Despite the appearance of accord at this first meeting of the commission and its women-run branches, there was conflict between the two groups. The women came to the meeting confident in the success they had already experienced in their regions. They had already proved their organizational acumen at the local level. The Woman's Central boasted 1,153 cooperating soldiers aid societies (or auxiliaries) and the other branches had successfully tapped local resources, swelling branch inventories and treasuries and convincing branch leaders of the power of their combined efforts. Rural women invested branch women with their confidence and believed them to be agents of the United States government and, in return, branch women worked hard and were committed to sustaining and maintaining the autonomy of women's wartime relief work. The men had early on foreseen the difficulties of dealing with a popular reformer such as Dorothea Dix and an ambitious professional woman such as Elizabeth Blackwell; now they began to see that the younger women at the branches were also outspoken, articulate, and often unwilling to compromise branch prerogatives. They were even willing to debate the issue of women nurses, something the commission executive board had thought already settled.

Branch women were dissatisfied with the treatment of women nurses in the field and held the commission responsible for failing to support them. From women nurses in hospitals and camps, branch women heard accounts of obstructionist officers and hostile army surgeons.[37] To make matters worse, the new commission-selected Surgeon General, William Hammond, made his general disapproval of women nurses clear, and launched his attack on Dorothea Dix's position as superintendent of women nurses almost immediately after his appointment.[38] Though branch women appear to have made no official appeal to the commission or the army on behalf of mistreated nurses, at the women's council the issue resurfaced.[39] Hammond began a meeting on the subject as if the future of women nurses had already been decided, explaining that he did not approve of women in military hospitals and that surgeons were reluctant to employ women as nurses and complaining that women nurses asked too many questions and did not adapt well to military protocol.[40] Clearly Hammond intended to use the opportunity of the women's council to make his case against the U.S. Army's employment of women nurses.

Although Hammond had met with little resistance from the individual women nurses he had spurned at the front, the women at the meeting—including Dix, Schuyler, May, Maria C. Grier (president of the Women's Pennsylvania Branch), and Abby Hopper Gibbons (an outspoken Quaker abolitionist from New York)—spoke in support of women nurses and challenged his obstructionism.[41] They reminded him that Dix was empowered by the Secretary of War to appoint women nurses. Abby May spoke up first, but the most passionate defense of the work of women nurses came from Dix. Because of Dix's disagreements with the commission, she had developed a close working relationship with the renegade Western Sanitary Commission and had found there the kind of support for female nursing and for her own leadership that she did not find in the USSC. Not easily discouraged, however, Dix came to Washington and, heartened by May's refusal to accept Hammond's estimation of the unruliness of women nurses, she once again stated her case. Dix recounted the many insults she and nurses recruited by the Woman's Central had met at the hands of army surgeons. If women nurses were undisciplined, Dix explained, it was because she lacked the power necessary to oversee their work: Once they were assigned, they were in the hands of the army surgeons, who generally neglected them.[42] Dix contrasted Hammond's resistance to female nursing and her powerlessness in dealing with the Army of the Potomac with the respect and appreciation afforded her and her recruits in the West, implying that, as head of the United States Army's Medical Department, Hammond's negative opinion of women nurses authorized their mistreatment by army officials at all levels. Speaking for his fellow army and USSC doctors, Dr. John Foster Jenkins argued that physicians did not welcome women nurses into their hospitals because a number of women who had volunteered were "unfit" for the job, and he reiterated Hammond's concerns about their inadequate training and discipline.[43]

Until this point, the interchange had been primarily between Hammond, Jenkins, and Dix, but with this remark, the two doctors had insulted May, Grier, and Gibbons, who had all seen service in the commission's hospital transport campaign, had witnessed the army's disrespect first-hand, and did not take kindly to Jenkins's estimation of the incompetence of women nurses. Dix countered that very few women who had offered their services as nurses turned out to be unfit. Gibbons also criticized Hammond's generalizations; she and Grier both argued that insubordination was not endemic to female nursing.[44] Gibbons and Grier suggested that the meeting consider how to improve the discipline of the nursing corps instead of dismissing the matter entirely. Perhaps an order from the Surgeon General, suggested May, might improve Dix's position and make it easier for the superintendent to supervise women nurses.

Unimpressed by the commission's attempt to present the issue of female nursing as closed, the women delegates offered the new Surgeon General spirited resistance. Following the lead of Elizabeth Blackwell, young commission women had at first been ambivalent about Dix's leadership. Dix's style relied heavily on a traditional view of women's superior morality and her selfless commitment to the prevention of suffering—a style reminiscent of an older form of benevolence that did not fit well with the new generation's efforts to build a closer, more equitable working relationship between the women and men of the commission. But when faced with increased army resistance and the realization that the commission had no intention of doing anything further for women interested in becoming nurses, the delegates backed Dix and collectively expressed their disappointment that the commission had been unable (or unwilling) to do more for her and other women nurses. Moreover, Surgeon General Hammond's preference for an obedient nursing corps comprised of Catholic sisters and convalescent soldiers threatened to obscure the distinguished service of Protestant women nurses in the first two years of the war. Any difference of opinion the delegates had with Dix paled in comparison to their differences with Hammond and the commission over the abandonment of women nurses. Since April, Hammond had exercised virtually unchecked power in the United States Army's Medical Department and the commission. This was perhaps the first organized resistance he faced, and, ironically, it probably confirmed his prejudices against women nurses, whom he often said talked and wrote too much to be effective.

It is not surprising, then, that nothing came of Hammond's meeting with Dix and branch representatives in Washington on the issue of women nurses, for he had sought neither their input nor their approval. The council meeting nonetheless revealed that, although by definition the branches were subordinate to the central commission, when branch women differed with their commission counterparts over a critical issue, they used their authority and their positions to contradict male authority. The women understood that their command over branch resources put them in a position to shape commission policy. In her official report to the commission after the meeting, Schuyler wrote that, "to enable the Commission to carry out this entire system it must have supplies, and for these supplies it is dependent upon its Branches."[45] And as long as their supply work was supporting the government's war efforts, branch women believed they were as justified in offering advice to the government as were commission men.[46]

More important, however, the confrontation reveals branch women's growing sense of themselves as female professionals and an appreciation for the responsibilities of their leadership positions. As young branch leaders grew confident in their own abilities and in their professionalism, they saw themselves as spokeswomen for female professionals generally. Their interest in women nurses had little to do with their own urge to care for wounded men; few branch women distinguished themselves as nurses during the war.[47] Nor did their decision to confront Hammond appear to be a response to appeals made by individual nurses. For branch women and their generation, nursing represented a frontier, a point at which women's aspirations ran up against an arbitrary boundary constructed to keep women out of the professions. Their own proposal to organize local women's soldiers aid societies met with little resistance from the first generation of men to consider themselves professional reformers because it was grounded in the well-traveled terrain of women's local reform efforts. Women attempting to enter medicine as professionals, however, fell victim not only to the separate spheres ideology that restricted women's nursing work to the domestic setting but also to male doctors on the defensive after years of professional infighting.[48] The problem of women nurses reminded young branch women that their own professional authority could be compromised unless they remained critical of how commission men exercised theirs.

While the issue of women nurses allowed some branch women to begin to test the limits of their new-found sense of collective authority, others came to the women's council meeting with confidence in their individual professional qualifications and their ability to represent the interests of local women. Mary Livermore and Jane Hoge, for instance, had been caring for soldiers in Chicago and St. Louis and raising money and supplies for the Western Sanitary Commission since the beginning of the war when they came to Washington to meet with branch women and commission representatives.[49] Working for the Western Sanitary Commission, resented by the USSC as a renegade venture, had made Livermore and Hoge cautious about aligning their network of midwestern soldiers aid societies too closely with the other commission branches; however, the two were careful to negotiate a relationship that recognized them as experts on the "North West region."[50]

In charge of an effective regional supply network, Livermore and Hoge came to Washington ready to pledge their support to the commission but determined to do so on their own terms. In return for the support of the two women, the commission agreed that Livermore and Hoge would organize their branch along whatever lines they believed best. This arrangement recognized their authority to command the resources of their region, but it also recognized their unique domestic situations. Both Livermore and Hoge were married and had households to look after, and neither had the financial means to commit themselves to the work like Schuyler and May. In fact, when they were invited to Washington for the women's council, Livermore and Hoge hesitated due to "almost insuperable obstacles of a domestic character."[51] And as they met with branch women from Boston and New York, Hoge and Livermore began to understand that they could not maintain work regimens similar to their branch counterparts without making arrangements for the care of their children and for their housekeeping. A Chicago colleague explained their situation to Olmsted as a characteristic of "our new Western cities." "We have not as with you men of retired wealth but of business capacity whose principles or sympathies impel them to engage in such enterprizes [sic]," he explained, "nor have we ladies of wealth who can afford to leave home duties and give their time to such purposes."[52] The two apparently presented their predicament to the commission during their Washington visit, for by the time they returned, they had come to an agreement with Olmsted. At the beginning of December, Livermore and Hoge began drawing a monthly salary that allowed them to hire domestic help to take their place at home while they worked at the Chicago branch offices.[53]

Once branch women became paid professionals, women's political culture had taken a very important step away from its antebellum dependence on the strictly voluntary labor of middle-class women. The commission's decision to pay women to run the Chicago branch is significant. Although some women may have been insulted by the suggestion that they be paid for their work, Livermore and Hoge were unequivocal about their financial needs and about the valuable work they could provide if comfortably compensated. When the commission was late in sending their salaries, for instance, Livermore addressed Olmsted directly, pointing out that the commission's delay "subjects us to some inconvenience."[54]

Livermore's frankness about her need for a salary stands in contrast to Amy Morris Bradley's experience in the Virginia peninsula in 1862. Like Livermore and Hoge, Bradley came from modest middle-class means, and like so many other unmarried northern women, she supported herself by teaching and relying on the beneficence of friends and family members.[55] Bradley served on USSC hospital transports throughout the peninsula campaign, where she faced some of the most gruesome scenes of the war. When a doctor Bradley was working with asked her why she did not draw the salary of a contract nurse, she was indignant. "To think that I poor, Amy Bradley, would come out here to work for money," she wrote her sister of her indignation. "[H]e got my opinion of him and a good many other things in very plain terms, I can assure you."[56] Yet Bradley was always struggling to support herself, and in the last year of the war, she accepted an individually arranged salary from the commission for the work she was doing with convalescent soldiers.[57]

Perhaps initially Bradley was willing to overlook the reality of her financial needs in a way that married women with children to look after could not.[58] Instead of admitting that she could use the money, Bradley was bound by Victorian notions of middle-class femininity that excluded women who worked for wages and those whose work outside the home was not merely an expression of their domesticity. Whatever her reason, the issue of working for pay that branch women raised would be an important one in the years following the war. The war effort made this a clear issue as activist women struggled to redefine the relationship of women to their society.

These were precisely the issues that Blackwell had foreseen in the formative days of the Woman's Central Association of Relief. In her original plans to develop a rigorous selection and training program for women interested in becoming nurses, Blackwell had insisted on securing a respectable wage for her trainees as recognition of their mastery of a level of medical training—an argument not unlike the one made by the commission for paying its members.[59] Blackwell's preference for paying women for their nursing work, like her resistance to the army's choice of Dix as superintendent of women nurses, reflected her commitment to medical professionalism for women and men, doctors and nurses, alike. Initial Woman's Central plans stated that Blackwell's registration committee would consider women of any class and background: "[M]any may be rich and many poor. Some may wish to go at their own charges, and others will require to be aided as to their expenses, and still others, for the loss of their time."[60] For the first three months, Blackwell paid her nurses out of the Woman's Central treasury.[61] After that, the army began paying women nurses forty cents a day plus rations, a rate that compelled Blackwell to suspend the work of the registration committee two months later because these "poor wages" contributed to the overall low esteem under which women nurses were held.[62]

Perhaps Blackwell also perceived a link between a class-specific femininity and the exclusion of all women from the professions—a situation that Bradley's predicament could attest to. The salary of nurses working under the auspices of the Woman's Central and the Sanitary Commission remained largely token, ensuring that, in the end, Dix's preference for middle- and upper-class volunteers prevailed, women who could afford to support themselves and who could turn their salaries into food and supplies for the men.[63] For women such as Amy Bradley, "the paltry sum of twelve dollars a month and rations," as she referred to it, was not enough to risk her reputation on, nor, as Blackwell saw it, was it enough to guarantee women nurses status as medical professionals.[64]

Where Blackwell was unable to obtain adequate sustenance and status for women nurses, women at the branches enjoyed more success.

The work of war relief required that branch women secure the best person for the job and then make whatever arrangements necessary to retain her. When May faced the possibility of losing one of her associate managers due to financial considerations, for instance, she arranged for the woman to be paid out of the treasury of the New England Women's Auxiliary Association.[65]

Behind the image of an organization espousing a middle-class division of labor which dictated that men were paid for their work and women were not, a few notable exceptions were made. The ideology of separate spheres specified that only men inhabited both the public and private spheres, and the commission ideal sought to preserve this separation. The real experiences of branch women, however, challenged the hegemony of this nineteenth-century gender ideology and threatened to implicate commission men in the process. It was, after all, Frederick Law Olmsted of the commission who brokered Livermore and Hoge's salary. Perhaps the reality of working with these professional women motivated commission men to consciously construct the organization's image in the traditional gendered terms of the commission seal's ministering angel, for they surely recognized the contradiction between their own rhetoric and reality.

Women who worked at and for commission branches put in long days at the office and considered their work there distinct from their lives at home. Livermore described her workday in the nineteenth-century language of separate spheres, yet, significantly, she saw herself as residing in both. After working until six or seven every evening, Livermore hailed a streetcar and began to unwind:

> It is as if I had left the world for a time, to refresh myself in a suburb of heaven. And only by a mental effort do I shut out the scenes I have left, and drop back for a time into my normal life—the life of a wife, mother and housekeeper. I try to forget the narratives of gunshot wounds, sabre strokes, battle and death, that have rained on me all day. This hour with my husband and children shall not be saddened.[66]

By separating their commission commitments from their family concerns, women at the branches entered "the world" of professional work, and, like skilled professionals, some negotiated to have their time compensated for. When they returned home, they resumed their former positions within their families and tried to forget the war they had left behind in the office.⁶⁷ The separate spheres ideology indicated that only men had the ability to separate work from home; now branch women sought a similar division in their lives.

After the Washington meeting, branch representatives returned to their fields with renewed energy. May finalized her recommendations for branch organization and stepped up her recruiting of associate managers in New England. In Philadelphia, Maria Grier became president of the Women's Pennsylvania Branch and Clara Moore became corresponding secretary.⁶⁸ In New York, Schuyler returned to her work with characteristic energy. In December she wrote Olmsted, "[M]y aim would be to have a Soldier's Aid Society tributary to the Commission in every town and village." With some of her canvassing responsibilities to be delegated to her regional associate managers, Schuyler spent several weeks paying personal visits to her many colleagues throughout the Woman's Central region. "I came home feeling the necessity of a much more thorough organization throughout our field and among our auxiliaries," she explained to Olmsted.⁶⁹ In January, the Woman's Central committee of correspondence and supply committee sent a survey out to more than 1,500 northern women, asking them about local sentiment, supply efforts, and knowledge of the Sanitary Commission.⁷⁰ From the returns, Schuyler and her associates learned of economic hard times and of the many shortages on the home front and that women everywhere wanted more frequent and regular news and information from the commission and the branches.⁷¹

In response to women's concerns, Schuyler took a number of steps to enhance the organizational and administrative system. In order to improve lines of communication, Schuyler sent Mary Hamilton to the central offices in Washington to act as Schuyler's "eyes and ears," passing along information to the branches directly instead of relying on commission sources.⁷² In addition to appointing associate managers to improve communication in the countryside, the Woman's Central arranged to have male lecturers tour the region under commission contract and branch oversight. May's Women's Auxiliary followed suit.⁷³ Significantly, Schuyler stipulated that lecturers were not to collect money for the commission, adding that "a collection should only be taken up by him for the benefit of the S[oldiers] A[id] Society of the place in which he speaks, should the managers request it. This keeps the money in the country to be expended in materials."[74] This arrangement reinforced the branch preference for respecting local autonomy; lecturers were explicitly instructed not to collect money for the commission treasury. The arrangement also began to answer local women's demands for more and direct news about commission operations.

After touring and surveying the Woman's Central region, Schuyler became convinced that the commission needed to develop its own regular publication. In her report to the commission of the survey results, Schuyler noted that "the printed matter issued by the Commission is received with the greatest interest." Circulars sent to the auxiliaries from the branches were "read aloud at the meetings, passed from house to house, and . . . generally read from the pulpit."[75] Schuyler's impressions about the needs of the "country people" for information persisted, and in September 1863, she approached Bellows with an idea for a commission publication. As Schuyler saw it, the journal ought to be a mixture of first-hand accounts from commissioners on the battlefield and in the hospitals, summaries of branch activities, and practical instruction to the families of discharged soldiers on such matters as how to apply for pensions and how to look after the health and comfort of invalid soldiers.[76] Schuyler recommended that the commission "invite contributions in prose and verse from the whole country" and intended the publication to be "a paper *of* the people and *for* the people." If they were successful at this publishing venture, the paper would circulate throughout the countryside, reaching urban and rural women alike through well-established reform networks. Reaching the home front with a consistent flow of reliable and useful information would allow the commission and its branches to "[m]erge the domestic interests of the people in the army."[77]

As inspired as Schuyler's proposal was, the first two issues of *The Sanitary Commission Bulletin* published in November contained little of what she thought her constituency wanted and much technical information about the commission bureaucracy. Later issues, however, reprinted selections from Florence Nightingale's popular *Notes on Nursing;* gave detailed information about obtaining pensions, furloughs, and back pay; and included patterns and instructions for sewing hospital clothing for wounded soldiers.[78] Accounts of sanitary fairs were mixed with letters from soldiers and from women on the home front. Though members of the commission executive board were the most regular *Bulletin* contributors, some issues contained contributions from the publication's broader readership. These contributions tried to speak directly to the experiences of Schuyler's "truest patriots," the women and men in the countryside. Mary Livermore, for instance, wrote a series of articles about the sacrifices of poor women from the West—farmers' wives and daughters who worked hard in the fields, seamstresses who gave their wages to the Chicago branch, and schoolgirls who scoured their villages for contributions.[79] At first the *Bulletin* included only sporadic notices from the branches, and the WCAR, for one, was unsatisfied with these arrangements. When Ellen Collins reminded the editors that the branches considered the paper "our organ" and as such expected that it should contain regular contributions from the branches, the editors invited the WCAR to contribute a regular column and eventually began soliciting input from the other branches as well.[80]

Although it never became the lively "paper of the people" that Schuyler envisioned, the *Bulletin* enjoyed a generous circulation and a wide, largely female readership. As Schuyler had anticipated, "the country people" read the *Bulletin* "with greater interest and intensity" than those "in the large cities."[81] Women read the journal aloud at local soldiers aid society meetings, except when "the nature of the work, or the noise of the sewing machines, prevents reading aloud."[82] Other societies circulated publications among their neighbors and associates who read them with intense interest. One local woman noted that a popular commission publication written by Georgeanna Woolsey, a nurse-veteran who served in a number of campaigns, was returned to her "at the end of the month . . . literally worn out."[83] Schuyler encouraged her constituents to share the *Bulletin* in the same manner, helping to ensure that the actual circulation of the publication exceeded the number of copies printed.[84] This broad circulation suggests that the journal reached women who might otherwise not have had access to Nightingale's work and other works popular among the urban middle class.

Branch women also sought ways to restructure the financing of their networks of local aid societies. Schuyler and May explored ways of shifting the financial burdens—buying material and arranging for freight, for instance—of the country auxiliaries onto the branches and their urban constituency. Because the branches preferred to provide the commission with homemade food and uniforms, Schuyler agreed to help remote affiliates pay freight, and she began to be won over to May's decision to use branch funds to buy material in bulk and to pass the savings on to rural auxiliaries.[85] These financial arrangements responded to the needs branch women had identified on the northern home front and to their commitment to help families and communities in addition to Union soldiers.

And starting with Chicago in the fall of 1863, the branches began holding sanitary fairs in major cities where they raised large amounts of money to help support rural auxiliaries.[86] Like the *Bulletin*, the flurry of sanitary fairs held in 1863–1864 were branch initiatives that caused some friction between branch women and commission men. Borrowing from the nineteenth-century charity bazaar and anti-slavery fair, sanitary fairs featured sales of locally made items and a variety of entertainment, including musical concerts and meals elaborately prepared and served by local women. Livermore and Hoge planned the first sanitary fair at the Northwestern Branch in Chicago in October 1863. Planning a two-week-long event was an enormous undertaking and promised to bring in substantial proceeds, so Livermore and Hoge were surprised at the commission's resistance to the proposal.[87] As a traditional form of local benevolence, the fairs were specifically intended to appeal to local sentiment; in this regard they were antithetical to the commission's commitment to the federal principle. The commission treasurer, George Strong, railed against the fairs in the *Bulletin*, noting that "large sums thus raised have been received by the branches" but that the benefit to the commission was only indirect. Branches used the money to buy material for their affiliates to make up clothing and other supplies and had "not as yet contributed a dollar to [the commission] treasury," he complained.[88] Indeed, the Chicago branch raised an impressive $80,000 at the fair, a success that inspired other branches to stage similar events.[89] In Boston in December, May and her colleagues planned a fair despite continued commission resistance. Annie Endicott, one of the Boston Sanitary Fair organizers, complained to May: "I cannot refrain from expressing my regret at the uniform course of the Executive with regard to the Fair—throwing—as it constantly has—discouragements in the way of conscientious workers in the great cause."[90]

Despite commission reluctance, the women persisted.[91] Alone among commission executives, Bloor supported the fair efforts of the branches and encouraged the women to invite colleagues at their sister branches to join in the festivities.[92] Bloor predicted that the events would help the branches broaden their constituency to include those who were skeptical of the commission's urban leadership and secular message. To May, he confided that he wished "these fairs all over the country may prove Sanitary revivals" and that they might appeal to those "[who] have a very particular predilection to [revivals]."[93] According to the commission, not only were the fair initiatives unacceptable acts of local autonomy, allowing women to use their commission affiliation to enrich their local treasuries, but the rest of the commission executives believed that encouraging such emotionalism was reckless and counterproductive to their vision of women acting under their own temperate paternal guidance.[94]

Women's accounts of the fairs attest to a growing sense of pride in the success of individual branches and an appreciation for the autonomy of women's work and local political culture. A shared interest in a traditional type of women's community activism connected branch women to each other and to the fairs. In the antebellum period, women used fairs and bazaars to support local ministers, anti-slavery activism, and community welfare networks. During the war, branch women used fairs as a way to mobilize local interest. Branch women traveled from fair to fair to support their friends and co-workers at the other branches and to strengthen the ties that bound them together in their work.

Unlike the *Bulletin*, the sanitary fairs were independent branch (and local auxiliary) ventures run almost exclusively by women.[95] Branch women did not worry that these renegade ventures violated commission men's ideas about centralization, for the fairs were consistent with their own priority of helping women help their communities. Comfortable in their leadership roles and in their independence from commission authority, women planned elaborate, long-running exhibits that were both lucrative and entertaining and that renewed people's interest in a war that had gone on much longer than anticipated. The vast sums of money raised at the fairs ensured that, despite disagreements, the commission would remain dependent on the branches as the main source of income.[96] Even Bellows, who had complained loudly and often about the fairs, reluctantly acknowledged in the final issue of the *Bulletin* that the commission was "chiefly indebted to the money created by the Fairs, which American women inaugurated and conducted."[97]

After the success of the sanitary fairs, branch women were more secure than ever in their positions of authority. As branch leaders, they supported—and were supported by—an expansive network of women workers, directed the relief efforts of their soldiers aid societies, and influenced the policy of a national relief operation. When individual commission men overlooked branch autonomy or attempted to challenge the authority of branch directors, they were reminded that the branches had well-developed protocols and chains of command; branch chairs were unwilling to compromise these prerogatives to yield to the whims of the commission.

WILLIAM HADLEY, a commission lecturer, learned this lesson when he interfered with the inner workings of the New England Women's Auxiliary Association on one of his tours through northern New England. The NEWAA arranged to have Hadley speak to audiences in New England about the status of commission operations. Because Hadley had already worked for Schuyler at the Woman's Central, he had surely been instructed to defer to the authority of the associate managers, as Schuyler had been careful to point out in her original arrangements.[98] Apparently he misunderstood the limits of his position, however, and proceeded to give instruction to NEWAA associate managers in Maine. When several of May's associate managers complained, May recognized Hadley's breach of authority and reminded him that he had not been instructed to do other than lecture and canvass for supplies. This was apparently not his first reprimand from May, for an obviously frustrated Hadley responded: "I might make apologies, but they would be useless. This is not my first offence [*sic*]." Recalling previous mistakes, Hadley's frustration turned to anger: "I have most conscientiously desired to *please* as well as serve the 'New England Women.' I have not succeeded, and feel no heart to try any more. I will, at least, endeavor to let their affairs alone."[99] Hadley claimed that he could no longer work for May as commission lecturer and tendered his resignation, adding curtly, "I have men to serve whom I can please, and to them I will hold myself responsible."[100]

Hadley's fit of pique seems misplaced, but in her reply May showed the poise and reserve of a seasoned administrator. May chose to ignore Hadley's hasty resignation and calmly explained her position to the lecturer by placing him in her shoes:

> If you had established business or other relations with a number of people, two years and more ago; and change was now proposed, I think you would feel that *you* were the one to effect the change with them, and not a third party, coming in between you and your friends, however interested he might be. Am I mistaken in this?[101]

But she also documented the incident, writing to Frederick Knapp, the commissioner ultimately in charge of lecturers, enclosing copies of the letters she had exchanged with Hadley. May regretted having bothered Knapp with the entire unfortunate affair, but, she admitted, she saw "no way to avoid it, under the circumstances."[102]

Recognizing that Hadley's bungling of his lecture contract threatened to compromise May's credibility in her region, Knapp responded swiftly. Knapp was "surprised and disturbed" at Hadley's letters to May and at how Hadley had dealt with her associate managers: "[T]here was a want of the courtesy, which as ladies they have a right to claim, and which as faithful laborers they have a right to expect that the Officers of the Commission will demand of all persons connected with our work who have occasion to refer to them."[103] Knapp also decided to ignore Hadley's impulsive and emotional retreat from service and explained in precise terms that, in the future, he expected Hadley to respect May's authority. One month later, however, when May reported that Hadley's "insolence to our Associates and, in a back handed fashion, ourselves" continued, the commission removed him.[104]

This brief incident gives some indication of the authority and respect May had come to command from the women at affiliated soldiers aid societies and from her commission colleagues. For three years, May worked diligently to find and appoint experienced women as associate managers and to establish trust with remote New England towns that were skeptical about the commission and suspicious of its urban leadership.[105] May learned early on that the commitment of her local affiliates to the commission was entirely dependent on their confidence in her leadership abilities and her respect for their autonomy. Once she convinced local soldiers aid societies to send their supplies and their support to the Women's Auxiliary, May and her branch colleagues had to strike a balance between catering to local needs and seeing to it that the Boston storehouse remained stocked. When Hadley, whom May invited to New England to help extend the influence of the NEWAA, strong-armed her associate managers and refused to recognize her authority over him, she responded professionally and decidedly. And recognizing that they stood to lose more by upsetting May and her colleagues at the NEWAA than by dismissing an agent with an inflated ego, the commission supported May unequivocally. Though Knapp referred to May and her colleagues as *both* "ladies" and "faithful laborers"—by definition, middle-class Victorian "ladies" were not "laborers"—he clearly believed that May's professional handling of the affair stood in contrast to Hadley's lack of professionalism.

Schuyler had a similar experience at the WCAR a few months later. In 1864, the commission dismissed Alfred Bloor, the USSC's liaison to the branches. For three years branch women had worked with Bloor amicably and had communicated with him about many things, including the planning of sanitary fairs and the content of the *Bulletin*. Although there were times when either Bloor or Schuyler thought it appropriate to remind the other of branch or commission protocol, Bloor worked well with the women at the branches.[106] A short time after Joseph Parrish took over for Bloor, he stumbled into a confrontation with Schuyler. In the first *Bulletin* published under his direction, Parrish asked associate managers to "call councils of their co-laborers" to renew the efforts to collect supplies from soldiers aid societies.[107] By all accounts, this was the first attempt made by a commissioner to direct the work of associate managers, and this affront to branch autonomy must have caught Schuyler by surprise. Two issues later, Parrish instructed associate managers to conduct a survey of their affiliated societies and forward the responses on to the branches.[108] In neither incident did Parrish make any effort to discuss his intentions with Schuyler, May, or any other branch director, and he seemed to be under the impression that his position as commission liaison to the branches gave him the authority to administer their work.

Although Schuyler might have been able to overlook Parrish's first breach of authority, she could not overlook the second. After meeting with her WCAR colleagues, Schuyler decided that Parrish's oversight could be addressed by "a personal interview and explanation" whenever such a meeting could be conveniently arranged.[109] Schuyler sent Parrish word that there were a number of issues she needed to discuss with him when he next visited New York. Before such a meeting took place, however, a new issue of the *Bulletin* reached Schuyler, containing the WCAR's semi-annual report. When Schuyler and her colleagues examined the report, they realized that Parrish had edited it without their consent.[110]

Parrish's careless disregard for Schuyler's authority and the autonomy of the branches had to be addressed before further incidents permanently undercut the work of the Woman's Central and threatened WCAR credibility among its constituency. This "was deliberate murder by our friend the Dr.," Schuyler wrote angrily to her assistant, Angie Post. "[S]hould we come to swords' points what a chance he will have of annoying me, by altering, cutting out [etc.] those same wonderful articles."[111] The preparation of annual and semi-annual reports was very involved, and it was tedious work that Schuyler dreaded. Seeing the results of her efforts handled so carelessly must have been very frustrating. Like May, however, Schuyler was determined to handle the matter in the most direct and professional manner she knew how.

On the same afternoon that Schuyler wrote angrily to Post, she wrote a long letter to Parrish, carefully tracing the history of cooperation between the Woman's Central and the commission. Assuming that because Parrish was new to the work and was simply misinformed, Schuyler was diplomatic but direct. She explained how Woman's Central resolutions had made it a fully independent branch of the commission and how the two organizations had cooperated through Bloor with a great deal of mutual success. When Schuyler broached the subject of associate managers and Parrish's indiscretions, however, she became more explicit. "I don't think you have any right to give any instructions to our Associate Managers," she explained, "it is a question of *authority*, which is involved ... my dear Dr."[112] As was the case in May's confrontation with Hadley, a commissioner had trod carelessly on the agreement between the women-run branches and their associate managers, and a branch woman moved swiftly and decidedly to correct the situation. Schuyler wanted Parrish to understand branch protocol and to appreciate and respect branch independence, but she also wanted to make it clear that, when it came to dealing with the Woman's Central and its well-organized female constituency, Parrish and his commission colleagues deferred to her. "After reposing sufficient confidence in the Branches to grant them certain powers," she explained, "[the commission] should be willing to trust them and allow them to carry out their own plans, believing that the Branches must best understand the people with whom they are in daily correspondence."[113]

Both incidents attest to branch women's sense of independence and professionalism and their commitment to the autonomy of women's war relief. They handled these conflicts with the composure and detachment of professionals. Schuyler, May, and their colleagues were becoming comfortable with the authority that came with administering a nationwide relief agency, and they understood that they needed to be vigilant about encroachments on that authority.

Branch women were part of an extended women's community, one that respected the value of women's work and that was built on a long tradition of women's community activism. Choosing to work within the confines of the male-run commission did not require young women to give up the values of that community, but they did have to manipulate a bureaucracy and learn how to manage male egos. By negotiating for salaries that recognized the value of their work, questioning government officials about their policies, fighting for improved conditions for women nurses, and responding to the indiscretions of their male colleagues cordially but professionally, these young women were learning to work with men and the male political process on terms that approached equality. In so doing, they were playing an integral role in the evolution of women's political and work culture.

Although branch women did not question the existence of separate spheres, they challenged men's exclusive right to exist in both. Young branch women did not demand entrance into the public sphere as "ladies" but as colleagues. In this way, they began to decrease the social distance between the men and women of the commission. In the process, they challenged Victorian society's resistance to women professionals and, with it, the conventional wisdom that women's work was impulsive and erratic, and hence in need of prudent male oversight. In fact, though he had much to gain from maintaining the fiction of commission women as self-sacrificing and disorderly domestic angels and worked hard to sustain it, even Henry Bellows could not help admitting that women's branch work exhibited "all the regularity of paid labor."[114] Branch women did not consider themselves to be ministering angels, as the commission seal would have the public believe. The actions of individual women such as Schuyler, May, Livermore, and Hoge threatened to upset the official image of the commission as an organization run by the selfless voluntary efforts of middle-class women and to perhaps reveal the real intentions of commission men who stood to lose the most from allowing the public to see beyond the myth.

V

"True Grit"

WOMEN AT THE FRONT

Nothing could have prepared Harriet Whetten to receive the Union prisoners of war who came aboard the *Spaulding* that night in July. The men released from Libby Prison in Richmond, Virginia, "were in a wretched condition," Whetten recalled, "their wounds full of maggots, their clothes full of vermin and nearly starved."[1] Though they had followed the progress of the war in their local newspapers before they left home, the women who volunteered to staff a fleet of river steamers in the summer of 1862 were shocked at the condition of the soldiers who were brought on board. Day after day, transport women treated soldiers who were abandoned in the malarial swamps of the Virginia peninsula and others who had lain on the battlefield for days without food or water in the unrelenting southern sun. "Mrs. John" Harris described the wounded that had lain on the battlefield for a week, "one dying of lock jaw, another of internal hemorrhage, and one raving in madness with the brain slowly oozing from his death wound."[2] Once the men were brought on board, the work of separating those who could be saved and those who could not began.

Often the sights below deck were worse than those on shore. Harris recorded the "fearful sights" she witnessed on her boat after a day "spent in operating." "In one pile," she estimated, "lay seventeen arms, hands, feet, and legs."[3] Harris saw the losses as not only an individual soldier's but his family's, too. "The loss of a strong arm or leg," she ght, "is a mother's loss," and each death reminded her of the "orphaned children and stricken widow" at home.[4] Committed to providing triage aboard boats filled with wounded and sick men, Whetten and her colleagues knew little of what went on on the battlefield. They saw only the enormous human costs.

Despite the horror, transport women managed to work effectively as informal triage nurses throughout the spring and summer of 1862. The hospital transport campaign began in April 1862, when General McClellan launched his offensive against the Confederate capital of Richmond, Virginia.[5] Using a team of government-owned river steamers, for three months the commission operated a primitive ambulance system, removing wounded and sick soldiers from the Virginia peninsula and transporting them to northern hospitals for treatment. Much of the work involved providing for soldiers who had been left behind on the battlefield as the fighting and armies moved elsewhere, finding them food and shelter, and making them as comfortable as possible until removal could be arranged. The commission intended to ensure "that every man had a good place to sleep in, and something hot to eat daily, and that the sickest had every essential that could have been given them in their own homes."[6]

Providing ambulance service during the peninsula campaign presented itself not only as a chance for the United States Sanitary Commission (USSC) men to serve the U.S. Army by providing direct relief to wounded soldiers but also as a unique opportunity to promote the organization. By stepping in to help the U.S. Army as it went further into the South, the commission proved once again that it was prepared to take on any new challenge the war presented and that commission men were organizational experts whose contributions were integral to the success of the Union war effort. Yet the commission's decision to appoint women nurses to serve on the boats was a departure from policy. Though Dr. Elizabeth Blackwell's original Woman's Central Association of Relief (WCAR) proposal was based on her plan to recruit, train, and assign a corps of trained women nurses, when commission men took the proposal to Washington, they largely abandoned the issue of nurses. At the time, establishing a secure position for nurses was tangential to the plans of Bellows and his fellow commissioners for social resurrection. In the face of continued army resistance to allowing women on the battlefield and in the field hospitals, any commitment to organizing a corps of female nurses had all but disappeared.

For Frederick Law Olmsted, the architect of the USSC's hospital transport campaign, however, employing women as nurses in the summer of 1862 presented itself as an opportunity that he could not pass up. Placing women on commission-operated vessels allowed Olmsted to tap into the domestic rhetoric of the middle-class home, a strategy that had worked well to garner support for his work on Central Park. In order to promote the park in 1857, Olmsted and his New York supporters likened public parks to the separate sphere of the middle-class home and promised to recreate the healing environment of that home in the public park, making it a place where working-class New Yorkers could relax and benefit from the polite company of the middle class and the elite.[7] Convinced of the ameliorative powers of the middle-class home, Olmsted saw his hospital transport campaign as an experiment in bringing the home to the battlefield.[8] Inviting women to nurse on the boats allowed the commission to portray these floating hospitals as homes away from home, where wounded and ill soldiers—like overworked workers in the city—could retreat and regain their health.

With this in mind, then, gender relations were conceived along middle-class lines in the campaign: Men were to negotiate with military authorities to plan the collection and transportation of the wounded while women were to ready the beds for the wounded and staff the kitchens.[9] Olmsted reassured female recruits that nurses on commission transports would have to answer only to male commissioners, not to the U.S. Army. The position of women nurses would be secure aboard commission transports, and middle-class and elite women would be shielded from the army's rough handling, much like the park visitors were spared the conflicts of the city. The domestic metaphor accurately reflected middle-class antebellum ideas of proper gender roles, and both men and women in the commission (albeit with different motives) began the hospital transport campaign expecting to replicate prewar gender relations on the boats.

The real experience working in battlefield triage, however, turned out to be something entirely different. Instead, women who came to

care for soldiers on the Virginia peninsula confronted scenes of profound suffering such as Whetten and Harris described that reminded
them they were far from home. The middle-class and elite women
who volunteered to staff these floating hospitals were, by all accounts,
women who ought to have deferred most readily to the domestic rhetoric, not to mention to the commission's chain of command. For transport women, however, authentic battlefield experience, much like the
cooperation between the USSC and its women-run branches, further
subverted the ideology of separate spheres and revealed the superfici-
ality of commission rhetoric celebrating women's domesticity. Faced
with wide-scale suffering that far exceeded their experience caring for
the ill in the domestic setting, transport volunteers fashioned new
standards of behavior for themselves and set their own standards of
care for the wounded soldiers.

In fact, the transport experiment validated military resistance to
having middle-class women serve as U.S. Army nurses on the grounds
that they were resistant to discipline and did not adapt well to military
protocol. Despite the commission's plans and the initial expectations
of women volunteers, transport women developed an alternative
agenda that was centered on providing immediate relief to suffering
soldiers. Transport women were torn between their own commitment
to caring for soldiers as individuals and the army's (and, at times, the
commission's) resistance to this kind of individualized care. They occasionally operated as if in an independent command structure, one
that rewarded creative solutions to the problems they faced daily
rather than obedience to military discipline and that made careful note
of individual wartime sacrifice. Under the rigors of hospital service,
women volunteers found the older notions of middle-class femininity
impossible to adhere to and inadequate to their tasks. After it became
clear that the volunteers would have to violate gender conventions,
they manipulated the domestic metaphor of campaign planners to jus-
tify their presence: If the boats were intended to be replicas of the
middle-class home, then women of their social stature not only be-
longed aboard but could make independent decisions about the well-
being of the wounded. Transport women made opportunistic use of
the gender constructs implicit in middle-class domesticity, discarding
the limits of class and gender one day and wielding them like a
weapon in the name of humanitarian expediency the next.

WITH the goal of bringing the healing powers of the middle-class home to the battlefield, Olmsted enlisted the aid of middle-class and elite women in his plans from the beginning. He approached Eliza Woolsey Howland and her sister Georgeanna (Georgy) Woolsey, both of New York City, about serving as nurse superintendents even before the government had approved his request for boats. And until hospital transports were attacked by Confederate snipers in July 1862, no one in the commission administration seriously questioned the need for women on the boats. One transport woman noted that boats were regularly prepared for duty by loading them with "everything necessary, including two ladies, two surgeons and blankets."[10]

Commission arguments for women's participation in the war effort rested on assumptions about women's aptitude in caring for others. In part, these assumptions reflected antebellum reality: Most of the ill and injured in prewar America were cared for by women in their homes and not in hospitals, which were considered asylums for the destitute and incurable. Women's healing expertise was acknowledged in the commission's *Manual of Directions*, a pamphlet containing simple recipes and instructions for preparing home remedies such as baths, sedatives, and stimulants; a newspaper editorial about the commission's hospital transport campaign remarked, "Whitewash and women on a hospital ship are both excellent disinfectants."[11] The Union Army recognized Florence Nightingale's work for the British Army in the Crimea and circulated her instructions to women interested in nursing.[12] The commission's use of prevailing gender ideology, however, reached its most rapturous height when describing not real women but the ideal Woman. In one commission publication, for instance, the author imagined a fictional conversation between Nightingale (who represented commission women) and a wounded soldier: "'Man,' said this brave true woman, 'where I am is "Home"; I bring with me its comforts and its care to the battle-field and camp, and all a mother's love shall tend your aching brow and stanch the oozing blood.' Thus an angel came and ministered unto him."[13] Though providing nurses for service on the battlefield was never the primary purpose of the organization, commission leaders found images of ministering angels particularly potent, especially because they contrasted so starkly with scenes of wartime suffering.

The commission's use of conventions of womanhood and its reference to women's real-life experiences as nurturers of the sick is not, perhaps, surprising. Olmsted, for instance, accounted for the general ill health of the U.S. Army when he estimated that "of this hundred thousand men, I suppose that not ten thousand were ever entirely without a mother's, sister's, or a wife's domestic care before."[14] What is remarkable, however, is that the commission, in emphasizing women's special skills and knowledge, painted a corresponding picture of male ineptitude. Edward Jarvis, a commission doctor from Boston, for example, criticized the army for leaving men to fend for themselves: "He who has never arranged, cared for, or cooked his own or any other food, who has never washed, mended, or swept is expected to understand and required to do these for himself or suffer the consequences of neglect."[15] Comments like Jarvis's contain an admission of women's control over men's health and well-being. Historians have noted how antebellum women's talents were often recognized in the breach—such as when widowers were suddenly left to care for a full household alone. Jarvis went beyond an admission that women contributed to domestic tranquillity, however, when he claimed men could neither perform nor "understand" women's traditional work in the home. By implication, then, inviting women to join this campaign put women's domestic powers at the disposal of the USSC transport crew and of the wounded soldiers for whom they cared.

The commission's reference to the middle-class ideology of womanhood attracted an unusual number of well-connected middle-class and elite women to the hospital transport campaign. These women were precisely the sort of volunteers that Blackwell would have resolutely turned away. Often, these self-described "ladies" were women of the urban bourgeoisie who had not distinguished themselves outside circumscribed social circles and had not been active in branch women's work to collect and distribute supplies; many of them had not even expressed an interest in undergoing the brief nurse training program Blackwell had conducted. The women, an article in the *Bulletin* reported, "belong nearly all to the most wealthy or most respectable families."[16] Louisa Lee Schuyler, for one, complained that women of this sort were notoriously fickle with their support of the commission.[17] For them, the day-to-day business of supporting the soldiers and their families had not served as an inspiration to donate their time, and contributing money seemed sufficient indication of their commitment to the war effort. Perhaps it was, in part, the chance to go south to rescue Union soldiers that drew these women from their comfortable surroundings to join the transports. Often their letters home reflected the desire to experience danger and included stories of their bravado, as when Harriet Whetten boarded a boat full of Confederate prisoners and described to a friend that she went down into the hold of the boat at sundown: "[I]n the midst of the crew of ruffianly looking fellows I felt as if I were in hell."[18] But they also seemed to find comfort in the promise of domestic security aboard the commission boats. Olmsted certainly had these women in mind when he reassured female recruits and their families that the women would at all times be protected and provided for by commission men. On commission boats, volunteers were guaranteed status as "ladies."[19]

With less than a day's notice, Eliza Howland and Georgy Woolsey reported for duty as "'nurses at large,' or matrons" aboard the first boat to come into the commission's hands.[20] In the next three months, other women volunteers joined them as nurse superintendents on board an ever-changing number of river steamers.[21] Among those who became permanent members of the transport team were Katharine Prescott Wormeley of Newport, Rhode Island; Christine Kean Griffin, Ellen Ruggles Strong, Caroline Lane, and Whetten, all of New York City; Helen Louise Gilson of Chelsea, Massachusetts; and Amy Morris Bradley of Kennebec, Maine.[22] Howland and Woolsey had successfully completed Blackwell's nurse training course in New York, but most women volunteers expected that their previous domestic experience provided them with all the skills they would need on the transports. It was surprising that women of their social status volunteered, the *Bulletin* article about the transports wrote, "because it could not be supposed that their former habits of comfort and luxury could prepare them for encountering the perils and privations which they must necessarily meet with in this field of labor."[23] Nonetheless, Eliza Bellows, who had suffered from a variety of nervous disorders before the war, found a cure in the purposeful activity of the campaign, which she felt prepared for by her antebellum life. In a letter to her son, Bellows explained her abilities in stoic terms: "I have some important qualifications for such business, which are chiefly, that I am not overcome by the sight of wounds and that I can live for a long time on very little food and almost no water."[24] In fact, perhaps

Bellows provided an insight into her own motivations for going to the front in an earlier letter when she admitted that she worried "that we are all effeminated by too luxurious and self-indulgent habits" and hoped that the war would "arouse our manhood and womanhood."[25]

Katharine Wormeley initially assumed that her work aboard the transports would "be very much that of a housekeeper."[26] Harriet Whetten reassured a friend that her commission duties would fall within the realm of middle-class domesticity.[27] "You must understand," Whetten predicted, "that there are men nurses and orderlies detailed, so that we volunteer ladies have nothing disagreeable to do."[28] Despite the commission's intentions, however, life aboard the transports turned out to be nothing like middle-class domestic relations. Women of privileged upbringing joined the transports because they believed that the controlled environment of the commission boats would guarantee their safety and the presence of commission men would protect their reputations—not to mention spare them the dirty work. One look at the condition of the men aboard the *Spaulding*, however, revealed the limits of such expectations. When faced with scenes such as Whetten and Harris described, many women returned home as quickly as they had left.[29] Yet some stayed and became accustomed to working tirelessly night and day below the cramped decks of the steamers. For those who stayed, any romantic visions they might have entertained about traveling to the South and witnessing battles first-hand dissolved in the dimly lit bowels of boats filled with suffering soldiers and scant supplies. As much as they and their families might have believed that commission men would shield them from these brutalities, transport volunteers witnessed some of the worst scenes of suffering of the war.

With little precedent to go by, transport women responded to commission rhetoric that celebrated women's ability to preserve men's health by trying to recreate the conditions of home on the boats. Even the attempt was no small feat; the boats were far from homelike. Harris described the conditions in the following manner: "There are eight hundred on board. Passage-ways, state-rooms, floors from the dark and foetid hold to the hurricane deck, were all more than filled; some on mattresses, some on blankets, others on straw." Worst of all were the ships' holds, where the lack of light added a surreal quality to the work. "It was like plunging into a vapor bath," Harris described her descent into one such hold, "so hot, close, and full of moisture."[30] Nonetheless, when time and conditions permitted, women strove valiantly to make the ships homey by putting their kitchens and quarters in order, setting makeshift dinner tables, and inviting women from other boats to "tea."

But usually transport women had little time to consider these domestic comforts. They often worked continuously for two or three days with minimal sleep and ate their meals standing up in the kitchen for lack of space. During days of heavy casualties, the boats offered the women no escape from the horrors; they worked, ate, and slept amid these scenes. Harris washed out her skirts one night, to rid them of "the mingled blood of Federal and Confederate soldiers which covered many portions of the floor." Then she lay down, "with the sick, wounded, and dying all around, and slept from sheer exhaustion, the last sounds falling upon my ear being groans from the operating room."[31] "For the first time in my life," remarked Eliza Bellows, "I have not known where I was to pass the night."[32] Aboard these cavernous boats, women could not tell night from day, so they marked their days by the number of mouths fed and beds made. Georgy Woolsey casually mentioned the Union surrender of New Orleans on May 1st, musing, "[W]hat is [the hour] to us so long as the beef tea is ready at the right moment?"[33] By Wormeley's estimate, the transport team in one three-day period recovered, treated, and transported close to 4,000 men. During these periods, Wormeley was not the only one who felt "like a cockroach, running familiarly as I do into all [the ship's] dark corners."[34] Though Wormeley and others took quinine as a preventive, they lived in fear of contracting malaria in the swampy Virginia delta.[35] Under such conditions, triage was emotionally and physically demanding.[36] Even Wormeley, whose letters usually reveal a carefully cultivated English stoicism, admitted "that it *is* wearing."[37]

Potent commission rhetoric and the occasional polite diversions the women engineered aside, transport women's real experiences collided with their preparation in mid-nineteenth-century domesticity. The women anticipated that they would supervise the work of male and female contract nurses, servants, and freed slaves, much as they supervised the work of domestics in their own homes, but in reality they found themselves doing much of the labor.[38] Though early in her work aboard the boats, Wormeley had assured her mother that her work was not unlike "arranging a doll's house," by the end of her first month, she noted that the women did less delegating and more of the actual work than they had originally anticipated. "You will see from my letters," Wormeley explained to a friend, "we women do more than is set down for us in the programme; for in fact, we do a little of everything."[39] They worked long hours making and remaking beds that were often difficult to reach, washing the faces and hands of hundreds of soldiers as they lay on the deck or in their beds; hauling buckets of water for cooking, cleaning, and laundering; and cooking endless gallons of beef tea, milk punch, and half a dozen kinds of gruel.[40]

The commission's intention of having transport women stand in for wives and mothers on the home front broke down as volunteers dealt with the strenuous and gruesome work of rescuing soldiers from the battlefield. For women on board commission transports, authentic experience opened a breach between those who were there and those who stayed home.[41] Volunteers became alienated and uneasy when they were reminded of the rituals of middle-class domesticity they had left behind. Hearing church bells gave Wormeley "a strange, distant feeling," and she and her comrades complained heartily when they experienced intervals of enforced leisure.[42] Unlike home-front women who experienced the war vicariously, transport volunteers could not sentimentalize the miseries of war. "We who are here, however, dare not let our minds, much less our imaginations, rest on suffering," explained Wormeley, "while *you* must rely on your imagination to project you into the state of things here."[43]

At first, transport women were reluctant to discard the essentials of feminine dress and manners that were as important to them at home as they were impractical on the boats, but these distinctions seemed unimportant after a few weeks on the peninsula.[44] At the beginning of the campaign, volunteers were distressed to learn that they were not allowed to wear hoops, ribbons, ruffles, and other such symbols of their gender and their class. One month into their tour of duty, however, Wormeley, the Woolseys, and their comrades gladly discarded the filthy dresses they had brought from home for the comfort of men's clothing. Transport women created their own "uniform" that included flannel shirts worn over skirts with "the collar open, sleeves rolled up, shirt tail out." The women called the shirts "Agnews," after

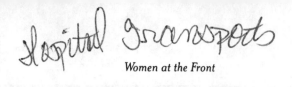

the doctor from whom they stole the first shirt.[45] Free from the material reminders of their status as ladies, women volunteers shed the polite deportment: They complained bitterly of the army's ill-preparedness and grew increasingly impatient with "loud-mouthed congressmen" and "philanthropic ladies" who made token visits to the boats.[46] At the very least, the intimate living and work arrangements on the boats made it difficult to adhere to these antebellum standards of respectability.[47] Unable to discern one day from the next, the transport women found that the importance of keeping up the habits of ladies became insignificant. No longer able to identify with the philanthropic ladies they had been, women volunteers looked for something else in themselves and in each other, something that made sense for their particular circumstances. Transport women came to appreciate one another for what Wormeley described as their "true grit."[48]

If women aboard the transports turned out to be imperfect stand-ins for the mothers and wives of soldiers, they were even worse at replicating the domestic subservience idealized in the middle-class home. Olmsted wanted women volunteers to work as if they were under official contract. Yet he seemed to be ambivalent about asking women to work with the regularity of men; he asked that no volunteer should come if she were not prepared "to act as if she were paid and [she] must be expected to be treated with the same discipline."[49] Despite the expectation that as workers under contract they would defer to the authority of the army and that as women they would comply with the wishes of commission men, together the volunteers experienced danger and overcame official intransigence with collective resistance. Faced with the prospect of preparing food for hundreds of wounded and ill soldiers without the benefit of a stove, Georgy Woolsey and her comrades located a stove in an officer's tent on shore and confiscated it. As they made their way back to the river, the women celebrated with "a triumphant procession [through town], waving . . . bits of stove-pipe and iron pot-covers."[50] The loyalty the women felt for each other and their shared commitment to caring for the soldiers took precedence over military protocol.

The independent command structure they operated under dictated that individual military rank was irrelevant when it came to providing relief to the many. "Our work," explained Wormeley, "requires us to

Katharine Prescott Wormeley in the hospital transport "uniform," including a men's flannel shirt that the women called an "Agnew." The Massachusetts Commandery Military Order of the Loyal Legion and the U.S. Army Military History Institute.

give life and some comfort to the many."[51] In order to do so, women volunteers developed alternative behavioral standards and encouraged each other to break rules and test the tolerance of their commission and military colleagues. "Kleptomania," Wormeley boasted, "is the prevailing disease among us. We think nothing of watching the proprietor of some nicety out of the way, and then pocketing the article."[52] Such behavior stood in direct conflict not only with antebellum standards of behavior but with military and commission protocol.

With confidence in their individual abilities and a consciousness of their collective strength, transport women began asserting themselves and speaking up about what they thought was best for the wounded soldiers, even if their decisions occasionally contradicted orders from commission or army authority. Sometimes the women simply made the most of the confusion that reigned on the transports, and other times their transgression was explicit. Transport women boarded boats and entered camps when they thought it was in the best interest of the soldiers.[53] Wormeley and a fellow transport volunteer left the *Wilson Small* "without orders and, indeed, without permission," to inspect a hospital on shore.[54] Such independence influenced women on the home front who heard about the brave adventures of transport women. Georgy's disregard for protocol on the peninsula encouraged similar behavior by her mother and sisters at home. When a general prevented Georgy and Eliza's sister Jane from getting to the wounded relative of a friend who had arrived in New York on a hospital transport, Jane plotted to "kidnap" the soldier.[55]

The intimacy that the women felt for each other as they worked together under such demanding circumstances helped them challenge a domestic hierarchy that placed arbitrary limits on their actions. On the ships the women developed an intense esprit de corps; as Whetten explained, "we have all grown to love each other like people shipwrecked."[56] The work of the transport women was so integrated that Wormeley described the women as "four fingers" of a hand.[57]

In their efforts to care for wounded and ill soldiers, transport women were just as comfortable exploiting their status as "ladies" among the men as they were unwilling to allow this social distinction to interfere with their attempts to care for the soldiers. One Sunday, for instance, when the women were beset by a group of "picknickers," as they derisively called visiting politicians and their wives, they asked the visitors if they would take a dying general home to his wife on their way back. When the congressmen refused on account of "the ladies," who accompanied them, Griffin secretly visited their wives as a fellow "lady" and met with no such resistance.[58]

Yet, as Wormeley's rhetoric shows, though they were willing to use the connection when it was convenient, transport women were becoming conscious of their war experiences separating them from "picknickers," or women and men who could only bear visiting "the clean, sweet, and fresh wards" on the boats.[59] On one stormy night Wormeley and Griffin decided to take a tug to pick up some wounded and bring them back to their steamer. But when they reached the men, the pilot of the tug, realizing the men suffered from typhoid, refused to take them aboard. He proved to be no match for the two women, for as Wormeley boasted later, "Mrs. Griffin and I looked at him. I did the terrible, and she the pathetic; and he abandoned the contest."[60]

At times, however, their upbringing in middle-class femininity threatened to get the better of them, and they struggled to control the emotions that overwhelmed them. Conventional sentimentality encouraged women and men to sympathize—empathize, even—with another's pain, but transport women recognized this as self-indulgent.[61] Wormeley admitted that "[t]o feel acutely at such times is merely selfish."[62] "No one knows what war is until they see this black side of it," Wormeley explained. "We may all sentimentalize over its possibilities . . . but it is as far from the reality as to read of pain is far from feeling it."[63] They were not always successful at maintaining the emotional control they needed to do the work. "The heavens are filled with blackness," Harris wrote in July, as malaria and dysentery began claiming the lives of one in every four soldiers fighting in the Chickahominy swamps.[64] The stress of the work likewise began to take its toll on Amy Morris Bradley after a month on the peninsula. She described the experience of receiving wounded from the Battle of Seven Pines on board the *Knickerbocker*:

> I shall never forget my feelings as one by one those mutilated forms were brought in on stretchers and carefully placed on those comfortable cots! What, said I, must I see human beings thus mangled? O, My God why is it? Why is it? For nearly an hour I could not get control of my feelings! But when the surgeon said, Miss Bradley, you

must not do so, but prepare to assist these poor fellows. I realized that tears must be choked back and the heart only know its own suffering! Action is the watchword of the hour![65]

Wormeley went through a similar epiphany the first time she treated a soldier with "a ghastly wound." The soldier asked her for something, and when Wormeley moved hastily to respond, she was advised by a commission colleague to "never be hurried or excited, or you are not fit to be here."[66] Faced with emotions that might have impeded their ability to care for the men, transport women fought an ongoing battle for self-control.

Living amidst the gruesome realities of a battle both sides seemed to be losing, sometimes all they could do was try to focus their thoughts elsewhere. After three sleepless days, for example, when Wormeley and other transport volunteers had treated close to 2,000 men, she wrote, "[l]ast night, shining over blood and agony, I saw a lunar rainbow;—it flashed upon my eyes as I passed an operating table, and raised them to avoid seeing anything as I passed."[67] Wormeley's attempt to avoid the gruesome sights on board her transport violated the antebellum expectation that women and men seek out authentic experience and identify with individual suffering. Wormeley did not allow herself to empathize with soldiers undergoing painful and disfiguring operations, for she was convinced that "[n]o one must come here who cannot put away all feeling. Do all you can, and be a machine,—that's the way to act; the only way."[68] For her, empathy was an element of an old sentimentality that women and men working under such conditions could ill afford.

Comments like Wormeley's have led historians to condemn the women of the commission's hospital transport campaign because they discarded their antebellum sensitivity to individual suffering for what George Frederickson calls "a stoical and fatalistic sense of the inevitability of large-scale suffering" that was promoted by the military.[69] Military reasoning held that experiencing pain was necessary for developing healthy masculine endurance and that philanthropic efforts to relieve individual suffering deprived soldiers of the strength which came from becoming inured to the pain of battle.[70] Commission protocol endorsed this reasoning. Throughout the war, the male military and commission bureaucracies launched an ambitious campaign to depersonalize suffering and to judge relief efforts by their efficiency, not by their humanitarian results. Frederickson suggests that Wormeley's insensitive remarks serve as a measure of the success of this joint campaign. Similarly, Lori Ginzberg singles out the transport women as examples of "a new style of benevolence," one that valued recognition by male co-workers more than it did women's experience in antebellum benevolence.[71] In choosing not to feel the pain of their patients, historians have concluded, transport women had become callous cogs in the wheels of an insensitive male bureaucracy.

But transport women's ambivalence about their feelings, however, suggests otherwise. Transport women were, perhaps, practitioners of a new style of benevolence. In the unprecedented circumstances of large-scale triage, transport women learned tough lessons about how best to care for the soldiers. Often the circumstances dictated that they put away their feelings until a leisure moment. But in trying to prevent themselves from feeling deeply, transport women were not simply looking for the acceptance of their male colleagues. They did not adhere blindly to military and commission standards of efficiency nor did they merely accept that this kind of large-scale suffering was unavoidable or, worse yet, necessary. For although they might have abandoned the antebellum culture of sentimentality, transport volunteers did not simply replace it with a callous bureaucratic approach to their work. They continued to care for the soldiers as individuals. When her ship took on heavy casualties, Whetten stood by a mortally wounded man who the ship's surgeons had decided was too near death to treat. At his request, Whetten held his hand until he died, "and for a few minutes after[,] [she] stood there, before anyone came, by the side of this rough bunk, and blessed God that the poor mangled chest palpitated with pain no longer."[72] Even Olmsted indulged his desire to give special care to individual soldiers, although as a commission representative he was enlisted in an effort to replace individualized attention with professional distance and as a man he felt he had to keep such emotionalism hidden. When no one was around to see him, Georgy Woolsey often caught Olmsted "sitting on the floor by a dying German, with his arm round his pillow—as nearly round his neck as possible—talking tenderly to him, and slipping away again quietly."[73] Transport women regretted the anonymity of soldiers' deaths, and Wormeley rejoiced when Georgy thought to "write the

names and regiments of the bad cases and fasten them to their clothing, so that if they are speechless when they reach other hands, they
may not die like dogs."[74]

Seeing each death as an individual sacrifice made transport women
highly critical of the care the men received in the hands of the U.S.
Army. Georgy complained bitterly when army personnel resisted the
women's efforts to give each soldier something to eat as he was
brought on board, for it took her and her comrades "but a minute's
delay to pour something down their throats and put oranges in their
hands, and saves them from exhaustion before food can be served
them."[75] But although the wisdom of taking extra time to identify a
wounded soldier and to give him something to eat was obvious to
Georgy and her comrades, it was not so to male military personnel.
In fact, such individual attention was antithetical to military protocol
not only because it was inefficient but even more because it was un-
manly.[76]

Like their peers at the commission branches, transport women preserved what they could of their antebellum habits and continued to
judge their own success based on the independent standard of care
that they shared. Indeed, they recognized these standards as particularly feminine, for when Olmsted seemed to be operating under similar principles, he was described in feminine terms by his colleagues.
Wormeley described Olmsted in the following manner: "His face is
generally very placid, with all the expressive delicacy of a woman's."[77]
And one of Olmsted's aides found similar feminine qualities in Olmsted when he wrote that "[He] has a deal of tact; as much as a
woman."[78] Similarly, transport women were assisted by male nurses
called Zouaves because of their Eastern-style uniforms consisting of
short jackets and loose-fitting pants. At first the women criticized the
Zouaves because of their feminine dress, but later they applauded
"their efficiency, their good sense, their gentleness" and believed that
their feminine dress "seemed to take them in some sort out of the
usual manners and ways of men."[79]

Their willingness to recognize the female qualities in their male colleagues attests to the chasm that was developing between commission
rhetoric celebrating the integrity of the separate spheres and the transport experience. Although commission volunteers knew that they
were not merely duplicating prewar domestic relations, however, it

was the men they left behind who understood most clearly the transformation that was taking place. The role reversal is important enough
to highlight. Although the image of the *male* soldier going off to war
and leaving his female relatives at home was the dominant one, for
some transport women, the roles were reversed.

Husbands of transport women who were also involved in commission work expressed this irony in plaintive letters to their absent wives.
George Strong was distressed that his wife's transport work had
caused her to be away from home on their May 15th wedding anniver-
sary. Strong's descriptions of his wife's life on the transports are a mixture of pouting and condescension, but his admiration was unmistak-
able. "Ellie enjoys her Bohemian life," he wrote, "[she] works hard,
sleeps profoundly, finds coarse fare appetizing, and has a good time
generally."[80] By mid-June, though, Strong began pressuring Ellie to
come home, sending his pleas by telegram, by mail, and through commission personnel, "entreating, conjuring, and commanding her to . . .
come straight home."[81] Despite George's efforts to cajole and to assert
husbandly prerogative, Ellie waited until the danger that Confederate
snipers would fire on the transports and the army's decision to repos-
sess commission boats caused a mass exodus of women from the
transports before she returned home to George.[82] Henry Bellows
might have sympathized with George Strong, for one evening during
his wife Eliza's brief service, he wrote, "I go home to-night—if a man
can be said to go *home*, who goes to nobody that is specially dear."[83]

Bellows accurately captured the import of women's service in the
hospital transport campaign with his self-pitying comment. The commission had conceived of women as bringing *home* to the front by
ministering to soldiers, little understanding the implications of official
rhetoric. The home, male commission leaders such as Strong and Bellows realized, was wherever women were. But in creating such a mo-
bile concept of home—one that in effect followed women—they were
forced to admit the supreme irony. In serving the soldiers, commission
women abandoned the responsibility traditionally assumed to be their
primary one.

From this perspective, the United States Sanitary Commission's attempt to use women as nurses in the controlled environment of U.S.
Army vessels and to capitalize on the metaphor of the properly or-
dered middle-class home was a failure. The women of the hospital

transport campaign successfully used the same rhetoric of middle-class domesticity to enlarge their sphere of influence during wartime. Although male commission leaders (and some women themselves) expected to recreate the model middle-class home on the transports, the rigors of hospital service transformed women's conceptions of their capabilities and the value of their work. Domestic metaphors eased the transition of women into the male realm of the battlefield, both for male commission leaders and for women and their concerned relatives, but once aboard the transports, women grew increasingly assertive and surprised even themselves with their resilience and strength. Transport women's service had been envisioned as bridging the gap from the home front to the war, yet in practice it also brought the battlefield to the home and to the women and men who stayed behind.

In July, several commission vessels were fired on despite their status as neutrals. In response, Olmsted decided not to place any more women on commission transports and he slowly began to demobilize the existing volunteers. "No more ladies or female nurses should be sent here," Olmsted wrote to Bellows, adding that he had "just learned that the *Arrowsmith* which followed us received ten bullets from rifles fired simultaneously from both banks."[84] Though Olmsted expressed concern only for the safety of the "ladies" on the boats, by the end of the month, the commission had left the Virginia peninsula entirely, returning the responsibility of transporting wounded and ill soldiers to the U.S. Army. Despite these dangers, however, transport women such as Wormeley and the Woolsey sisters stayed aboard the boats until the very end of the commission's service.[85]

In the end, what drew the women of the commission's hospital transport campaign together was their commitment to a standard of care that differed from that of the military they served. These women of mostly privileged upbringing served under arguably some of the most trying circumstances of the Civil War and survived the unsafe and often unsanitary conditions they encountered below the cramped decks of river steamers. Yet at the end of her transport experience, Wormeley described the time as a period when "we worked together under the deepest feelings, and to the extent of our powers, shoulder to shoulder, helping each other to the best of our ability, no one failing or hindering another."[86] The intimacy that the women felt for each other as they worked together under such demanding circumstances helped them challenge a domestic hierarchy that placed arbitrary limits on their actions. They learned to respect each other not for their manners, their obedience to military protocol, or their deference to commission prerogatives but for their resourcefulness and their commitment to the soldiers they served. On boats that were far from home and far from homelike, elite and middle-class women came to work as "ladies" aboard the commission-run transports. In the end they stayed together for the standard of care they agreed the men deserved. Together they could see to it that the men did not "die like dogs."

Because the commission's hospital transport campaign came early in the war, it had the potential to change the way women and men experienced the war. As David Blight has argued in his work on one young Union soldier, "[W]e can glimpse in this tiny corner of the war the enormous potential of the human transformations at work."[87] After living and working under altered domestic arrangements on the commission ships and identifying so closely with women of similar backgrounds, transport women underwent profound transformations and were reintroduced into the comforts of home with difficulty. In fact, some chose not to return. Whetten and Bradley, for instance, chose to work on army boats, staying in the peninsula longer than did Olmsted and the other male commission volunteers.[88] In that regard, these two women had much in common with Civil War soldiers, many of whom chose to re-enlist after their original contracts expired rather than face readjustment to civilian life.[89] When Wormeley and Howland returned to civilian life, they both described a period of readjustment, during which they felt out of place and disconnected from others. While Wormeley and other transport veterans went back to the women's work of collecting supplies for soldiers at the front, it is not difficult to imagine that during this time they felt they had more in common with veteran soldiers than they did with the members of their own household or their sewing circle. This period of readjustment varied and must have been difficult for some women, such as Strong and Bellows, who returned to husbands who had stayed home. Like women in twentieth-century wars, these women chose to give up the trappings of middle-class domesticity "for the duration." When the immediate need for their services had passed, some were not ready simply to resume the anonymity of their former status as Victorian matrons. On the day of her return from Virginia, for example, a Mrs.

Balestier insisted that her husband write a letter to correct an insulting error in a New York newspaper. The paper reported that Mrs. Balestier and a female associate were returning on the *Daniel Webster* as "passengers" instead of as "matrons at large," and Mrs. Balestier wanted to establish that "except when prevented by sea-sickness, she and Miss Butler . . . performed all the duties required of them as nurses."[90] Though she was identified in print only by her husband's last name, Mrs. Balestier wanted to be sure that those who knew her were aware of her distinguished wartime service. Like so many veterans, Mrs. Balestier had not expected a heroine's welcome—she only wanted the recognition she thought she had earned.

"Descendants of Heroic Mothers"

COMMISSION WOMEN
LOOK TO THE FUTURE

On Sunday, January 3, 1864, the front page of the *New York Times* reported the brutal death of a Brooklyn woman at the hands of an uniformed soldier. Bridget Dailey left her home Saturday evening "for the purpose of getting some groceries for Sunday." When Dailey did not return, her ten-year-old daughter went in search of her and found her bleeding to death on the street. Witnesses reported "a man dressed in the uniform of a U.S. soldier" leaving the scene. The coroner determined the cause of death to be a stab wound to the abdomen. The soldier was still at large, and no mention was made of the fate of Dailey's daughter.[1]

A murder was gruesome news for the *Times* to report in a holiday edition of the paper, usually packed with news from the front. Though the end of the war was nowhere in sight, the paper engaged in some speculation about the dangers of returning soldiers at this early date, speculation that the story of Bridget Dailey's murder surely fed. Most references to the plight of Union veterans were sympathetic and pleaded with New Yorkers to help the "starving, friendless soldiers [who] are daily passing through our streets."[2] Some even proposed plans for helping soldiers through organized rather than personalized relief. In February, for instance, "some fifty gentlemen interested, who are among our very first citizens" met to plan a home for disabled soldiers.[3]

The commission executive board was inexplicably absent from the public debate about what to do with the returning soldiers. By the time the civilian population was preparing for the influx of unemployed and invalid veterans, commission men were limiting USSC operations to projects already underway. Faced with increased government resistance to commission plans and disinterest among the members of the executive board, the USSC board decided not to take part in the demobilization.

Branch women placed no such limits on their work. Encouraged by their successful independent ventures, branch women did not shy away from providing assistance to returning soldiers or committing to work that would take them beyond demobilization. Because their work was based on grassroots women's networks that touched families and communities throughout the North and West, it did not require a friendly reception from Washington. May, Schuyler, and their colleagues were committed to sustaining women's local welfare networks that had done as much to support families and communities as the soldiers. Now, soldiers, many of them sick and invalid, were going home to communities that were not prepared to support them. As the end of the war drew near, the branches directed their attention toward the information and supply needs of the families of returning soldiers. And though the branches were mostly dissolved by the end of 1865, the connections made between the branches and their many and dispersed auxiliary societies were not hastily dismantled. As part of a new political culture, women saw beyond the demands of a single campaign and embraced the need for their continued collaborative efforts on behalf of their communities and what Abby May called their "sisterhood of States." With an eye toward future and even more ambitious enterprises, Schuyler, May, and their branch colleagues encouraged auxiliaries to keep meeting and kept the door open for a renewal of their work together.

IN the spring following Bridget Dailey's grisly murder there was enough general apprehension about the return of the troops that the *Times* ran a series of editorials criticizing those who warned "what a dangerous body this army would be to the country at large if ever it achieved victory in the South."[4] In particular, the paper attacked critics, domestic and foreign, who advised that U.S. soldiers be used as mercenaries for wars in Europe and Mexico because they were capable of little other "than doing duty as soldiers of fortune, or mercenary bravos for the disorganized States of the world."[5] To those who dreaded the effects of "a million or more of men trained in arms, let loose upon the community," the editors recommended they do whatever they could "to give them place and practical aid in the pursuits and professions which they may desire to enter."[6]

Whether northerners feared or pitied war veterans, newspapers began carrying stories of their imminent return early in 1865.[7] Veterans congregated in northern cities, and many faced difficulties finding work due partly to their youth and inexperience and partly to civilian distrust of soldiers.[8] From Chicago, Mary Livermore described the feelings of many:

> An army of a million soldiers who had been trained to waste, burn, destroy, ravage, and slaughter, and who had been practicing what they had been taught for three or four years, had been disbanded, and the men sent to their homes. Would they resume their former law-obeying, law-abiding habits, and melt away into the peaceful haunts of industry?[9]

Indeed, in the first two years after the war, former soldiers were implicated in an urban crime wave that had many northerners denouncing the war all over again.[10] But even outside of the urban areas, women's branch affiliates spoke of communities that were ill-equipped to handle the war's end. A woman at the New England Women's Auxiliary Association's (NEWAA) North Bridgewater affiliate expressed the town's fear of "profane, idle and filthy" soldiers and worried that "there is not so much interest felt by the community in their return as there was in their departure."[11]

For the men of the commission, the arrival of the veterans in northern cities should have threatened the return to the social disorder that had compelled them into the service of the commission in the first place. They had begun the enterprise as an experiment in reclaiming their social status by reaching out to the Union soldier, and through him to the working classes of the city, and so the prospect of soldiers returning from the war en masse might have been an irresistible call to action. With the structure of the commission in place, the bureaucracy could have easily been converted to provide the "regular, systematic provision" for the veterans that the readership of the *Times* began calling for in 1864.[12] Commission men might have taken to the work of providing temporary support for needy soldiers as a way of exercising the benign influence bourgeois New Yorkers believed effective in preventing the kind of disorder Bridget Dailey's death signaled.

But at USSC offices in Washington there was no indication that the organization would take up the challenge. For most of 1864, Bellows traveled with his family in California.[13] In his absence, commission operations almost fell apart as commission men fought with one another and blamed one another for the organization's problems.[14] Since Olmsted's resignation the previous fall, others had begun to express discontent with the commission, and by 1864, the situation was aggravated by general war-weariness. "The Washington office is utterly insubordinate and unruly," Strong grumbled during Bellows's absence.[15] When Bellows returned in the fall, his commission responsibilities seemed to weigh on him heavily. In November, he wrote to his son Russell, "I am already more pressed with work than ever, since my return."[16] Bellows was preoccupied with plans for an American Unitarian Association meeting in January and complained that commission work had become "methodical and unambitious."[17] With his chief officers fighting among themselves, Bellows felt that he "ought to give *all* instead of *half* my time to it," but at the same time he was relieved that he had other pressing matters to take up his time and that his colleagues were willing to pick up the administrative slack.[18]

Despite the leadership void and a lackluster commitment to the organization's mission, commission men were not without vision. For almost three years, Frederick Knapp had cared for furloughed and discharged soldiers passing through Washington on their way home, and he was well aware of the difficulties of reintroducing soldiers into civilian life. Due in part to USSC lobbying, the army sent the pay of most soldiers home to their families to prevent "improvident expenditure" and to see to "the wants of those dependent on them," leaving soldiers with no money to get home when they left their regiments.[19] As they passed through the capital, soldiers fell victim to all sorts of mischief and often remained in the city instead of seeking out the commission's help to get home.[20] Knapp's experience with soldiers released from duty convinced him that the commission needed to commit to a plan for looking after them when they were released from service.[21] Early in 1864, Knapp launched an ambitious campaign to convince USSC executives to open sanitariums to house disabled soldiers.[22]

But Knapp found little support for his plans to extend the commission's work beyond the end of the war. Bellows and his executive board had very little of their original enthusiasm left and seemed bent on wrapping up the work. Early on in the war, commission men had begun to think about what role their organization would play in the war's aftermath. A commission report written by Bellows and published in 1862 estimated that if the war ended in a year:

> not less than a hundred thousand men, of impaired vigor, maimed or broken in body and spirit, will be thrown on the country. Add to this a tide of another hundred thousand men, demoralized for civil life by military habits, and it is easy to see what a trial to the order, industry, and security of society, and what a burden to its already strained resources, there is in store for us.[23]

Since making these estimates of the heavy burden of demobilization, the commission had entertained proposals for postwar institutions to care for veterans and potential directions for USSC work after the war.[24] Events that began to unfold in 1864 and 1865 would seem to have proven their prognostications correct. Bellows even recognized the problem, describing the demobilization later in the following manner: "We saw in our cities all the suffering of invalidism, all the beggary and want of war, just at its close, passing before us at one review."[25] Despite the commission's early interest in expanding the work to include veterans, though, Knapp's proposals fell on deaf ears. In May 1864, a proposal for the construction of a sanitarium was brought before the executive board and dismissed.[26] Though the proposal was for just one small sanitarium, a far cry from the ambitious plans Knapp had for a network of such institutions, Strong opposed the measure "because this is not among our legitimate functions."[27] Bellows also rejected the suggestions of Knapp and others that commission duties be expanded.[28]

But it was perhaps not just a lack of commitment that made commission men reticent about accepting the challenge of a postwar role.

The USSC suffered a series of setbacks in its third year that reminded the executive board of the tenuousness of the organization's official standing. Early in the year, U.S. General William Tecumseh Sherman stopped the commission from using military transportation to get supplies to the front, and when his southern offensive picked up pace in the fall, he forbade any civilians, including commission agents, from accompanying the troops to Atlanta.[29] In August, the army investigated and dismissed Surgeon General Hammond, a move that was as much a condemnation of the commission as it was of Hammond, for Hammond's appointment had been the first step in the commission's ambitious campaign to overhaul the United States Army's Medical Department. Strong, Bellows, and their colleagues could do little to stop the attack on Hammond, but privately they fumed about the insult to the commission's credibility. The little they did to defend Hammond served only to jeopardize relations with Secretary of War Stanton, who was tired of the commission's criticisms of army medical practices, and the commission had to work hard not to lose access to the army entirely.[30] Perhaps Knapp's ambitions raised the specter of further rejection by the military bureaucracy. By 1864, commission operations were shrinking, and those in charge were unwilling to draw any further official attention to their operations.

While their commission colleagues complained and looked forward to the end of their work, branch women extended their reach. In 1864, the sanitary fairs staged at the branches peaked, and chairwomen proudly recorded the success of their supply- and money-raising efforts. "And still a third year dawned upon us, and found our labors not one whit diminished, and the interest as great as it had ever been," Abby May described the work of the NEWAA. Though the initial enthusiasm was gone, she noted, it had been replaced by "a depth and power of purpose that we felt sure would outlast the war, no matter how long it might continue." Counting more than 1,050 societies as affiliates of the Women's Auxiliary, May was optimistic about the future of "our little sisterhood of States."[31] Three hundred associate managers and delegates attended the NEWAA's annual meeting in December, far exceeding attendance records in previous years. In Boston, delegates discussed May's plan for sending out lecturers to share their experiences at the front with the women at home. In New York, Louisa Lee Schuyler hosted an equally successful meeting.[32]

By the time Schuyler and her delegates met in New York in November 1864, the WCAR had been operating under its articles of
reorganization for one year. Schuyler was pursuing a rigorous canvassing plan that included getting commission lecturers to "luke-
warm" areas.[33] "We must keep our shoulders to the wheel," Angelina
Post, Schuyler's assistant, advised an associate manager at the end of
the year.[34] According to the reorganization plan, submitted to and
approved by the commission the previous fall, the Woman's Central
began operating in two entirely new venues in 1864. The special relief
committee was created to "extend to invalid and discharged soldiers
sympathy, aid and advice, to impart to them such information with
regard to their special needs." The visiting committee was created to
"visit sick and wounded soldiers, the relatives and friends of members
of auxiliary societies, who may be in Hospital in and near this city."[35]

Mary Livermore had begun visiting the poor wives of soldiers in
1863, and from her experiences we can get an idea of what the WCAR
women faced when they launched this initiative in New York in
1864.[36] On her visits into the working-class neighborhoods of Chicago, Livermore found desperate immigrant and black women with
children to care for with no or inadequate support from their soldier
husbands, living in crowded and rat-infested basement tenements,
sacrificing their health by working long hours washing clothes or
scrubbing floors, leaving their young children unattended while they
worked. The Chicago branch brought food and fuel to these women,
sought medical care for them and their children, raised money to pay
for their back rent, and helped pay for burials when they or one of
their unfortunate children succumbed to the unhealthy conditions of
nineteenth-century urban life. To Livermore, the young wives and
widows of Union soldiers were the forgotten casualties of the war.
"No one knew them until suffering had done its dreadful work on
the young soldier's widow," Livermore explained on learning of the
death of one such woman.[37] The combined significance of these new
venues meant that the WCAR and the other branches had already
taken steps early in 1864 that the commission vacillated about for
months longer. Schuyler, Livermore, and their colleagues were committed to seeing to the needs of the returned soldiers and their families
and did not wait for the commission to take the lead.

By committing to the care of returning soldiers and reaching out to provide direct assistance to their unfortunate families, branch women were clearly shaping their own agenda as they built the basis for their postwar activities. By 1864, their vision of war relief had expanded to begin to ask difficult questions about the long-term consequences of the economic and social displacement that accompanied the war. What would happen to the families of soldiers who did not return from the front or who did so as invalids? What about the women and children who had compromised their health to work in wartime industries? Though the U.S. government had passed legislation in July 1862 providing for the care of the widows and orphans of soldiers, many potential beneficiaries did not qualify or failed to apply for such benefits. At a time when the U.S. government was only marginally committed to caring for these people, branch women were actively seeking ways to answer their pressing needs and advocating for an expansion of state services.[38]

By the third year of their cooperation, the USSC and the branches were clearly moving in different directions. As the commission's field operations contracted, the executive board became reluctant to adjust the work to answer the changing needs of the soldiers. Privately, commission men looked forward to the end of the war, as much for their own sake as for the soldiers. Members of the commission executive board began making their individual postwar plans, and some decided to leave the commission before the work was complete. Since the draft riots of 1863, Bellows, Strong, and Olmsted had increasingly invested their hopes for social resurrection in the Union League Club, a private club created to foster loyalty in the urban bourgeoisie. Olmsted described the Union League Club's membership as "the hereditary natural aristocracy."[39] As one historian has argued, instead of looking for ways of coming into closer contact with the working classes of the city, and hence educating them about the benevolence of the middle and upper classes, the Union League Club reached out to the black riot victims, "a model deferential working class," in order to "counteract working-class disloyalty publicly by exhibiting an ideal relationship between the classes."[40] Unconvinced of their ability to permanently influence the government bureaucracy or alter the course of class relations through the ambitious USSC program, commission men retreated to the safety of a private club, where they chose projects that could be carefully and closely administered and staged public events that dramatized their philanthropy.[41]

Emboldened by the success of their independent initiatives and their growing sense of themselves as professionals committed to careers in public service, branch women accelerated their operations in the final year of the war. In addition to visiting convalescent soldiers in hospitals and in their homes, the WCAR stepped up the fund-matching policy, received a financial commitment to that project from the commission, participated more actively in the publication of the *Bulletin*, organized a visit to the front for a group of associate managers, and planned a Grand Council meeting in New York in the fall.[42] May took a short break from her work, and Schuyler sent her assistant Angie Post away to rest in the summer of 1864.[43] But work at the NEWAA and the WCAR continued as usual. Despite expressing concern for Post's health, Schuyler kept her assistant abreast of WCAR activities and delegated work to her during her break.[44] Throughout the summer, Schuyler kept her colleagues at the WCAR busy. Post wrote to Bellows's daughter, Annie, during the Bellows family's extended stay in the West, and explained that Schuyler had given her enough work to keep her occupied all summer. Post was envious of the fun that her young friend Annie reported having in California, but, she added, "[t]here is one thing though that I would not like and that is to be quite so far from Grant's army!"[45]

With the activities of the WCAR expanding, Schuyler and her colleagues relied even more heavily on associate managers to canvass their regions. In June, Schuyler visited associate managers throughout her territory and in Cincinnati, Chicago, Louisville, and Cleveland.[46] At this late date, some associate managers were able to achieve remarkable success in communities that were surely weary of the repeated calls on their benevolence. From Elmira, New York, Mrs. Charles Stuart, WCAR associate manager, sent details of her efforts to organize soldiers aid societies in Elmira and neighboring towns in the winter of 1864–1865. Following a branch policy established at the beginning of the war, Stuart first approached women known for their benevolence work and then solicited the support of the churches in town. In Elmira, Stuart was proud to report that the ten churches in town, "including the Roman Catholic," collectively agreed to lend their support to the commission and to close their doors once every three months to allow all their members to gather in one place and hear of the work of the commission.[47]

Although Schuyler and her colleagues looked forward to the end of the war, the organizational structure of the WCAR was at its peak in the final few months.[48] At the local level, both Schuyler and May could count on the work of a competent crew of associate managers and a loyal network of soldiers aid societies. At the branch offices, their effective leadership was supplemented by a group of professional women associates who had more than three years' experience under their belts. Since the beginning, women leaders had consistently insisted on the autonomy of the branches and had earned the respect of commission men. For almost four years, the NEWAA and the WCAR had planned and administered independent initiatives, often without consulting the commission or against the explicit wishes of commission personnel, and they defended their choices based on what was clearly a distinct agenda. As the war drew to a close, branch decisions continued to be made in the best interests of the network of affiliated community societies and women-run branches rather than on the indifference of a disillusioned commission executive board. Though the commission operation was disintegrating, the women's infrastructure stood strong.

Early in 1865, with the defeat of the South imminent, branches began inquiring about providing information and support for returning soldiers. In May, the USSC responded in a circular advising branches and affiliated soldiers aid societies to keep operating until July 4, when further instructions would be given. In the meantime, the circular suggested that women in their groups devise ways of protecting returned soldiers from "inducements to idleness and dissipation," turn every branch and soldiers aid society into a "Bureau of Information and Employment," gather names and data about all veterans in their towns, and help dispense information about the benefits available to them.[49] The commission offered women no official role in the organization's demobilization plans, though the circular vaguely referred to commission plans to possibly open asylums for disabled soldiers. Despite these instructions, or perhaps in response to them, May wrote to Bellows later in the month to ask for more explicit instruction and to suggest that the NEWAA begin processing pension claims for veterans. Bellows's response was a long and eloquent defense of "the spontaneous, public, unofficial character of the ministry rendered to the sick and wounded through the war," laissez-faire government, and a decentralized approach to caring for disabled soldiers.[50] This "treatise," as Bellows referred to his lengthy reply, had more to do with his and his fellow commissioners' changes of heart than it had to do with May's request for advice on processing pensions. The branches looked to the end of the war as a means of extending their influence and finding new work for the women in their network, but the commission responded with reticence and retraction.

Receiving no further direction from the commission and no indication of what would be asked of them in the way of supplies or work after July 4, Schuyler took matters into her own hands. In June, Schuyler sent word out to her affiliates advising them to be prepared to help disabled soldiers find employment, to give families of deceased soldiers advice about collecting claims, and to supply and assist general hospitals that anticipated an influx of convalescent soldiers in their area. She advised societies that were seeking a national arena for their work to consider affiliating themselves with the "Freedmen's Association."[51] Though he agreed with Schuyler's advice in sentiment, Dr. Joseph Parrish, the commission liaison to the branches, was a little concerned that she had decided to give instruction to her affiliates before the commission made its July 4 announcement. "Is it not the wiser way," Parrish asked, "to let the official notice of the Board . . . be sent to the Branches and their constituents, before any body else acts?" He did not want the commission machinery, "vast and harmonious as it is, [turned over] to any organization less Catholic [sic] or national than itself."[52] Schuyler thanked Parrish for his advice, but as the decisions had already been made by the WCAR Board and the word had gone out to their affiliates, she explained, there was little she could do.[53]

When the branches and soldiers aid societies finally received the long-awaited July 4 circular, they must have been disappointed. No further mention was made of the commission's long-term plans, and the women were told that there would be no further need for their assistance. The circular explained that the USSC had some 127 claim offices to collect the pensions and back pay of soldiers and expected that project to mark the end of the commission's work with the sol-

diers. Worse yet, the commission would not involve the branches in
this work. "[T]here will be no probable necessity for addressing the
women of the country," the commission authors added, so the
branches and soldiers aid societies ought to consider their work done.
The authors extended their heartfelt thanks to the vast women's network that had sustained it for more than four years and asked that
branch women forward any remaining supplies and cash promptly to
the commission.[54]

At best, these instructions were dismissive. Commission women at
the branches and at local soldiers aid societies had waited to find out
how they would be included in the commission's demobilization
plans, only to be told that they were no longer needed. They had
proven themselves capable of doing relief work on both the local and
regional level and had managed to work effectively within the commission bureaucracy. While branch and local women had at times differed with each other and, more often, with commission men, together they had provided critical support for the soldiers and their
families. To have their cooperation end so unceremoniously had to
have been insulting. The July 4 instructions seem to indicate that the
commission executive board believed that the wartime working arrangements that had brought middle-class men and women together
in a relationship that had been more equitable than was possible in
their separate ventures before the war would not be carried over into
the postwar years. Presumably, Bellows and the commission executive
board expected that women would return to their prewar domestic
roles and would limit themselves once again to local reform work.
With commission men in retreat, it stood to reason that commission
women would follow.

Despite the commission's thought that this would be its final word
to the branches, weeks later the WCAR and the NEWAA pressed the
commission to let women take part in the processing of claims. On
July 13, Schuyler asked that Parrish look into the possibility; Parrish
liked the idea. "The Commission must rely upon the devoted industry
of the women of the Country, to make the work as complete as it can
possibly be," he responded.[55] Though the NEWAA had already been
approached by the Freedmen's Association about the possibility of
collaboration, May held out for the possibility of working with the
commission further. Parrish met with May and her colleagues in Bos-

ton and learned that six claim agencies were opening in Massachusetts. He reported back to the commission that "the women however, are of the opinion, that the whole work of the Claims offices, could be as well done by them, as by the more expensive plans now in operation."[56]

In part, branch women's demand for an official role in the processing of pension claims reflected the reality of the work they were already conducting. Branch women had been assisting women and veterans seeking information and advice about pensions and had helped individuals prepare these claims since at least 1862. But by 1865, branch women were no longer politically naive. Surely they appreciated the potential influence they might wield by becoming involved in the dispensation of Civil War pensions and welcomed the opportunity to continue their wartime agenda of providing relief that lived up to their distinct standards of care.[57]

Parrish found similar resolution throughout the New England region. Societies affiliated with the NEWAA continued to meet and plan. "In no case have the Societies formally disbanded," he explained.[58] With money left in their treasuries, affiliated societies saw no reason to demobilize. At the local level, soldiers aid societies made a variety of decisions about how to use the remaining funds. Some societies had already begun sending money and supplies to the Freedmen's Association, such as the society in Portland, Maine, and still others were considering such an affiliation. The women of North Bridgewater, Massachusetts, on the other hand, used their $500 to buy a government bond, to be used when "the Commission sounds the note for future work." Parrish found "a little Society in this county with two hundred dollars to spare," which they had decided to spend erecting "a monument to the memory of the soldiers who have died from their town."[59] Parrish was convinced that this was not the only town that decided to use money collected in the name of the USSC for the purposes of expressing local pride.

Ironically, this is precisely the kind of local sentiment that the commission had tried to combat. At the same time, however, branch policies had fostered an independence in their affiliates that allowed them to make decisions based on what local representatives believed was best for the community. With the end of the war near, Parrish's survey of soldiers aid societies indicated the persistence of local autonomy and serves as a measure of the success of branch women's modes of organization. May's and Schuyler's policies had encouraged local women to keep meeting in their societies throughout the war, despite economic hardships and familial responsibilities. They had worked hard to preserve the integrity and guarantee the continuity of the network of soldiers aid societies. Branch policies had not sought to replace local with national loyalties, for their affiliates had made it clear to them that without local loyalty, national loyalty would not exist.[60] Believing that the strength of the national relief effort rested in the regular meetings of the local societies, the branches had cultivated an allegiance that outlived the national crisis. "They preserve with an honorable degree of pride their organizations, and continue to meet," Parrish observed, adding that "[w]ithout exception, the opinion has been expressed, that the longer they have worked together, the more attached they have become to the work and to each other."[61] Clearly this new political culture had made possible the survival of women's grassroots activism, but it had also revealed the possibilities of linking local concerns to a national effort. The women who were part of this culture did not retreat as readily as men involved in similar work during the war.

Though their war work was clearly drawing to a close, women at the branches and at the auxiliaries wanted to maintain the connection. Pressed by the commission to complete final reports and close up their accounts as quickly as possible, however, May, Schuyler, and their colleagues at the branches worked feverishly through the summer months to fulfill their responsibilities to the commission. Any plans they had for new directions for their work had to wait until they completed detailed financial and statistical reports to the USSC. Early in the summer, Schuyler began showing the strains of four years of hard work, and friends and family pressured her to look after her health. In June she hoped to wind "up quickly and thoroughly" to prevent the WCAR's lingering on in uselessness.[62] She left any future incarnation of the organization to Ellen Collins, who planned to work for the Freedmen's Bureau.[63] By August, though, Schuyler was moved by the desperation of the returning soldiers and the needs of their families to consider forming a new society, "making the nucleous [*sic*] of it from as many of our old members, as could be got together." She did not foresee that the women would "work in the driving way we have been" and anticipated that it would not require living "a one-ideaed life," as had the commission work. While in June she was excited about her family's pending trip to Europe, in August Schuyler was reluctant to go and tried to convince herself that she would "enjoy it when I get there." "I am sorry too, to leave the country just now—there seems so much to do," she confided to Post.[64] Schuyler continued working late nights well into the fall, and just days before she and her family left for Europe she still wrote and sent materials to her associate managers.[65]

The WCAR Board declared July 3 to be their last official day to receive and process supplies from auxiliary societies. Letters and supplies "poured in all throughout the last week," leaving Schuyler and a diminished staff with much to sort out and reflect on.[66] From throughout their region, women wrote emotional letters to Schuyler and her staff about how much they would miss their connection with women at the branches and expressed hopes of working together again. "We are all feeling the break-up very deeply," Schuyler wrote, adding "[i]t is worth a dozen years of hard work—this ending."[67] The Blackwells attended the final meeting of the WCAR Board so that Schuyler could recognize their work selecting and "training a band of one hundred women nurses for our Army Hospitals."[68] In a series of resolutions prepared by Schuyler, branch women expressed their gratitude to all those they had worked with over the years. Schuyler once called the hard-working women in the rural and marginal soldiers aid societies—those women who rarely sent money but who always contributed what they could—"the truest patriots," and now she saved the WCAR's highest compliments for these women, whose steady work throughout the war had impressed her most. To the soldiers aid societies, Schuyler offered the following words of praise:

> Henceforth the Women of America are banded [*sic*] in town and country, as men are from city and field. We have wrought, and thought and prayed together, as our soldiers have fought, and bled, and conquered, shoulder to shoulder; and from this hour, the Womanhood of our country is knit in a common bond, which the softening influences of Peace must not, and shall not weaken or dissolve.[69]

With the end of their official connection rapidly approaching, Schuyler expressed women's collective resolve in martial language—

like the soldiers in the field, their work had brought them together in an unprecedented way. Her message seemed to foretell of postwar efforts, such as the renewed temperance campaign, a "crusade" that allowed women to call up their wartime connections and to once again strengthen their local efforts by linking them to a national campaign. Though the immediate demand for their collective action was coming to an end, the calls of a close sisterhood with their fellow workers did not.

Despite their efforts to finish up the work, Schuyler and her colleagues did so with difficulty. Four years of work to build an extended community of women, with whom they had developed a mutual confidence and respect and from whom they learned of the many difficulties facing families and communities in wartime, did not come to an end with Schuyler's eloquent words. And perhaps no one knew that better than Schuyler herself; hence her reluctance to take a well-deserved vacation and her obsession with the work in the days before she left. In several late-night letters to Angie Post in October and November 1865, Schuyler recounted the minutiae of the final days of the WCAR and explained in agonizing detail how she wanted the papers of the organization to be gathered and preserved.[70] She wanted to take photos of her associate managers with her to Europe and tried to collect them in the final few weeks before her departure.[71] Schuyler planned to meet with the members of the WCAR on October 12 and 13 for "the first social meeting of the late members."[72]

Closing up the accounts of the WCAR gave Schuyler and her staff a new perspective from which to view the work the organization had done for the commission. The USSC had already arranged for the history of the organization to be written, and for the last issue of the *Bulletin* the commission gathered expressions of gratitude from branches and soldiers aid societies for the opportunity to work in such a noble cause. Various societies contributed letters of appreciation, and Parrish filled the pages of the *Bulletin* with glowing accounts of the commission's largesse. Schuyler and her Woman's Central colleagues, however, decided to use this last issue of the *Bulletin* to publish the WCAR's final report and to reprint resolutions thanking the Blackwells, the associate managers, and the soldiers aid societies. In the final report, the WCAR Board thanked the men of the commission for the "harmonious character of our intercourse" but admitted to "a little lurking pride—we may as well confess it—that the Commission itself is, in some sense, an offshoot of our own Association."[73] Clearly, the women of the WCAR were looking back over the work and reflecting on how the history of the cooperation would be written. Reaching out to the Blackwells (whom the commission had long ago shunned) one more time and reminding readers that the USSC would not have come into being had it not been for the women's initiative suggest that Schuyler and the WCAR Board remembered clearly that the effort to systematize women's benevolence was not simply the handiwork of a group of prominent urban male philanthropists. The WCAR Board was not entirely comfortable having the Woman's Central remembered as merely the commission's "oldest Branch of Supply," and in their final published statements they made this clear.[74] Branch women had worked hard throughout the war to keep the lines of supply from the countryside open. Now they asserted their primacy as relief professionals.

At the NEWAA, May sent out similar words to her many affiliated societies. In a short report that summed up her work of organizing women in the New England area, May traced the growth of the Women's Auxiliary from 475 aid societies at the end of one year to more than 1,000 three years later.[75] Each year the Women's Auxiliary raised more money than the last and spent more of it buying material to support the industrial department that paid needy women to make army clothing.[76] She praised her associate managers for helping to bring together the disparate interests of their communities

> like the patchwork quilts made of many colors, and by many hands, but wrought, at last, into a whole beauty and of use, which have gone from your homes and Aid Societies, to carry comfort to the weary sufferers of our great army.

May assured her readers that the women of the country will never "again become idle spectators in the life of our country." "The destiny of America," May added, "must be wrought out by her women as well as her men."[77] The NEWAA's contribution to the final *Bulletin* wished the commission a fond farewell, but like other women's societies, the Women's Auxiliary was determined to continue the work of seeing to the needs of soldiers and freedmen.[78] During the war, May had not lived as "one-ideaed" a life as had Schuyler. As early as 1863, May had balanced her branch work with a position on the board of the Friends of the Colored Troops, an organization that sent supplies to men serving in the black regiments of Massachusetts and helped support their families in their absence, and she moved easily into the work of the Freedmen's Bureau when her commission responsibilities began to ease.[79] In 1864, May joined the Social Science League, a progressive organization in Boston that, as would the American Social Science Association, would take up the work of urban reform.[80] It was no surprise, then, that the Women's Auxiliary offices did not close down until March 31, 1866, and that May and her colleagues continued their work for nine months after the commission had closed its doors.[81]

Though Schuyler was not as prepared as May to extend the work of the WCAR much beyond the life of the commission, her final expressions to the Woman's Central associates and to the commission public were a rejection of the notion that the WCAR had simply acted as a subordinate to the male commission executive board.[82] The actions and parting messages of the women leaders are testaments to their sense of independence and professionalism. Women at the branches had effectively galvanized the support of diverse women throughout the North and had asserted themselves as the professional equals of men. Though they relied on the commission's access to military intelligence and its ability to address the political powers in Washington, women's branch leadership was not dependent on the good will of middle-class men. Branch leaders were inheritors of a long tradition of women's autonomous local politics, a heritage that had made it possible for them to reach out to women very different from themselves and that had guided their interactions with commission men. The women of the Soldiers' Aid Society of New Haven believed themselves to be the worthy "descendants of heroic mothers."[83] They likened their own work during the Civil War to the work of their mothers during the War for Independence, and, in so doing, bequeathed the tradition of women's independent activism to their daughters and to the generations of women that would follow. For women leaders, the war did not so much mark an end to this type of local activism as it indicated the continuing possibilities of linking local efforts together again in a national agenda.

Extending the Sisterhood

COMMISSION WOMEN
IN THE GILDED AGE

*I*n 1872, when Louisa Lee Schuyler returned to New York after seven years in Europe, the city was a crowded place, teeming with immigrants and workers.[1] The destitution, corruption, and conflict that greeted Schuyler on her return to the city were enough to drive away even the most devoted of reformers. In the years after the war, cities had become modernized, offering inhabitants the benefits of urban services such as professional fire and police protection, public transportation, and basic sanitation and health facilities. Increasingly, however, urban government was the domain of machine politics, and public institutions were run by patronage and political appointees. And though the war had precipitated an industrial boom in the North that had made some Americans rich, economic growth had ground to a halt in a depression that sent thousands of people out of work by the winter of 1873–1874.

Members of Schuyler's urban elite looked with equal disdain at machine politicians who got rich from graft and at the homeless and unemployed who gravitated to urban centers looking for work and assistance. Machine politicians provided relief to their urban constituents in times of need, but most of Schuyler's contemporaries were reluctant to have money indiscriminately distributed to people who were out of work. Indeed, her former colleague, Henry Bellows, expressed this postwar belief when in 1865 he suggested that poverty might be prevented "by encouraging self-respect & self-reliance, & by withholding careless Relief."[2] Members of the late-nineteenth-century elite and middle class, such as Bellows, had lost much of their antebellum perfectionism and were beginning to see social inequality as endemic. In the Gilded Age, the urban elite relieved their consciences of any moral responsibility to the working class and the poor by arguing that charity was bad for the poor because it discouraged work. Working-class people responded to the general disregard for their plight with mounting militancy, culminating in a wave of strikes that crippled cities throughout the country in 1877.

People of Schuyler's generation and social standing did not venture much past upper-class neighborhoods where they nurtured a careful ignorance of social conditions. In the years leading up to and during the war, people young and old had engaged in heated arguments over political matters such as secession and abolition; in the Gilded Age distraction was more palatable than engagement. A general pessimism about the government's ability to rise above corruption exacerbated the elite's disillusionment with the postwar status quo. The atmosphere was inhospitable to far-reaching private reform initiatives, and even the most visionary antebellum reformers had little faith in the government's ability to care for those in need.

Despite the moral torpor, Lou Schuyler wasted no time in getting to work. Within months of her return, Schuyler spearheaded a campaign to improve the care of the indigent in the city's poorhouses and began to gather support for the creation of a nurse training school in New York. Within a year, Schuyler was lobbying state lawmakers for funding and for legislation to reform public institutions and had launched her career on a path that would run up against the city's powerful political machines.

This was no accident. Lou Schuyler and her colleagues at the other women-run commission branches had become political insiders through their war work. After years of distinguished service supplying the U.S. Army with support critical to winning the war, Lou Schuyler, Abby May, Mary Livermore, and the other women leaders were not ready to retire to private life nor were they willing to allow the government they had helped save to be turned over to political opportunists.

Cooperation with the commission provided the war generation of women with critical experience in aligning politically prominent men to a woman's cause and in manipulating a male-run bureaucracy. The commission served as training ground for women such as Schuyler, May, and Livermore who would build careers on the organizational acumen and political savvy they perfected during the war. And as members of a transitional women's political culture, women who worked for the commission during the war set important precedents for women's reform in the postwar era. After the war, women's organizations such as the Woman's Christian Temperance Union (WCTU) made a clean break from male domination, yet they worked with male-led labor unions and agrarian populists to form progressive political alliances.[3] The postwar careers of Schuyler, May, and Livermore indicate that there are connections between this first generation of professional reformers and the emergence of the WCTU and women's independent reform agendas in the Progressive Era.

But the war generation emerged from their commission experience with more than the organizational skills and political wherewithal to remain effective reformers in the postwar years. The motivation behind the WCAR's initial call to arms in 1861 was the understanding that the U.S. government had a responsibility to care for its soldiers and soldiers' families. As they traveled the countryside collecting supplies for the soldiers, commission women witnessed first-hand how hard women worked to support their families without male wage earners. The war provided commission women with insight into the lives of working-class and rural women, and they became convinced that the government should be doing more to help marginal families. During the war they had honed political skills and had begun to introduce women's concerns about the high costs of war borne by the northern home front. In the postwar years, women leaders continued to be motivated by similar convictions. Unlike their male colleagues and many of their social counterparts, they did not hide behind the safety of Gilded Age rhetoric about the inevitability of social inequality and the suffering that naturally accompanied it, nor did they surrender to cynicism about the impotence of government in the face of machine politics. Whether they lobbied for the reform of public institutions, helped former slaves gain access to federal relief programs, or sought pensions and public support for working women and their children, the war generation's initiatives exhibited a maturing commitment to collective political action and to the idea that the state

The Woman's Christian Temperance Union began as women launched spontaneous crusades to shut down saloons throughout the Midwest. The crusading female figures in this illustration are comparable to the angel used in the Sanitary Commission's promotional literature. Library of Congress.

responsibility for its charges. Though they have often ssed as elite women reacting against an increasingly diverse society by attempting to implement programs of social control, this argument accepts Gilded Age reform rhetoric at the cost of a more judicious look at these women as independent agents and as professional political activists. The climax of wartime women's careers came in the Progressive Era, when women's political culture combined grassroots initiatives with federal efficacy and enlisted the state in meeting the needs of its dependents. The war marked their emergence into public life; the postwar years enabled women leaders to mature as advocates of the rights of women and their families and as proponents of a more morally conscious state.

LOU SCHUYLER was thirty-five years old when she returned from Europe, and she considered herself an accomplished professional reformer. Whereas ten years earlier Henry Bellows had had to persuade Schuyler to participate in the work of the United States Sanitary Commission, now she set her own reform agenda and followed nobody's lead. In 1871, after reading reports of the squalid conditions under which the state's poor and infirm were incarcerated, Schuyler began visiting hospitals, asylums, and poorhouses in New York, institutions that continued to operate as the last resort for the city's destitute and that were notorious for their corrupt administration. Often she found her access to these public institutions blocked by politicians who were anxious about her intentions. Schuyler was no stranger to this sort of obstructionism, for politicians and army doctors had resisted women's entry into army camps and military hospitals during the war. Women had proven themselves in virtually every venue during the war, but professional jealousies and prejudices about women being exposed to the promiscuous—mixed by class, ethnicity, and gender—living arrangements in the state's institutions remained unaltered. Schuyler persisted, however, and after conducting detailed inspections of the facilities, interviewing inmates, and finding evidence of poor administration and neglect, she decided to act.[4]

Horrified by what she saw in New York state poorhouses, mental institutions, and city hospitals, Schuyler began organizing visiting committees to inspect the facilities and report violations to the proper authorities. "It was a question of humane treatment for thousands," she recalled years later.[5] In 1872, Schuyler created the State Charities Aid Association (SCAA) to coordinate the work of these visiting committees, and she served as SCAA president. As had been her policy at the WCAR, Schuyler relied on associate managers—in many cases, the same women who had served in the WCAR during the war—to take local initiatives under the aegis of the SCAA while she conducted organized lobbying from the central offices in the city.[6] Enlisting the support of former commission colleagues such as Emily Blackwell, Frederick Law Olmsted, and Jane Woolsey, Schuyler described the purpose of the SCAA: "[W]e are men and women working together . . . with the one object of helping and elevating our poorer classes."[7] Although this thought highlights the paternalism of the SCAA, the association took up the antebellum humanitarian crusades of Dorothea Dix and was informed by the war generation's ongoing attempt to answer difficult questions about the causes and effects of poverty. Rather than rely on a passionate expression of moral outrage as had Dix, however, Lou Schuyler based her demands for reform on statistics and other scientific data compiled from a careful inspection of the institutions. Schuyler received assistance from influential friends such as Charles Loring Brace, the founder of the Children's Aid Society, and Josephine Shaw Lowell, a politically powerful woman in New York and a leader in the scientific charity movement. In 1875, the State Charities Aid Association was responsible for passing legislation that removed children from the state poorhouses and arranged to have them cared for in private homes, and the organization continued to lobby to have the mentally ill cared for in more appropriate settings.[8]

Creating a system to monitor the management of the state's hospitals, prisons, and almshouses allowed Schuyler and her colleagues to do more than express their concern for the inmates of the city poorhouses. The SCAA was a direct attack on the system of patronage that put inept and corrupt people in charge of such institutions, where they took money from the taxpayers and neglected the people in their care.[9] As Schuyler saw it, the state had as much responsibility to care for children, the indigent, and the insane in the postwar years as it had had toward the soldiers and displaced persons in its care during the war.

During the war the WCAR and later the USSC had stood as constant reminders to the American people and the U.S. government that the needs of the people in its care were not being fulfilled and that in some cases army doctors, quartermasters, or other government officials were as much to blame for the neglect as were any institutional flaws. Now the SCAA put political appointees on notice that the public would hold them accountable for the level of care they provided at state hospitals and poorhouses and for the way public money was spent. This challenge was similar to the one Schuyler and other branch women had posed to the claims of commission men that they had exclusive rights to determine how to spend public money. The SCAA venture serves as a measure of Schuyler's maturing political skills, for here she challenged the machine politicians who appointed men to run these institutions in return for patronage. The SCAA asserted the right of private citizens to monitor poorhouses and state hospitals and established Schuyler as an able political lobbyist.

In the same year that she launched the SCAA, Lou Schuyler began work on a piece of unfinished commission business—the training of women as professional nurses. In 1873, Schuyler's SCAA opened the Bellevue Training School for Nurses, the first nurse training school in the country at Bellevue Hospital in New York. To do so, Schuyler marshalled all of her resources, including a group of women veterans of the WCAR and the USSC's hospital transport campaign.[10]

In their work at Bellevue, Schuyler and the SCAA looked to Florence Nightingale for practical advice on opening a nurse training school, for Nightingale was responsible for opening the first such schools in England. The decisions made by the women administering the school also show the lasting influence of Dr. Elizabeth Blackwell's ideas about science and health reform and the need for trained women professionals to improve the standard of care given in public hospitals where men held a monopoly on medical care. In addition to training women to be professional nurses, then, the Bellevue School began to restructure the public hospital to provide better care for its patients. The school, for instance, forced doctors to recognize that women had health needs that differed from men's, and the results were an improved consciousness and standard of care for female patients.

In fact, in the name of providing improved care for poor women in city hospitals, Schuyler's SCAA launched what must have been perceived by the New York medical community as an attack on their professional integrity. Though the number of women earning medical degrees continued to grow in the United States in the postwar years, male doctors continued to put up stubborn resistance to women who cared for their patients. At the beginning of the war this prejudice had informed the calculated decision by New York doctors to eject Elizabeth Blackwell from their plans to form a commission to look into the health and medical care of U.S. Army soldiers. Now, in an ironic turn of events, the sister of two of Blackwell's former nurses outmaneuvered the doctors. Under the leadership of Abby Howland Woolsey, chair of the SCAA's special committee at Bellevue Hospital, the committee removed expectant and new mothers from the surgical wards of the hospital where many were dying from puerperal fever.[11] Once they were removed from the promiscuous accommodations at the city hospital, relocated to a special maternity hospital, and placed under the care of nurses trained at the Bellevue School, the women patients experienced a dramatic improvement in health and survival.[12]

Doctors at the hospital, however, resisted the SCAA and the nursing school's appropriation of the maternity wards because students at the medical school regularly held clinics in the wards. Woolsey pulled off a real coup, then, when she removed this critical teaching resource and replaced male doctors with female nurses. As the sister of two veterans of the USSC's hospital transport campaign and of the wars between army doctors and wartime nurses, Woolsey was perhaps unmoved by the resistance to her effort to improve the standard of care women received in the public hospital. In any case, Schuyler had long ago established that her independent initiatives would not be compromised by professional male jealousies.

After her work for the commission during the war, the initiatives she pursued in the postwar years show Schuyler's growing interest in public welfare. Schuyler was now working to find ways of meeting the needs of a diverse urban population, much as Blackwell had been doing at her New York Infirmary before the war. In the process, Schuyler was becoming a part of the political process, learning how to propose and pass legislation, how to hold elected officials up to public scrutiny, and how to play political factions off one another to the public's benefit. In fact, Schuyler's SCAA exercised such political clout that it was likened to a well-oiled political machine. An SCAA colleague recalled, for instance, the response of the New York medical community to the SCAA's elimination of the maternity wards at Bellevue Hospital. "The most distinguished doctors in New York," she recalled, treated "us as if we were Tammany politicians trying to rob them of their fees."[13] The comparison was not entirely unfounded. Schuyler was not accustomed to losing. When she or one of her initiatives met with resistance, Schuyler put into motion a network of personal and political alliances. And when Schuyler could not persuade her detractors to give in, this discreet circle of influential New York "friends" did.[14] In the case of Bellevue Hospital, Schuyler's friends included doctors who were familiar with her and other SCAA women's work for the USSC and who shared the SCAA's vision of hospital reform. In other SCAA campaigns, Schuyler applied political pressure by organizing voters who promised to support politicians friendly to her initiatives. "I think we must make the Senators understand," Schuyler intimated in 1881, for instance, when an SCAA bill was pending before the New York state legislature, "that the Assn [SCAA] represents *the people,* and that the Assn is stronger than the [State Board of Charities] [emphasis in original]."[15] To those who attempted to stand in her way, resisting Schuyler must have seemed as formidable as challenging Tammany Hall.

Louisa Lee Schuyler's political career was long and the extent of her influence was broad.[16] Although her public advocacy would never again involve her in an initiative that organized along gender-specific lines or one that reached out to rural and working-class women as anything other than the beneficiaries of her work, Schuyler was the outspoken leader of every reform she undertook and she actively recruited women to take leadership roles in her organizations. Her SCAA work to establish a system of medical training for women nurses in New York indicates that Schuyler had emerged from her commission work with a commitment to promoting women in the professions and a vision of advocating for improved medical care for women and children. Certainly she had been influenced by Elizabeth Blackwell's thoughts about health reform and her direction in the early days of the WCAR. As part of the circle of young women who gravitated toward Blackwell's initiative during the war, Schuyler had launched her political career when men of her class were suffering from political disenchantment and disenfranchisement. But whereas Blackwell was dismissed because her nurse training proposal threat-

ened the male medical establishment, Schuyler headed a powerful political lobby of women that could not be as easily outflanked as Blackwell had been. Schuyler had not only time but powerful friends on
her side when she launched her Bellevue Nursing School initiative in
the postwar years. Blackwell might have been disregarded as a maver-
ick twelve years earlier, but the same New York establishment had a
harder time ignoring Schuyler who, like others in her generation, had
proven herself as a persistent and politically connected professional
committed to the care of the city's less fortunate, especially women
and children. And though Schuyler did all that she did without en-
dorsing women's rights or suffrage—what Blackwell would have
called "an anti-man movement"—her initiatives opened up opportunities for women to become medical professionals and to take charge
of the political process.

These were interests that Schuyler and Abby May shared. In the
postwar years, May became even more focused on women's rights and
worked to find ways that middle-class and working-class women
could collaborate to improve urban conditions in Boston. In 1866,
May continued the special relief work of the New England Women's
Auxiliary Association, caring for returned soldiers and their families;
served as chair of the New England Freedman's Association's committee on teachers; and became president of the New England Woman's
Suffrage Association. Her suffrage activism carried over into her work
for the New England Women's Club and her directorship of the new
Association for the Advancement of Women in New York.[17]

Like Schuyler, May was an effective lobbyist who became even
more intimately involved in the political process after the war. In the
1870s, May was the first woman elected to the Boston School Committee, helped get a bill passed in Massachusetts that allowed women
to vote for the school committee, and was eventually appointed to the
State Board of Education. As a member of the State Board, May was in
charge of overseeing the normal schools in Massachusetts and became
involved in the preparation of public school teachers.[18] She too was
involved in reform that served to improve the conditions of mostly
middle-class women like herself, but in her school and dress reform
work, May focused on what she saw as the responsibilities of middle-
class women to women of more modest means. She consistently argued that excessiveness in dress and display not only was demeaning

to middle-class women who should be involved in meaningful work but also was an unfair standard of femininity to be held up for working-class women to aspire to.[19] Once women dressed simply and in such a way as to allow them to engage in work, May recommended that they find some. Like Caroline Healey Dall, a prominent Boston health reformer and feminist with whom May was associated, May believed that women needed productive labor to be free from "disease, depression, and moral idiocy."[20]

It was women and their work that interested May and the other founding members of the Women's Educational and Industrial Union (WEIU) in Boston in 1877. The organization, which began in 1871 as the Woman's Education Association, attracted prominent women with established public careers, such as Julia Ward Howe and Mary Livermore, and women who had distinguished themselves in the professions.[21] The WEIU proposed "to increase fellowship among women and to promote the best practical methods for securing their educational, industrial and social advancement."[22] In 1873, the WEIU oversaw the opening of the Boston Training School for Nurses at Massachusetts General Hospital.[23] In this early initiative, the WEIU surely benefited from May's experience. May was no stranger to the professional jealousies of the medical community in Boston, for she had worked with Dr. Marie Zakrzewska when Zakrzewska was seeking approval for a nurse training school at the New England Hospital for Women and Children before the war.[24] Her own stint in the hospital transport campaign in the summer of 1862 had impressed May with the need to have women trained as professional nurses. Like Schuyler, then, May saw nurse training as unfinished business, and the WEIU offered May the opportunity to finish it.

More than simply promoting women in the professions, the union was committed to fostering connections between middle-class women and working-class and immigrant women based on their shared experience as women—the kind of gender solidarity May and other wartime leaders had promoted during the war. The WEIU held vocational training classes for women and provided a number of social services such as legal aid, health education, and free medical treatment for needy and working women. WEIU women launched the school lunch program in Boston's public schools and kept control of that program well into the twentieth century. The organization investigated the industrial conditions under which women worked throughout the state of Massachusetts and reported its findings to the State House, recalling the war generation's concern for the plight of women working in wartime industries.

The WEIU did more than simply reach out to the working class and the poor in the city of Boston, as did Schuyler's SCAA in New York. It expressly opened up its membership to all women, promising to bring women of different classes closer together and giving women of all backgrounds the opportunity to take a positive role in social change in the city.[25] The WEIU provided a safe space at its central location in downtown Boston for working women and others to meet for lunch, conversation, or instruction and offered a variety of inexpensive meals for working women and their families. Describing the many projects the WEIU undertook to ameliorate conditions for the working classes in the city and the corresponding number of buildings the union came to occupy, historian Sarah Deutsch has suggested that by the turn of the century, the WEIU had "turned Boylston Street in downtown Boston into virtually a woman's mile."[26] At the WEIU complex, working women and others sought advice and assistance with employment, obtained medical care for themselves and their children, and received pure milk for their youngest children. WEIU women used their strategic location to lobby state and city lawmakers to subsidize and later to adopt many of these programs.[27] Postwar initiatives such as the WEIU helped turn the state into an engine of positive social change. In this way, the WEIU left a lasting influence on the city with its vision of an activist state and its commitment to making working people part of the solution to urban problems.

Although perhaps not a political powerhouse like Schuyler, May's career was steadily built on the foundations of her commission work. Like Schuyler, she had had reservations about her abilities at the beginning of the war. In her postwar career, however, May acted independently, confidently, and effectively to launch ambitious and original initiatives and use her own personal and political success to open up educational and occupational opportunities for others. May was committed to expanding educational and employment opportunities for women of all classes, establishing effective training programs for women professionals, and encouraging cross-class collaboration among women to foster positive urban change. In order to achieve these goals, May used a variety of approaches. Although May came from a family of prominent social reformers and activists, the war had provided her the opportunity to try out her own skills and test her stamina. Certainly she continued to make use of the personal connections she had forged with Boston abolitionists, health reformers, and feminists, but May also branched out to capitalize on professional relationships she had developed with women and men in her commission work. Like others of her generation, May's political skills matured during the war and the postwar years, as did her commitment to fighting for women's rights.

Mary Livermore, too, was a tireless advocate for women when her commission career was over. In Iowa in 1863, she had been terrified when asked to speak about her work for the commission before a packed hall of soldiers aid society members, politicians, and local military heroes, protesting that she "had never attempted a public address to a promiscuous audience."[28] Coerced into going up on stage, Livermore proved herself an effective speaker. Livermore's lecture career took off in the 1870s, allowing her husband and her to give up their newspaper business in Chicago and move back to New England.[29] In Boston, Livermore became the long-term president of the Massachusetts chapter of the Woman's Christian Temperance Union and, with May, served as an officer of the Association for the Advancement of Women.[30] She supported her family in the postwar years with her public speaking engagements.

Livermore began her suffrage activism after the war, claiming to have been converted to the cause by her wartime work. "During the war," she recalled, "I became aware that a large portion of the nation's work was badly done, or not done at all, because woman was not recognized as a factor in the political world."[31] The ballot was critical to improving conditions for all women, Livermore explained, for she "saw how women are degraded by disfranchisement, and, in the eyes of men, are lowered to the level of the pauper, the convict, the idiot, and the lunatic, are put in the same category with them, and with their own infant children."[32] In fact, although the national WCTU hesitated to officially advocate women's suffrage until the 1880s, under Livermore's leadership, the Massachusetts chapter was pushing for municipal suffrage as early as 1877, and the chapter's executive committee had submitted a petition in favor of a constitutional amendment.[33]

Through organizations such as the American Social Science Association and the WEIU, both Livermore and May balanced women's rights activism with an interest in helping working women and their families and in advocating for women's right to labor during the Progressive Era.[34] Livermore's work for the WCTU perhaps best illustrates how she and others of her generation had come to see women's rights as necessary in order to promote an entire package of social reforms designed to ameliorate the urban conditions that fostered class conflict and in order to bring women's concerns to the political forefront. What started as a moral campaign against saloons and liquor interests in the winter of 1873 became the Woman's Christian Temperance Union in the summer of 1874, an organization with a broad agenda of women's issues that became the first mass women's movement.[35]

According to Ruth Bordin, in 1892 the WCTU boasted a membership role of 150,000.[36] Yet despite its broad appeal and its widely ranging agenda of social reform, the WCTU is often overlooked because the organization was neither consistently nor exclusively committed to women's suffrage.[37] But as Bordin explains, it was the WCTU that made women's suffrage a popular grassroots issue, and, more than suffrage, the WCTU advocated wide-ranging social reform and encouraged women to take control of all aspects of their lives. Instead of limiting itself to the vote or to temperance, even, the WCTU spoke out against domestic violence, provided child care and other services for working women and their children, lobbied for free kindergartens, and joined forces with the Knights of Labor to fight for shorter workdays and safer work conditions.[38] In the end, the WCTU was not simply an organization that sought to end liquor consumption. Rather, it represented a wholescale critique of social inequalities and the institutions that sought to preserve them. Like the WEIU, the WCTU fought what women perceived to be the ill effects of urbanization and industrialization and it empowered women to work for substantive social change.

From this perspective, it makes sense that women such as Frances Willard, long-term president of the WCTU, and Mary Livermore moved easily into Christian Socialism in the 1880s.[39] As advocates of a broad spectrum of reform initiatives benefiting working women and their families and as critics of the degrading conditions brought on by postwar urbanization and unchecked industrial growth, Livermore and other women leaders saw in Edward Bellamy's vision a state that reflected their goals. Livermore served as president of both the Boston Nationalist Club and the Society of Christian Socialists, two of the many clubs that sprang up to advocate this late-nineteenth-century brand of American socialism.[40] For a woman such as Livermore who had spent the better part of her adult life seeking solutions to the many issues facing women, workers, and their families, socialism's promise of social transformation offered an attractive alternative to incremental reform.

In linking feminism to socialism, Livermore and others sought to go beyond antebellum bourgeois health reformers who, like Blackwell, likened a healthy society to a happy marriage—a delicate balance of masculine and feminine sensibilities. They envisioned a society that recognized the equality of the sexes, and in so doing, solved many of the social problems of late-nineteenth-century America. More than her former commission colleagues Schuyler and May, Livermore understood that answering difficult questions about women, their families, and their work required substantive social change. And enlisting the state as a positive force in that change was not only possible but desirable.

The evolution of the careers of Schuyler, May, and Livermore provides a basis for re-establishing the connections between the war generation of women and the generation of professional women activists that came of age during the Progressive Era. Certainly it is no exaggeration to say that the Progressive Era was the heyday of nineteenth-century women's public political work and culture, for during this period middle-class college-educated women launched a myriad of reform initiatives that forever altered the way government was conceived.

Historian Paula Baker has called the process by which social policy—traditionally women's domain—became public policy the "domestication of politics."[41] For it was women's, rather than men's, political culture, Kathryn Kish Sklar explains, that was poised to form coalitions that profoundly challenged state and federal government to make positive social change.[42] In the last decades of the nineteenth century, female-dominated institutions such as reform associations, women's clubs, and settlement houses provided an autonomous base from which women could pitch a variety of successful political battles. Women such as settlement house resident Florence Kelley, who organized working-class and middle-class women to fight for protective labor legislation and who became the factory inspector for the state of Illinois, indicate the potent possibilities of the gender-specific autonomy achieved by women activists during this period.[43]

But, as Sklar also points out in an essay on Hull House, women were able to achieve success in the Progressive Era not only by drawing on the strength of these female institutions but also by leaving those institutions to engage in the male political arena.[44] Women activists in the Progressive Era drew from antebellum separate spheres ideology and the notion of women's moral superiority in building these female institutions; they could thank the war generation for their willingness to use these notions to trespass into the sphere of postbellum politics. But wartime leaders were more than mere trespassers—they were masters of the kind of coalition politics that achieved positive social and political change in the postwar years.

In fact, the postwar careers of Schuyler, May, and Livermore suggest that it was the Civil War that provided them with both the impetus and the opportunity to begin to address women's concerns outside of the local context—to begin to look beyond what was traditionally considered women's sphere of influence. The war allowed Schuyler and her colleagues to see how hard rural and working-class women worked to support their families and how little assistance was offered them. Commission women saw how the economic crisis of the war upset already fragile family economies, yet they were consistently moved by the willingness of economically marginal women to sacrifice even more to preserve the Union. The sisterhood of states wartime women had built with women across the North did not fall apart in the postwar years. On the contrary, when the war was over, wartime leaders anticipated that the end of the political crisis would not usher in an end to the economic crisis. In fact, in the postwar years, industrialization and urbanization accelerated the economic dislocation initiated by the war, as industries that had experienced unprecedented expansion during the war continued to grow. In the war's aftermath, then, wartime leaders sympathized with those who had been marginalized by the transition from local to centralized economies, particu-

larly women and children. In their experience, problems of this magnitude required more than private benevolence and local solutions—
they required coordinated efforts and political action. But this time,
instead of waiting for their male contemporaries to endorse the initiatives that they believed would begin to address the needs they had
identified, wartime women leaders moved on their own initiatives.

Conclusion

*H*ad Schuyler turned her final report into a narrative history, as did May, she might very well have begun it the way she did a *Bulletin* article in February 1865. "Nearly four years ago we began life as an association," Schuyler recalled, "in a little room ... [that] contained two tables, one desk, half a dozen chairs, and a map on the wall."[1] From these humble beginnings Schuyler and her branch colleagues turned a scattered constituency of soldiers aid societies into a dynamic network of relief that sponsored a novel effort to train women as professional nurses, provided information and advice to soldiers' families, brought quality supplies from the home front to the soldiers, and helped support community welfare programs that aided economically marginal families whose male wage earners were absent.

Though the women who ran the commission branches had all been involved in local reform work before the war, they were young and inexperienced compared to many of the women who ran community welfare networks. And they found no adequate antebellum model of an organization that was national in scope yet based on a broad, yet locally flexible, agenda. By midcentury, men's organizations were primarily based on white men's shared access to centralized sources of political power—a model that offered little to women. Women's conventional public activism, on the other hand, was highly varied and local and relied on the moral reputation of local leaders and a personal nnection to the recipients of aid. Even the American Female Moral Reform Society (AFMRS), an organization with a national agenda and a diverse set of objectives, was still very much shaped by women's experiences in evangelical religion, and participation was determined by denominational loyalties.[2] The unique conditions of a protracted war that accentuated women's economic and social isolation when it might have brought them together in concern for the soldiers demanded a more catholic approach. "We had to feel our way very carefully," Schuyler remembered, admitting that "we were all very ignorant that first summer, and made blunders enough." But they persisted, and as the work grew, they kept pace, "learning from experience and daily requirement."[3] Branch women made the most of the resources available to them, and in the end they combined elements of women's and men's political culture that spoke to their particular needs and those of their generation.

Young women of the war generation sought an approach that would command the resources of local women at the same time that it commanded the respect of politically influential middle-class men. They claimed the authority to consolidate and administer women's localized reform and to help determine the shape of a powerful wartime relief agency. Faced with the unprecedented circumstances of a modern war, this generation of women was not content to rely solely on the methods of their mothers nor were they willing to count on the beneficence of their brothers. Branch women such as Schuyler, May, and Livermore were part of a transitional political culture that stood between those women who had sought reform and a political voice through local means and those who would effectively link local concerns to national movements. Unlike previous generations of women activists who relied on their ability to influence politics indirectly, women leaders in the commission engaged in the political process directly.

To do so, women leaders first had to come to terms with how their diverse female constituency experienced the war. Reaching out to women in remote rural areas and in more industrialized towns, branch women learned how wartime inflation and shortages of staples affected families and communities. Women experienced the war, like they did most things, in local terms. Branch women also learned that despite personal hardships women everywhere remained committed to their local benevolence work and to helping the needy in their own towns. Recognizing the potential of this local momentum, Schuyler, May, and their colleagues helped support local efforts in exchange for a commitment to contributing to the branches. They did not ask women to trade local loyalty for loyalty to the commission. Instead, branch leaders used local societies as lenses to focus women's energy on a cause that demanded a unified (national) response. Branch women could not forget that the real circumstances of women's lives provided the greatest challenge to the creation of an imagined community of women that extended beyond the limits of class and local geography. This approach made the most of local resources and respected women's commitment to their families and their neighbors.

In the process of courting local loyalties, branch leaders protected the autonomy of women's benevolence work and asserted their right to determine how money raised by the northern home front was spent. Branch women kept local community-based reform from being absorbed into a men's organization. Local women held branch women accountable to a system of female values that had long determined the shape of community reform efforts: They demanded discriminate use of home-front contributions, preferred investing in homemade instead of ready-made clothing for the soldiers, and believed that a working woman deserved a wage that reflected her responsibilities to her family.[4] In exchange for adhering to these terms, branch women expected to be treated like professionals. As professionals, Schuyler, May, and their branch colleagues expected to be able to use the products of the female home front at their own discretion.

Previous generations of women activists had found power in their ability to condemn the all-male political process and to sympathize with the victims of the commercial marketplace, but the war generation was willing to effect change by a more direct approach. Engaging in a cooperative venture with middle-class men that gave them access to political power did not require that branch women give up the sex-segregated autonomy of women's political culture nor did it signal their adoption of male values. Within the commission bureaucracy, women of Schuyler and May's generation commanded the respect of commission men by appealing to them as colleagues, not as "ladies" or moral superiors. Without abandoning sex-specific appeals and a separatist strategy, women at the commission branches adopted the

rhetoric and tactics of male professionals and acted in distinctly political ways.⁵ At the same time, they rejected the notions that women's
societies were strictly subordinate and dependent on male leadership,
that women's work could be sacrificed to wartime expediency, and
that working women's wages should be determined by middle-class
profit motives. Claiming authority as professionals and political
actors, branch leaders asserted the collective economic and political
power of an extended cross-class female community, engaged in the
decision-making process of a distinctly political organization, and
proved themselves capable of sustaining the work over an extended
period of time.

For women at the commission branches, the work provided a secular alternative to evangelical reform, yet it made no overtly political
demands as did the suffrage movement. Before the war, women's suffrage was still very much a minority reform movement. Though most
were not active in suffrage before the war—including women such as
May and Livermore who would become vocal suffrage activists in the
postwar years—women everywhere organized along gender-specific
lines after the war. At the same time that women leaders had demanded that they be considered professional equals to men in their
commission work, they never gave up claims to a particular feminine
morality and consistently advocated gender solidarity. This claim had
remained implicit in branch claims on behalf of working women and
had allowed middle-class women to go to such "promiscuous" places
as the army camp and the working-class tenement.

Members of this transitional political culture liked having it both
ways. At times they adhered to a strategy based on the antebellum
concept of gender difference, and at others they demanded to be received as the equals of men. Schuyler, for instance, was a highly effective lobbyist and an invincible politician who sponsored legislative solutions to urban poverty and to the poor treatment of the indigent
insane, but she presented herself as a selfless, apolitical humanitarian
reformer. Postwar suffragists such as May and Livermore were openly
critical of the male-dominated political world even as they sought to
gain entrance to it. "The state," May wrote in the *Woman's Advocate*
in 1868, "has proven itself void of all positive worth. . . . It has made
one man rich at the expense of a thousand."⁶ Livermore recalled that
the war opened her eyes to the many evils of women's legal inequality,

and she and other women's rights advocates spoke of the need for a parallel development of the sexes.

At the same time, Livermore was president of the Woman's Christian Temperance Union, a crusade in which women attacked male immorality. In a behavior that prefigured women's activism during the Progressive Era, May and Livermore balanced their calls for equal rights with efforts to protect working women and their children from the exploitation of the marketplace and to speak out for women's right to labor.[7] Perhaps claims to professional equality during the war offered some women access to male power structures where they discovered new possibilities for the exercise of a more broadly based moral authority in the postwar years. Whether or not women organizers believed in a particular feminine morality, it remained a valuable organizational tool. Recognizing the power in local women's community-driven moral reform, women leaders understood that the problems of the modern, urban, and industrial society in which they lived required political solutions. The organizations they formed and the reforms they spearheaded during their lifetimes had distinctly political agendas. And in order to achieve them, women leaders experimented with a form of coalition politics to further their interests, an approach that demonstrated the potential to enlist the support of like-minded men on issues of mutual interest. This same strategy would allow women to form nationwide grassroots lobbies and to work effectively with men and the male political process during the Progressive Era.[8]

Indeed, these women appear to fit comfortably into a "middle ground" that George Fredrickson criticizes the war generation for overlooking. Lumping together middle-class women and men who worked for the commission during the war, Fredrickson condemns them for giving up the localized, optimistic, humanitarian reform of the prewar years for elitist postwar efforts that were highly centralized and institutionalized and that were pessimistic about human potential. Except in only two cases, Fredrickson concludes, the war generation did not subscribe to "a social philosophy grounded in the belief that science, organization, and planning could be enlisted on the side of humanitarian reform."[9] Indeed, when Richard Hofstadter looked at men such as Bellows, Strong, and Olmsted in the postwar years, he found a class of disaffected and isolated "Mugwumps"—overwhelmingly urban, middle-class men from established families who perceived themselves to be victims of a collapsing social hierarchy that made them equally as "hysterical" about working-class activism as they were of the "crass materialism" of the industrial giants.[10]

These interpretations assume that men and women reacted the same to the experience of the war and got the same things out of the commission cooperation. Schuyler's SCAA, according to Fredrickson, is an example of how the "sanitary experience" left northerners deeply conservative and pessimistic about the possibilities of individual and state-sponsored reform.[11] Yet though Schuyler sought support from prominent and influential men and women in New York for her long-term pursuit of legislation to protect the indigent, the insane, and children—rather than the grassroots support that had made the WCAR work—her campaigns were not driven by a sense of pessimism nor were they defined by a need to regain lost social status. Indeed, Schuyler devoted her postwar career to challenging the state to take responsibility for its weakest members. And Fredrickson's conclusions seem to fit May's and Livermore's careers even less comfortably. May's and Livermore's postwar careers not only reveal a blossoming commitment to feminism but also an evolving vision of a state that would incorporate traditionally feminine concerns such as the health and well-being of women and families and the economic security and cooperation of all classes. Moreover, Fredrickson's argument is inconsistent with what we know of highly successful postwar women's organizations such as the WCTU. Many women who had enjoyed the camaraderie of their work for commission branches and had found the connection to a national organization with a political agenda empowering joined the temperance crusade after the war. In the WCTU, local chapters were encouraged to take up any number of causes— from temperance to suffrage, from fighting violence against women to speaking out against war, from helping working women and children to speaking out against the exploitation of industrial workers.[12] Although women's participation in the crusade was determined in part by their middle-class status, the WCTU's organization was distinctly female, and its broad agenda reached well beyond the movement's middle-class membership.

A closer look at the commission, one that pays attention to the subtle differences between the experience of men and women in the commission leadership, suggests a more nuanced estimation of the experiment. With few exceptions, middle-class men, such as those who had led the commission, remained in social isolation until the Progressive Era, when a new generation emerged that was willing to challenge the social conservatism and insularity of their fathers.[13] For some middle-class men of the war generation, public activism proved to be only for the duration, for once the immediate emergency of the war was over, they retreated to privacy. As we look closely at women's involvement in the United States Sanitary Commission, we can conclude that women's reform underwent no such dramatic redefinition. Following their commission work, middle-class women leaders embraced the challenge of finding progressive initiatives that would ameliorate the social unrest of the postwar years, while commission men retreated to a conservative, defensive stance. Commission women's experience taught them to seek help from men in achieving political solutions to the problems of the day, and it allowed their daughters to eschew male leadership in their own independent initiatives.

Notes

PREFACE

1 Charles J. Stillé, *History of the United States Sanitary Commission: Being the General Report of Its Work During the War of the Rebellion* (Philadelphia: J. B. Lippincott, 1866).

2 The International Red Cross was established in Geneva in 1864. Walter Donald Kring, *Henry Whitney Bellows* (Boston: Skinner House, 1979), 421–422.

3 For a brief discussion of the writing of the *History,* see William Quentin Maxwell's *Lincoln's Fifth Wheel: The Political History of the United States Sanitary Commission* (New York: Longmans, Green, & Co., 1956), 310.

4 Stillé, *History,* vi, iv.

5 For example: "Its influence, therefore, extended far beyond . . . relief on the battlefield, and the constant efforts it made to inculcate a National spirit in the care of the soldier, produced an effect, both in the Army and the country at large, which powerfully contributed to the success of the National arms." Ibid., 151.

6 Ibid., 30.

7 In *The Search for Order, 1877–1920* (New York: Hill and Wang, 1967), Robert Wiebe argues that the war and its aftermath marked a fundamental shift in American values that was orchestrated by the urban elite. Wiebe's work is useful in understanding the appeal the commission model would have in the postwar era, as he suggests that "America in the late nineteenth century was a society without a core." The small-town values of the earlier period were no longer appropriate to the increasingly urban, industrial, ethnically, and socially diverse society. Wiebe, 12.

8 See George Fredrickson's discussion of the "strenuous" nationalism promoted by northern intellectuals, including the "sanitary elite." Fredrickson, *The Inner Civil War: Northern Intellectuals and the Crisis of the Union* (New York: Harper and Row, 1965).

9 In *Yankee Leviathan: The Origins of Central State Authority in America, 1859–1877* (Cambridge: Cambridge University Press, 1990), Richard Bensel discusses the weakness of American nationalism before the war and argues that, in the end, the South was more successful at exercising central state authority than was the North. Stephen Skowronek argues that the USSC was a propaganda instrument of New England intellectuals, who were offering their services to help solve what they saw as "a crisis of institutional authority." *Building a New American State: The Expansion of National Administrative Capacities, 1877–1920* (Cambridge: Cambridge University Press, 1982), 53.

10 Historians have largely dismissed the long-held assumption that the Civil War was "a poor man's fight." Maris Vinovskis found that while working-class men in Newburyport were not more likely to enlist in the war, they were more likely to be killed or wounded. Vinovskis, "Have Social Historians Lost the Civil War?" in *Toward a Social History of the American Civil War,* ed. Maris Vinovskis (Cambridge: Cambridge University Press, 1990), 12–21.

11 A few of the historians who have considered this phenomenon and its consequences are Fredrickson, *Inner Civil War;* Wiebe, *Search for Order;* and John Sproat, *"The Best Men": Liberal Reformers in the Gilded Age* (New York: Oxford University Press, 1968). Following the lead of Fredrickson's *Inner Civil War,* many historians have explored the ways in which the men of the "old patrician class" used the United States Sanitary Commission to widen their social and political influence in the wake of challenges to their hegemony by the working class and the new bourgeoisie. Though he does not refer to the Sanitary Commission specifically, Wiebe looks at how these men successfully introduced new bureaucratic-minded values in the postwar era as a means of social control. The anti-heroes in Sproat's work feared mass movements and held stubbornly to the belief that "the best men" should govern. In the end, the hopelessly outdated ideals of the liberals assured that their efforts to clean up the city would fail.

 More recently, Iver Bernstein considers the political and social dissension of the period through the prism of the New York City draft riots of 1863, when nouveau riche Democrat industrialists and disgruntled patrician Republicans came to blows over how to respond to and to interpret the working-class draft riots. Bernstein, *The New York City Draft Riots: Their Significance for American Society and Politics in the Age of the Civil War* (New York: Oxford University Press, 1990).

12 Mary Poovey found the same thing in depictions of Florence Nightingale. Poovey, "A Housewifely Woman: The Social Construction of Florence Nightingale," in *Uneven Developments: The Ideological Work of Gender in Mid-Victorian England* (Chicago: University of Chicago Press, 1988), 172.

13 It is worth noting that it might also have been useful to make the commission an angel because it allowed commissioners to reassure the U.S. government that the USSC would remain strictly subordinate to military authority. The army was often resentful of the USSC and complained that commissioners exercised too much power. See Katharine Prescott Wormeley, *The United States Sanitary Commission: A Sketch of Its Purposes and Work* (Boston: Little, Brown and Company, 1863). Wormeley explains that the USSC proudly maintained the

"strictest subordination" to the government. Wormeley, *United States Sanitary Commission,* 20–22.

14 "The Origin, Organization, and Working of the Woman's Central Association of Relief," October 12, 1861, *Documents of the United States Sanitary Commission* (hereafter *Documents*), vol. I, #32 (New York: n.p., 1866), 5. Wormeley, *United States Sanitary Commission,* 2.

15 Bellows quoted in Fredrickson, *Inner Civil War,* 106.

16 Frederick Knapp, "Plain Answers to Plain Questions," *The Sanitary Commission Bulletin* 10 (March 15, 1864): 289.

 Carroll Smith-Rosenberg argues that through natural language and imagery, "the bourgeoisie seeks to merge its identity with that of the nation . . . to depict interests and behavior that are class-specific as 'natural' or patriotic." Smith-Rosenberg, *Disorderly Conduct: Visions of Gender in Victorian America* (New York: Alfred A. Knopf, 1985), 50.

17 The commission angel is not unlike the crusading women of the Woman's Christian Temperance Union in the 1870s. See chapter 7.

INTRODUCTION

1 For Willard's prairie fire analogy, see Ruth Bordin, *Woman and Temperance: The Quest for Power and Liberty, 1873–1900* (New Brunswick, N.J.: Rutgers University Press, 1990), 15ff.

2 For critical treatments of women's mid-nineteenth-century reform efforts, see, for instance, Christine Stansell, *City of Women: Sex and Class in New York, 1789–1860* (Chicago: University of Illinois Press, 1987); Suzanne Lebsock, *The Free Women of Petersburg: Status and Culture in a Southern Town, 1784–1860* (New York: W. W. Norton & Co., 1984); and Lori Ginzberg, *Women and the Work of Benevolence: Morality, Politics, and Class in the Nineteenth-Century United States* (New Haven: Yale University Press, 1990).

3 Good but dated collections of women's wartime experiences, including women involved with the USSC, are as follows: Sylvia Dannett, *Noble Women of the North* (New York: Thomas Yoseloff, 1959); Marjorie Barstow Greenbie, *Lincoln's Daughters of Mercy* (New York: G. P. Putnam's Sons, 1944); Mary Elizabeth Massey, *Bonnet Brigades* (New York: Knopf, 1966); Agatha Young McDowell, *The Women and the Crisis: Women of the North in the Civil War* (New York: Oblensky, 1959).

4 Readers interested in some of these new directions should begin with the excellent collection of essays in *Divided Houses: Gender and the Civil War,* ed. Catherine Clinton and Nina Silber (New York: Oxford University Press, 1992). Elizabeth Leonard's *Yankee Women: Gender Battles in the Civil War* (New York: W. W. Norton, 1994) brings together the accounts of a volunteer nurse, the leader of a local soldiers aid society, and a female doctor. Megan McClintock examines the ties that developed between American families and the federal government through the administration of veterans' pensions in "Civil War Pensions and the Reconstruction of Union Families," *Journal of American History* 83 (September 1996): 456–480. Drew Gilpen Faust's *Mothers of Invention: Women of the Slaveholding South in the American Civil War* (New York: Random

House, 1996) is the most recent work on southern white women. Jacqueline Jones's *Labor of Love, Labor of Sorrow: Black Women, Work, and the Family, From Slavery to the Present* (New York: Vintage, 1986) is a good overview of black women's experiences.

5 Estimate from Maxwell, *Lincoln's Fifth Wheel*, 296. In 1865, the USSC estimated that there were 32,000 affiliated soldiers aid societies. *USSC Bulletin* (June 1, 1865): 1188.

6 Wormeley, *United States Sanitary Commission*, 53.

7 The Female Moral Reform Society was founded in 1834 and became the American Female Reform Society in 1839. Carroll Smith-Rosenberg, "Beauty, the Beast, and the Militant Woman: A Case Study in Sex Roles and Social Stress in Jacksonian America," in *Disorderly Conduct*, 120. The WCTU was founded in 1874. Bordin, *Woman and Temperance*, 3–4.

8 Peter J. Parish, *The American Civil War* (London: Eyre Methuen, 1975), 340–363; Phillip Shaw Paludan, *"A People's Contest": The Union and the Civil War* (New York: Harper & Row, 1988), 182. Paludan also notes that in 1863, although wages increased by 50–60 percent, prices went up almost 100 percent. Rents and fuel also went up dramatically.

9 LLS to FLO, May 20, 1863, United States Sanitary Commission Papers (hereafter USSC Papers), Box 955, Astor, Lennox, and Tilden Foundation Collection, NYPL, Rare Books and Manuscripts Division. LLS to USSC, "Results of the Survey," April 1, 1863, USSC Papers, Box 667–670, NYPL.

10 Abigail Williams May, New England Women's Auxiliary Association "Final Report," USSC Papers, Box 992, NYPL, 11.

11 See Kathryn Kish Sklar, "The Historical Foundations of Women's Power in the Creation of the American Welfare State, 1830–1930," in *Mothers of a New World*, ed. Seth Koven and Sonya Michel (New York: Routledge, 1993), 43–93; Paula Baker, "The Domestication of Politics: Women and American Political Society, 1780–1920," *American Historical Review* 89 (June 1984), 620–647; Barbara Epstein, *The Politics of Domesticity: Women, Evangelism, and Temperance in Nineteenth-Century America* (Middletown, Conn.: Wesleyan University Press, 1981).

12 See, for instance, Maxwell on Bellows in *Lincoln's Fifth Wheel*, 316.

13 Maxwell, *Lincoln's Fifth Wheel*, 302.

14 Ibid.

15 None of the members of the commission executive board escapes Fredrickson's critical eye. See, for example, on Bellows, Fredrickson, *Inner Civil War*, 100, 103, 109ff.; on Stillé, 101, 104; on Olmsted, 101. Many of the USSC men turn up again in Thomas Haskell's *The Emergence of Professional Social Science* (Chicago: University of Illinois Press, 1977), where Haskell finds them leading the social science movement and trying once again to establish the hegemony of their class by promoting the value of professional social science.

16 Fredrickson, *Inner Civil War*, 87.

17 Rejean Attie, "'A Swindling Concern': The United States Sanitary Commission and the Northern Female Public, 1861–1865" (Ph.D. diss., Columbia University, 1987). Attie's book based on her dissertation, *Patriotic Toil: Northern Women and the American Civil War* (Ithaca, N.Y.: Cornell University Press, 1998), was published as this manuscript was nearing completion.

18 For other modern works dealing with the commission and related subjects, see the following: Bonnie Blustein, "'To Increase the Efficiency of the Medical Department': A New Approach to U.S. Civil War Medicine," *Civil War History* 33 (March 1987); Kristie Ross, "'Women are needed here': Northern Protestant Women as Nurses During the Civil War, 1861–1865" (Ph.D. diss., Columbia University, 1993); Jane Schultz, "The Inhospitable Hospital: Gender and Professionalism in Civil War Medicine," *Signs* 17 (Winter 1992): 363–392; Jane Schultz, "Women at the Front: Gender and Genre in the Literature of the American Civil War" (Ph.D. diss., University of Michigan, 1988); Nina Bennett Smith, "The Women Who Went to the War: The Union Army Nurse in the Civil War" (Ph.D. diss., Northwestern University, 1981); Ann Douglas Wood, "The War Within a War: Women Nurses in the Union Army," *Civil War History* 18 (September 1972): 197–212.

Among the many contemporary anthologies of women's wartime contributions that include accounts of commission women, see Josiah Benton, *What Women Did for the War, and What the War Did for Women*, Memorial Day Address Delivered before the Soldiers Club at Wellesley, Mass., May 30, 1894 (Boston: n.p., 1894); L. P. Brockett and Mary C. Vaughan, *Woman's Work in the Civil War: A Record of Heroism, Patriotism and Patience* (Philadelphia: Zeigler, McCurdy & Co., 1867); Frank Moore, *Women of the War, Their Heroism and Self-Sacrifice* (Hartford, Conn.: S. S. Scranton & Co., 1866). Individuals involved with the commission published their own accounts/letters after the war, and the modern Frederick Law Olmsted, George Templeton Strong, Henry Whitney Bellows collections and biographies are also useful.

19 Ginzberg, *Women and the Work of Benevolence*, 11–35.

20 Elizabeth Leonard comes to different conclusions about how gender relations were changed by the commission and the war in general. In *Yankee Women*, Leonard concludes that women's and men's interactions in the war caused a "friction" that was relieved when "women persisted and as men backed down, coming to appreciate and even depend upon women's contributions under the circumstances, learning to relinquish power." Leonard, 198.

21 Sara Evans, *Born for Liberty: A History of Women in America* (New York: Free Press, 1989), 101.

CHAPTER I

1 Mary A. Livermore, *My Story of the War: A Woman's Narrative of Four Years Personal Experience as Nurse in the Union Army, and in Relief Work at Home, in Hospitals, Camps, and at the Front, During the War of the Rebellion* (1888; reprint, New York: De Capo Press, 1995), 91.

2 Livermore, *My Story of the War*, 91.

3 In *The Tribute Book: A Record of the Munificence, Self-Sacrifice and Patriotism of the American People* (New York: Derby & Miller, 1865), Frank Goodrich claims that there were two ladies aid societies that met on April 15, the day President Lincoln issued his call for 75,000 volunteers, one in Bridgeport, Connecticut, and one in Charlestown, Massachusetts. Goodrich, 70.

4 Abby Howland Woolsey to Eliza Woolsey Howland, April 19, 1861, *Letters of a Family During the War for the Union, 1861–1865*, vol. 1, eds. Georgeanna Woolsey Bacon and Eliza Woolsey Howland (New York: Printed for private distribution, 1899), 42.

5 April 18, 1861, *The Diary of George Templeton Strong*, ed. Thomas Pressly (Seattle, Wash.: University of Washington Press, 1988), 188.

6 Jane Stuart Woolsey to "A Friend in Paris," May 10, 1861, *Letters of a Family*, vol. 1, 66.

7 *Diary of George Templeton Strong*, April 16, 1861, 186.

8 Strong Diary, Typescript, III, August 29, 1862, 255, Butler Library (hereafter BL), Columbia University. Strong paid $1,100 for a draft substitute, of whom he said, "The big Dutchman therewith purchased looked as if he could do good service." Strong Diary, III, September 2, 1864, 284.

9 *The Papers of Frederick Law Olmsted*, Volume IV: *Defending the Union*, ed. Jane Turner Censer (Baltimore, Md.: The Johns Hopkins University Press, 1986), 117–118. Olmsted briefly considered volunteering for the navy, asking his father to "take care of my wife and children." *Papers of Frederick Law Olmsted*, vol. III, 342.

10 Livermore, *My Story of the War*, 110.

11 See, for instance, Stephen Crane, *The Red Badge of Courage* (1894; reprint, Toronto: Random House, 1954).

12 In *All the Daring of the Soldier: Women of the Civil War Armies*, Elizabeth Leonard estimates that somewhere between 500 and 1,000 women actually *did* enlist as men. See chapter 5 notes. (New York: W. W. Norton and Company, 1999).

13 Carroll Smith-Rosenberg, *Disorderly Conduct: Visions of Gender in Victorian America* (New York: Oxford University Press, 1985), 126.

14 New York Dispensary for Poor Women and Children, "First Annual Report," Blackwell Family Papers (hereafter BFP), microfilm reel #2, Schlesinger Library (SL), Radcliffe College. Dr. Elizabeth Blackwell, *Pioneer Work for Women* (London: J. M. Dent and Sons, Ltd., 1895), 168–169.

15 Blackwell was very particular about what she considered regular (and appropriate) medical training. For instance, well before mainstream medical schools admitted women, alternative medical schools such as those advocating hydropathy encouraged women to apply and female medical schools were established in Boston and Philadelphia in the early 1860s. Preferring to continue to press existing institutions to open their doors, Blackwell didn't think much of these alternatives, calling hydropathy "quack" medicine and female medical schools "silly schemes." Elizabeth Blackwell to Emily Blackwell, January 23, 1855, 3. BFP, reel 3. Elizabeth Blackwell to Barbara Bodichon, January 14, 1861, Elizabeth Blackwell Papers (hereafter EBP), BL, Columbia University. For information about alternative medical schools, see William Leach, *True Love and Perfect Union: The Feminist Reform of Sex and Society* (Middletown, Conn.: Wesleyan University Press, 1989).

16 Blackwell, *Pioneer Work*, 183–184. It is interesting that the first doctor Blackwell employed as a sanitary visitor was an African American man.

17 Leach, *True Love*.

18 Florence Nightingale is largely credited with popularizing these ideas, but domestic advice manuals had been making many of the same recommendations for years.

19 Dix launched successful efforts in Massachusetts, Rhode Island, New York, New Jersey, Pennsylvania, Kentucky, Maryland, Ohio, Illinois, Mississippi, Alabama, Tennessee, and North Carolina. Her momentum slowed only in 1854 when President Pierce vetoed the land reform bill she had initiated. David Gollaher, *Voice for the Mad: The Life of Dorothea Dix* (New York: The Free Press, 1995).

20 Dorothea Dix to Anne E. Heath, April 20, 1861, Dorothea Dix Papers (DP), Houghton Library (HL), Harvard University. This and a series of letters appear to be missing from Houghton. But it is quoted in Gollaher, *Voice for the Mad*, 397, and in Helen Marshall's earlier *Dorothea Dix: Forgotten Samaritan* (New York: Russell and Russell, 1967), 202–203.

21 For women and the Second Great Awakening, see Barbara Welter, "The Cult of True Womanhood: 1800–1860," and other essays in *Dimity Convictions: The American Woman in the Nineteenth Century* (Athens: Ohio University Press, 1976); Mary Ryan, *Cradle of the Middle Class: The Family in Oneida County, New York, 1790–1865* (Cambridge: Cambridge University Press, 1981); and Smith-Rosenberg, *Disorderly Conduct.*

22 Though these campaigns were aimed at combating "male" vices, clearly, they—temperance crusaders, in particular—often equated these vices with immigrants and the working classes.

23 Gollaher, *Voice for the Mad*, 142. Dix's moral outrage was often merciless, and doctors often paid a heavy price for her intervention.

24 Ryan describes this phenomenon best: "A father in a Victorian parlor was something of a bull in a china shop, somewhat ill at ease with the gentle virtues enshrined there." Ryan, *Cradle of the Middle Class*, 232.

25 Blackwell, *Pioneer Work*, 22.

26 In a letter to her sister Emily, who was studying medicine in Paris, for instance, Blackwell advised her against disguising herself as a man to gain entrance into the hospital, suggesting that she not "overestimate the benefits of disguise" and that Emily needed "influential men [to] take an interest in you and give you chances." Elizabeth Blackwell to Emily Blackwell, July 24, 1854, BFP, reel 3.

27 Blackwell to family, December 24, 1850, in Blackwell, *Pioneer Work*, 145.

28 Among the early "friends" of the New York Infirmary was Dr. Valentine Mott, who would also serve as the WCAR president when the USSC was formed. Ibid., 169. In 1868, the New York Infirmary became a medical college and continued to function as such until Cornell University opened its doors to women in 1899. Elizabeth H. Thomson, "Elizabeth Blackwell," in *Notable American Women*, vol. 1, ed. Edward T. James, Janet Wilson James, and Paul Boyer (Cambridge, Mass.: Belknap Press of Harvard University Press, 1971), 164.

29 The organization began as the New York Female Moral Reform Society, and in 1839 it became the American Female Moral Reform Society. Smith-Rosenberg, *Disorderly Conduct*, 120. See also Ryan, *Cradle of the Middle Class.*

30 Leach, *True Love*, 13.

31 Blackwell to Barbara Bodichon, June 5, 1861, EBP, BL.

32 Blackwell to Barbara Bodichon, April 23, 1861, EBP, BL.

33 Ibid.

34 Blackwell to Bodichon, June 5, 1861, EBP, BL.

35 Blackwell quotes from her journal conversations with Nightingale beginning in at least 1850 and continuing through the Civil War years. References to their hospital plans appear often. Blackwell, *Pioneer Work,* 150, 175–176ff.

36 See, for instance, Florence Nightingale's *Notes on Nursing: What It Is, and What It Is Not,* which was originally published in England in 1859 and in the United States in 1860. Due to its popularity, the book was reissued often and continues to be. The version I use below was published in Edinburgh in 1980. (Edinburgh: Churchill Livingstone, 1980).

37 Nightingale, *Notes on Nursing,* 101ff.

38 Ibid., v.

39 Blackwell to Bodichon, September 25, 1855, EBP, BL. This citation must have been misdated by the microfilm editor, for *Notes* was not even published in England until 1859. In 1855, Nightingale was still in the Crimea and Blackwell was in New York, so it is very unlikely that the doctor was looking at an early copy of the manual. In 1858–1859, though, Blackwell was in England working on opening a hospital and she met with her "old friend" often. See, for instance, Elizabeth Blackwell to Emily Blackwell, February 1859, in Blackwell, *Pioneer Work,* 175–176.

40 Nightingale to John Stuart Mill, September 12, 1860. Quoted in Martha Vicinus and Bea Nergaard, ed., *Ever Yours, Florence Nightingale: Selected Letters* (Cambridge: Harvard University Press, 1990), 210. Nightingale makes similar remarks in *Notes on Nursing,* when she refers to women's urge to do "all that men do, including the medical and other professions" as "jargon." Nightingale, 111–112. Blackwell noted this "little sneer" but didn't appear to take offense. Blackwell to Bodichon, September 25, 1855 (1859?), EBP. Lois Monteiro explains this fundamental disagreement as an early example of the debate between feminists who focus on women's fundamental differences from men and those who fight for a fundamental equality. Monteiro, "On Separate Roads: Florence Nightingale and Elizabeth Blackwell," *Signs* 9 (Spring 1984): 520–533.

In *Sympathy and Science: Women Physicians in American Medicine* (New York: Oxford University Press, 1985), Regina Morantz-Sanchez suggests that the first generation of women doctors had a vision of medicine that differed significantly from that of men doctors, one that was based in traditional holistic practices of midwifery and women healers and was at odds with male medical practices.

41 Welter, "The Cult of True Womanhood."

42 Nancy Cott, *The Bonds of True Womanhood: "Woman's Sphere" in New England, 1780–1835* (New Haven, Conn.: Yale University Press, 1977). Carroll Smith-Rosenberg has shown that women lived in a female world where they developed intense relationships with other women, where they participated in distinct rituals, and where men were relative strangers. Smith-Rosenberg, "The Female World of Love and Ritual: Relations Between Women in Nineteenth-Century America," *Signs* 1 (1975): 1–30.

43 Paula Baker, "The Domestication of Politics: Women and American Political

Society, 1780–1920," *American Historical Review* 89 (June 1984): 620–647. For women's antebellum temperance work, see Ryan, *Cradle of the Middle Class.*

44 Leach, *True Love and Perfect Union,* 26. In a sermon delivered on April 21, 1861, Bellows began to develop an organic social theory, in which he envisioned the nation as "the total social being incarnate in a political unit, having common organs and functions; a living body, with a head and a heart . . . with a common consciousness." Henry Whitney Bellows, *The State and the Nation—Sacred to Christian Citizens, A Sermon Preached on April 21, 1861* (New York: 1861), 6, 7.

45 Eliza Bellows to Russell Bellows, April 14, 1861, Henry Whitney Bellows Papers (BP), Massachusetts Historical Society (MHS).

46 Henry Whitney Bellows (HWB) to Stillé, November 15, 1865, BP, MHS.

47 James M. McPherson, *What They Fought For, 1861–1865* (New York: Doubleday, 1995).

48 At forty-seven, Bellows was not necessarily too old to consider active service himself. In fact, on April 28th, a member of the Central Park Commission offered Bellows a position as "fighting Chaplain—of a Squadron of Cavalry to be composed of gentlemen, who are anxious to go into active service." George Manning Jr. to HWB, April 28, 1861, BP, MHS. Bellows forwarded the letter to his son and added a note that seems to indicate that he had not considered the offers to fight seriously: "I send this as a curious commentary of the times. . . . It is the second overture of this sort I've rec'd!" HWB to Russell Bellows, April 1861, BP, MHS.

49 Fredrickson, *Inner Civil War.*

50 Although the antebellum era was long considered "the age of equality" or "the age of the common man," historians generally agree that the period was notable for increasing inequalities in wealth. Edward Pessen, *Riches, Class, and Power Before the Civil War* (Lexington, Mass.: Heath, 1973). In fact, Edward Pessen found that wealth was becoming much more concentrated throughout the antebellum era. In 1828, for example, the richest 4 percent of the population of New York City owned almost half of the wealth; by 1845 they owned 66 percent. (Pessen suspected that his estimates were conservative, suggesting that in fact the wealthiest 4 percent owned closer to 80 percent of the city's actual wealth.) And in Boston, 86 percent of the population owned 14 percent of the wealth in 1833 and less than 5 percent by 1848. The situation was similar in all the northern cities Pessen studied. Pessen, *Riches,* 35, 39.

The "egalitarian thesis" downplayed the existence of distinct classes in antebellum America and implied that Americans were overwhelmingly middle class. Yet the tax records Pessen examined clearly indicate that a few families in each city enjoyed sizable fortunes. In view of the rapidly changing economy, members of the exclusive northern elite protected their wealth through strategic marriages and family alliances that allowed them to weather the temporary fluctuations of the marketplace. Betty Farrell, for example, has two excellent chapters on this domestic maneuvering among Boston Brahmins, entitled "Kinship Networks and Economic Alliances" and "Kin-Keeping and Marriage Ties," in *Elite Families: Class and Power in Nineteenth-Century Boston* (Albany, N.Y.: SUNY Press, 1993).

51 For Knickerbocker resettlement, see, for instance, Edward Spann, *The New Metropolis: New York City, 1840–1857* (New York: Columbia, 1981). For Brahmin

resettlement, see Thomas O'Connor, *Bibles, Brahmins, and Bosses: A Short History of Boston* (Boston: Boston Public Library, 1991).

52 Bernstein, *New York City Draft Riots*, 148–150. See also Alan Dawley, *Class and Community: The Industrial Revolution in Lynn* (Cambridge, Mass.: Harvard University Press, 1982) for the great shoemaker strike of 1860.

53 Spann, *New Metropolis*, 253–255.

54 O'Connor, *Bibles*, 147, 124–125.

55 Among those who socialized in the same circles and lived (or aspired to) on the same streets as the urban elite was a class I will refer to as the middle class. Though the term is imprecise, it refers to that equally imprecise group of middle-class professionals, intellectuals, and merchants who aspired to the status of the Astors and the Lenoxes of New York or the Lawrences and Lowells of New England. The middle class was a somewhat more fluid class that often included that small but significant number of immigrants and working-class Americans who were, in fact, "self-made"—those who were often disparaged by the native middle class as "nouveau riche." Some women and men involved in the Sanitary Commission and its affiliates clearly made a comfortable living, but none experienced financial security comparable to the urban elite. Although a few might arguably be included in this more exclusive category and might more accurately be termed upper class or elite, they were only marginally so compared to the company they kept. Though Strong was a lawyer in a respected Wall Street law firm when he became treasurer of the United States Sanitary Commission, for instance, he faced economic uncertainty and recognized that his comfortable bourgeois status came from his marriage to Ellen Ruggles (Ellie). Henry Whitney Bellows worked his way through Harvard Divinity School and relied on the well-wishes of his bourgeois parishioners and the relatives of his wife, Eliza Townsend, daughter of a wealthy New York merchant, to support his family. Donald Walter Kring, *Henry Whitney Bellows* (Boston: Skinner House, 1979), 30–34. When Frederick Law Olmsted joined the commission ranks as general secretary, he was just beginning his career as a landscape architect, the third in a series of careers he had experimented with. Olmsted did not attend college, and he eventually decided to resign his commission post for financial reasons. Based on this evidence, then, the majority of those involved in the commission and related war relief societies can be considered middle class.

56 Allan Nevins and Milton Halsey Thomas, eds., *The Diary of George Templeton Strong*, Volume III: *The Civil War, 1860–1865*, January 11, 1860 (New York: Octagon Books, 1974), 4.

57 HWB to Eliza Bellows Dorr [sister], December 12, 1860, BP, MHS.

58 Frederick Law Olmsted (FLO) to Brace, December 28, 1859, in *The Papers of Frederick Law Olmsted*, Volume 2: *Slavery and the South, 1852–1857*, ed. Charles E. Beveridge, Charles Capen McLaughlin, and David Schuyler (Baltimore, Md.: Johns Hopkins University Press, 1981), 235–236. See Stansell, *City of Women*, for a look at Brace's work with the Children's Aid Society.

    A conversation with a southern slave owner in 1859 convinced Olmsted that the system of "*laisser aller*" made northerners "a low, prejudiced, party enslaved and material people," and he realized that the "poor need an education to refinement and taste and the mental and moral capital of gentlemen." Though he believed the North's "free labor" was superior to southern slavery, he also felt that the absence of a genteel influence over ordinary laborers in the North left them slaves to profit and pawns of political intrigue. FLO to Brace, December 28, 1859, *Papers of Frederick Law Olmsted,* vol. 2, 234.

59 HWB to Eliza Bellows [wife], May 16, 1861, BP, MHS.

60 Olmsted quoted by William Henry Lyon, *Frederick Newman Knapp: Sixth Minister of the First Parish in Brookline 1847–1915: A Sermon Preached in the First Parish Meeting House November 22, 1903 by William H. Lyon, D.D.* (Brookline, Mass.: The Parish, 1904).

61 See Olmsted's "Report on the Demoralization of the Volunteers," September 5, 1861, *Papers of Frederick Law Olmsted,* vol. 4, 153–198.

62 Olmsted, "Report of General Secretary to the Secretary of War," December 9, 1861, *Documents,* vol. I, #40, 28.

63 HWB to Stillé, November 15, 1865, BP, MHS.

64 Henry Whitney Bellows, Introduction to Brockett and Vaughan, *Woman's Work in the Civil War,* 64.

CHAPTER II

1 Florence Nightingale, *Notes on Nursing: What It Is, and What It Is Not* (1860; reprint, New York: Churchill Livingstone, 1980), 102.

2 Nightingale, *Notes on Nursing,* 12.

3 Wormeley, *United States Sanitary Commission,* 3.

4 Estelle Freedman, "Separatism as Strategy: Female Institution Building and American Feminism, 1870–1930," *Feminist Studies* 5 (Fall 1979): 512–529.

5 Blackwell, *Pioneer Work,* 169.

6 "The Origin, Organization, and Working of the Woman's Central Association of Relief," *Documents,* vol. I, #32, 7.

7 Blackwell, *Pioneer Work,* 189–190.

8 Ibid. Two men also attended the meeting: Henry Whitney Bellows and Dr. Elisha Harris, Superintendent of Hospitals at Staten Island.

9 "Origin," 10–24.

10 "Origin," 6.

11 "Ladies' Military Relief Meeting at the Cooper Institute," *New York Tribune,* 30 April 1861, in "Origin," *Documents,* vol. I, #32; *New York Herald,* 30 April 1861, 4–5; *New York Times,* 30 April 1861, 3, 8. On p. 3, the *Times* reported "between two and three thousand ladies" attended. On p. 8, the number was "about two thousand." The *Herald* reported "upwards of 3,000 brave and philanthropic ladies assembled."

12 Bellows's speech quoted in *New York Herald,* 30 April 1861, 5.

13 Henry Whitney Bellows, *The United States Sanitary Commission* (New York: Johnson's Universal Encyclopedia, 1877). The WCAR members who accompanied Bellows to Washington were all physicians: Dr. Elisha Harris, Dr. W. H. Van Buren, and Dr. Harsen. "Origins," *Documents,* vol. I, #32, 18.

14 On May 16, Bellows wrote to his wife that the delegation met with Dix first, before addressing the "bigger bugs," as Bellows described members of Lincoln's administration. HWB to Eliza Bellows, May 16, 1861, BP, MHS.

15 Dix to Anne E. Heath, April 20, 1861, DP.

16 Helen Marshall notes references to Dix's arrival in Washington in the April 19 diary entries of both of President Lincoln's secretaries—John Nicolay and John Hay. Marshall, *Dorothea Dix*, 201–203.

17 Dix to Heath, April 20, 1861, in Marshall, *Dorothea Dix*, 203.

18 Letter dated May 29, 1861, in *Boston Transcript*, 6 June 1861.

19 In fact, Acting Surgeon General Wood was in contact with Dix almost immediately (beginning on April 23), asking for her help with nurses for hospitals in Washington and with supplying soldiers with havelocks (head cover meant for hot climates—U.S. soldiers usually refused to wear them) and other items of clothing. Wood also asked Dix to set up a receiving station to process contributions. Marshall, *Dorothea Dix*, 204–209.

20 Gollaher, *Voice for the Mad*, 399–403.

21 Before returning to the United States, Dix tried to meet Nightingale at her family's home in England but was turned away because Nightingale was too ill. Gollaher, *Voice for the Mad*, 401. On her reading Nightingale, see Gollaher, 403. In a letter to William Rathbone (a friend of Nightingale's and Dix's) from Turkey, Dix described Nightingale's work in the military hospitals at Scutari. Dix to William Rathbone, 1855, DP.

22 On April 23, Cameron gave Dix the power "to select and assign women to general or permanent military hospitals." Gollaher, *Voice for the Mad*, 406. Dix's official commission, however, would not come until June 10. Marshall, *Dorothea Dix*, 203.

23 In Bellows's second letter to Eliza from Washington, for instance, the reverend was giddy with excitement about meeting President Lincoln and bragged about how warmly received they had been. Although Bellows was convinced it was his *"white cravat"* that opened doors, he also mentioned that he did not know "which end is my head and at which my feet," mentioned his "dizziness" being in "connexion with the primal [*sic?*] foundations of power," and even called himself "your Generalissimo." HWB to Eliza Bellows, May 20, 1861, BP, MHS. Without Dix's help, Bellows would not have gotten far.

24 Blackwell learned on April 26th that Dorothea Dix was already in Washington trying to convince the administration to appoint her to head a committee to register and train nurses. Dix sent Blackwell a letter asking Blackwell to join her. Greenbie, *Lincoln's Daughters*, 60–65.

25 Dix had passes to military hospitals and camps. On May 28, for instance, she was issued a pass from Simon Cameron to Fortress Monroe, and she received similar passes from President Lincoln, Charles Sumner, E. M. Stanton, and Generals Mansfield and Meigs throughout the war. DP.

26 HWB to Eliza Bellows, May 21, 1861, BP, MHS.

27 "Origin," *Documents*, vol. I, #32, 5–6.

28 Ibid., 8. This proposal is rather vague and general, but it gives some indication of the beginning of the concept of a sanitary commission, mentioning concern for the health of the troops and asking for the appointment of "a mixed Commission of civilians." Besides the nurses, the only other specific request it makes of the Secretary of War is for "a new rigor in the inspection of volunteers" in order to eliminate men who were too young, too old, or physically unfit for duty. Ibid., 7–8.

29 "An Address to the Secretary of War," *Documents*, vol. I, #1, May 18, 1861, 1.

The delegation's initial contacts with officials in Washington were discouraging, for the aged Surgeon General Clement Finley and Army Medical Director Charles Stuart Tripler did not look kindly on the meddlings of "sensation preachers, village doctors, and strong-minded women." Quoted in George Worthington Adams, *Doctors in Blue: The Medical History of the Union Army in the Civil War* (New York: H. Schuman, 1952), 73.

30 HWB to Eliza Bellows, May 21, 1861, BP, MHS.

31 Bellows wrote to Eliza, "Miss Dix implores me not to leave just at this moment." HWB to Eliza Bellows, May 21, 1861, BP, MHS.

32 Emphasis in the original. HWB to Eliza Bellows, May 20, 1861, BP, MHS. Bellows mentions that "[t]he Surgeon General of the Army has suddenly died, making a most providential opening for a new man who will accept our suggestions and carry them out." HWB to Eliza Bellows, May 20, 1861, BP, MHS. This statement is confusing. The USSC launched a campaign to remove Surgeon General Finley (64 years old) in the fall of 1861. Perhaps Bellows was referring to Army Medical Director Tripler who received Bellows's advances with similar ingratitude. Tripler was replaced by Jonathan K. Letterman.

33 "Origin," *Documents*, vol. I, #32, 18.

34 In the most comprehensive modern history of the United States Sanitary Commission, William Quentin Maxwell suggests that Bellows and Elisha Harris, a New York doctor who had been selected by the WCAR to go with Bellows, came up with the idea for a sanitary commission on the train on the way to Washington. Maxwell, *Lincoln's Fifth Wheel*, 5–6.

35 "Origin," *Documents*, vol. I, #32, 19.

36 Henry Whitney Bellows, *Speech of the Rev. Dr. Bellows, President of the United States Sanitary Commission: Made at the Academy of Music, Philadelphia, Tuesday Evening, February 24, 1863* (Philadelphia: C. Sherman, Son and Co., 1863), 20.

37 Wormeley, *United States Sanitary Commission*, 17.

On June 13, 1861, four days after Cameron prepared the order for the creation of the United States Sanitary Commission, President Lincoln reluctantly approved the measure. Though Bellows and his Washington delegation had worked for a month to draw up a proposal that would appease government apprehensions about accepting the support of a civilian relief operation, Lincoln feared the commission would be merely "a fifth wheel to the coach." The administration had surrendered to pressures from Bellows and his delegation, but the President and the army were convinced that they would be able to provide adequate supplies and support for the troops without the help of well-meaning but meddlesome civilians. Maxwell, *Lincoln's Fifth Wheel*, 8.

38 "Origin," *Documents*, vol. I, #32, 15.

39 Schuyler quoted in Greenbie, *Lincoln's Daughters*, 66.

40 Elizabeth Blackwell to Barbara Bodichon, April 23, 1861, EBP, BL. Elizabeth Blackwell to Barbara Bodichon, n.d. 1861, EBP, BL.

41 "Origin," *Documents*, vol. I, #32, 24–25. Blackwell explains that the nursing qualifications were based on those outlined in a letter from Dix, "Miss Nightingale's invaluable experience in army-nursing," and "the testimony of military surgeons."

42 Ibid., 24–25.

43 The WCAR's original appeal explained Blackwell's commitment to considering all qualified candidates: "Of these, many may be rich and many poor. Some may wish to go at their own charges, and others will require to be aided as to their expenses, and still others, for the loss of their time. But the best nurses should be sent, irrespective of these distinctions—as only the best are economical on any terms." Ibid., 8. Dix's requirements appear on pp. 24–28.

44 Ibid., 8.

45 Ibid., 26.

46 This description was included in a report filed by the WCAR in October 1861. Ibid., 28.

47 Ibid., 29.

48 Blackwell to Bodichon, June 5, 1861, EBP, BL.

49 Eliza Howland Schuyler to HWB, June 1861, July 1, 1861, July 5, 1861, and HWB to Eliza Howland Schuyler, June 24, 1861. USSC Papers, Box 954.

50 FLO to WCAR, September 10, 1861, USSC Papers, Box 833. The text of the resolution is reprinted in "Origin," *Documents,* vol. I, #32, 22–23.

51 HWB to RB, June 11, 1861, BP, MHS; FLO to HWB, June 1, 1861, *Papers of Frederick Law Olmsted,* vol. 4, 117–118. In fact, in April Bellows mentioned to Olmsted that he would find a way to include Olmsted in his plans. HWB to FLO, April 29, 1861, *Papers of Frederick Law Olmsted,* vol. 3, 330. Prospects looked grim to Olmsted, though, as he wrote family and friends a few days later, "There is not yet one dollar in the Treasury of the Sanitary Commission and I can not anticipate with any confidence what it will be in my power to do." FLO to Dr. Robert Tomes, June 25, 1861, USSC Papers, Box 833. Olmsted made identical remarks to his father in a letter on the following day. FLO to John Olmsted, June 26, 1861, *Papers of Frederick Law Olmsted,* vol. 4, 120.

52 Gollaher, *Voice for the Mad,* 406.

53 See, for instance, "Female Nurses in Hospitals," *American Medical Times* (13 September 1862): 149–150.

54 Blackwell to Bodichon, June 5, 1861, EBP, BL.

55 Ibid.

56 FLO to HWB, September 25, 1861, *Papers of Frederick Law Olmsted,* vol. 4, 202.

57 "Origin," *Documents,* vol. I, #32, 28.

58 The "Wilson Bill," as it was eventually called, was passed in a special legislative session in April 1862. Blustein, "'To Increase the Efficiency of the Medical Department.'" Strong referred to the Medical Bureau as "an invertebrate organism." Nevins and Thomas, eds., *Diary of George Templeton Strong,* vol. 3, September 23, 1861, 182.

59 Ibid., August 2, 1861, 173–174.

60 Ibid., September 23, 1861, 182.

61 Ibid.

62 Louisa Lee Schuyler to Alfred Bloor (FLO's assistant), September 18, 1861, USSC Papers, Box 833.

63 FLO to Dix, October 24, 1861, USSC Papers, Box 833.

64 Ibid.

65 Bloor to Dix, December 4, 1861, USSC Papers, Box 833.
66 Nevins and Thomas, eds., *Diary of George Templeton Strong*, vol. 3, September 23, 1861, 182.
67 John C. Frémont to Dix, August 21, 1861, DP.
68 HWB to Secretary of War, September 26, 1861, USSC Papers, Box 833.
69 Bloor to various WCAR women, October 1861–December 1861, USSC Papers, Box 833.
70 "Female Nurses in Hospitals," *American Medical Times* (13 September 1862): 149–150.
71 Gollaher, *Voice for the Mad*, 417–418.
72 FLO to HWB, July 4, 1863. *Papers of Frederick Law Olmsted*, vol. 4, 640. The full quote is even more damning: "but I am sure that [McClellan] is no more to be compared with such men as Rosecrans and Grant, for handling an American army in the wilderness of the South than Miss Dix is to be compared with Miss Nightingale in the work of reforming military hospitals."
73 Both seemed to use Nightingale, to some degree, as a reference point for their own work. Blackwell indicates that she wrote Nightingale and asked her assistance. Blackwell was relieved in the end that Nightingale refused, for Blackwell believed that Nightingale's ill health would have made such a cooperation ill-advised. Blackwell to Bodichon, December 30, 1861, EBP, BL. Dix waited impatiently for Nightingale's work on hospital reorganization to be published in the United States, for as she wrote to Elizabeth Rathbone, "I greatly wish to obtain copies." Dix to Rathbone, April 23, 1862, DP.
74 "Origin," *Documents*, vol. I, #32, 43, 20.
75 Louisa Lee Schuyler, *Forty-Three Years Ago, or The Early Days of the State Charities Aid Association, 1872–1915* (New York: United Charities Building, 1915), Louisa Lee Schuyler Papers (LLSP), NYHS, 5–6.

CHAPTER III

1 At the end of the war, various ladies aid societies disagreed over which one of them was organized first. In *The Tribute Book*, Frank Goodrich tries to clear the matter up, giving that distinction to the women of Bridgeport, Connecticut, who met on April 15, the day after President Lincoln's call for troops. Although the women of Charlestown, Massachusetts, came up with the idea for the Bunker Hill Aid Society on the same day, they did not sign an official roll until April 19. Goodrich, 70–73.
2 "Origin," *Documents*, vol. I, #32, 31.
3 WCAR Circular, January 13, 1863, USSC Papers, Box 669.
4 Eliza Howland Schuyler (LLS's mother, who worked for the WCAR on and off as her health would allow) to HWB, July 1, 1861, USSC Papers, Box 954.
5 Henry Whitney Bellows, "To the Loyal Women of America," United States Sanitary Commission, October 1, 1861, in "Origin," *Documents*, vol. I, #32, 35–39.
6 "Articles of Organization. Woman's Central Association for the Sick and Wounded of the Army," April 30, 1861, in "Origin," *Documents*, vol. I, #32, 14–15.

7 Fredrickson, *Inner Civil War;* Bernstein, *New York City Draft Riots;* Wiebe, *Search for Order.*

8 Ginzberg, *Women and the Work of Benevolence;* Attie, "A Swindling Concern." Elizabeth Leonard comes to different conclusions about how gender relations were changed by the commission and the war in general. She concludes that women's and men's interactions in the war caused a "friction" that was relieved when "women persisted and as men backed down, coming to appreciate and even depend upon women's contributions under the circumstances, learning to relinquish power" (*Yankee Women,* 198). My conclusions come closest to Leonard's than to those of other historians. For other modern works dealing with the commission, see the following: Blustein, "To Increase the Efficiency"; Maxwell, *Lincoln's Fifth Wheel;* Ross, "'Women are needed here'"; Schultz, "The Inhospitable Hospital" and "Women at the Front"; Smith, "The Women Who Went to the War"; and Wood, "The War Within a War." Among the many anthologies of women's wartime contributions that include accounts of commission women, see Benton, *What Women Did for the War, and What the War Did for Women;* Brockett and Vaughan, *Woman's Work in the Civil War;* Dannett, *Noble Women of the North;* Greenbie, *Lincoln's Daughters;* Massey, *Bonnet Brigades;* McDowell, *The Women and the Crisis;* and Moore, *Women of the War.* Individuals involved with the commission published their own accounts and letters after the war, and the modern Frederick Law Olmsted, George Templeton Strong, Henry Whitney Bellows collections and biographies are also useful.

9 See also Stansell, *City of Women;* Lebsock, *Free Women of Petersburg.*

10 In fact my research suggests that the commission was uncomfortably dependent on women's good will throughout the war.

11 FLO to WCAR, September 10, 1861, USSC Papers, Box 833. The text of the resolution is reprinted in "Origin," *Documents,* vol. I, #32, 22–23.

12 Eliza Howland Schuyler (Louisa Lee Schuyler's mother) to HWB, July 1, 1861, USSC Papers, Box 954.

13 See, for instance, Ryan, *Cradle of the Middle Class.*

14 Smith-Rosenberg, *Disorderly Conduct,* 121. In her essay "Business Heads and Sympathizing Hearts: The Women of the Providence Employment Society, 1837–1858," Susan Porter Benson makes a similar argument about this more local reform society. *Journal of Social History* 12 (Winter 1978): 302–312.

15 While some have questioned this conclusion, most historians agree that women became aware of their own oppression through their anti-slavery activism. For those who have questioned this assumption, see, for instance, Ellen Carol DuBois, *Feminism and Suffrage: The Emergence of an Independent Women's Movement in America, 1848–1869* (Ithaca, N.Y.: Cornell University Press, 1978); Gerda Lerner, *The Majority Finds Its Past: Placing Women in History* (New York: Oxford University Press, 1979); and Baker, "Domestication of Politics," 620–647.

16 Baker describes the late nineteenth century as "the golden age of partisan politics." Ibid., 635.

17 See, for instance, Bordin, *Woman and Temperance;* Peggy Pascoe, *Relations of Rescue: The Search for Female Moral Authority in the American West, 1874–1939* (New York: Oxford University Press, 1990); and Mari Jo Buhle, *Women and American Socialism, 1870–1920* (Urbana: University of Illinois Press, 1981). Bor-

din's work on the WCTU is the definitive history of this postwar temperance society, Pascoe looks at women's missionary organizations, and Buhle considers the connections between groups such as the WCTU and socialist organizations.

18 Eliza Schuyler, Louisa's mother, wanted the position for herself. But even before Eliza Schuyler's health forced her to resign, Bellows had already convinced Louisa to take over, and Louisa had already been acting as de facto chair. Mrs. George Schuyler to HWB, May 2, 1861–May 5, 1861, BP, MHS. Though I assume Louisa's parents had something to say in the matter, all the records indicate that she directed the WCAR because Bellows encouraged her to do so. See, for example, *Louisa Lee Schuyler, 1837–1926* (New York: The National Committee for the Prevention of Blindness, 1927); Robert D. Cross, "The Philanthropic Contribution of Louisa Lee Schuyler," *Social Service Review* 35 (September 1961): 290–301; and Robert Cross, "Louisa Lee Schuyler," in *Notable American Women*, ed. James et al., vol. 2, 244–246.

19 Schuyler, *Forty-Three Years Ago*, 5–6.

20 Ibid.

21 Ginzberg, *Women and the Work of Benevolence*, 142–143. Ginzberg estimates that Post was in her twenties when she worked for the WCAR.

22 Ednah Dow Cheney, *Memoirs of Lucretia Crocker and Abby W. May* (Boston: Massachusetts School Suffrage Association, 1893); Shirley Phillips Ingebritsen, "Abigail Williams May," in *Notable American Women*, ed. James et al., vol. 2, 513–515; and Mary A. Livermore, "Massachusetts Women in the Civil War," in *Massachusetts in the Army and Navy During the War of 1861–1865*, ed. Thomas Wentworth Higginson, vol. 2 (Boston: Wright and Potter, 1895), 593.

23 Cheney, *Memoirs*, 12.

24 Abigail Williams May mentions the first NEWAA meeting in a November 28, 1861, diary entry. May-Goddard Papers (MGP), SL.

25 There are notable exceptions to this rule. Of the women with positions equal to that of Schuyler and May in the USSC, Mary Livermore and Jane Hoge, the women who ran the Chicago branch, were married and had families and Livermore led an active postwar career, holding leadership positions in organizations such as the Woman's Christian Temperance Union. Mark Skinner to FLO, December 11, 1862, and Mary Livermore to FLO, April 19, 1863, USSC Papers, Box 953. For women's search for "an entirely female domesticity" in the postwar years, see Kathryn Kish Sklar, *Catherine Beecher: A Study in American Domesticity* (New York: W. W. Norton, 1976), 167.

26 In her essay "Female Support Networks and Political Activism: Lillian Wald, Crystal Eastman, Emma Goldman," Blanche Wiesen Cook dismisses the uninformed but long-held assumption that women chose careers as a consolation for "an unmarried, childless, career-cloistered life." In *Women's America: Refocusing the Past*, 3d ed., ed. Linda Kerber and Jane Sherron De Hart (New York: Oxford University Press, 1991), 306–325.

27 Blackwell recorded having explicitly chosen a career over marriage. For the others, how the decision was made is not as clear. Both Blackwell and May adopted female children and Dix tried to, a decision that suggests that they wanted families, if not necessarily marriage.

28 Smith-Rosenberg, *Disorderly Conduct*, 53–76.

29 Cheney, *Memoirs*, 9.

30 Winifred Hathaway, "Louisa Lee Schuyler—Her Personality," in *Louisa Lee Schuyler,* 19.

31 May's diary mentions several meetings with Schuyler, including March 14 and 15 when the two had their photos taken. May Diary, MGP. In addition, there were at least three annual meetings of the various branches that they both attended.

    In one of her letters to May, Schuyler refers to herself as "Lou." Although I have found many of Schuyler's letters to May, I have not been as fortunate with May's letters to Schuyler. New England Women's Auxiliary Association Papers (NEWAA Papers), MHS.

32 Emphasis in the original. LLS to Angelina Post, June 8, 1864, Louisa Lee Schuyler Papers (LLS Papers), New York Historical Society (NYHS).

33 See Correspondent from Bangor, Maine, to AWM, December 14, 1862, NEWAA Papers, MHS; Laura Savage, Utica, New York, to LLS, February 9, 1863, LLS Papers, NYHS; Correspondent from Sanquoit, New York, to LLS, May 25, 1863, USSC Papers, Box 667.

34 Alfred Bloor to WCAR, September 21, 1861, re: "winter clothing" and "bedding"; October 2, 1861, re: "bed sacks"; October 5, 1861, re: "bed ticks" and "hospital clothing"; October 14, 1861, re: "slippers," USSC Papers, Box 833. Bloor wrote Schuyler twice a week, informing her of the army's supply needs and of commission intelligence from Washington. For the next three years, Bloor acted as commission liaison, carrying on an extensive correspondence with Schuyler, May, and the women in charge of branches in Chicago, Philadelphia, and other cities throughout the North and West. Alfred Bloor to LLS, September 14, 1861, USSC Papers, Box 833.

    Due to conflicting reports, it is difficult to ascertain how many official branches existed. New York, Boston, and Chicago seem to have been the principal branches, but there may have been up to ten such branches in all. Jane Hoge, *The Boys in Blue; or Heroes of the "Rank and File"* (New York: E. B. Treat & Co., 1867).

35 In Boston, May prepared for the imminent arrival of one of these "floating hospitals" at Chelsea and called on the "Women of New England" to send money and supplies to the NEWAA to provide for the sick and wounded men returning from the southern battlefields. AWM, unidentified Boston newspaper clipping, 2 June 1862, USSC Papers, Box 667–670.

36 By December 1862, Schuyler's WCAR had 1,153 auxiliary societies and May's NEWAA boasted 475 affiliates. LLS's Report to WCAR President Valentine Mott, December 1, 1862, USSC Papers, Box 954; AWM, Final Report of the NEWAA, USSC Papers, Box 992.

37 See LLS to various correspondents, Schuyler letter copy book, December 1862, USSC Papers, Box 667.

38 See reference to the USSC as a "Christless philosophy," unidentified Philadelphia newspaper article, 19 June 1864, NEWAA Papers.

39 WCAR Survey, January 13, 1863, USSC Papers, Box 667. Bound survey responses, USSC Papers, Box 669.

40 Ibid. The survey questions include the following: "1st. What is the state of feeling which exists in your community in regard to the Commission? 2d. Is the broad, federal principle upon which it is based thoroughly understood? 3d.

What reports, if any, prejudicial to the Commission are in circulation in your neighborhood? And what difficulties have you to contend with?" Schuyler ought to have been pleased with the 16 percent return rate; she received 243 responses to the survey.

41 For instance, LLS counted 235 responses to a letter sent in March 1863. LLS Report, April 1, 1863, USSC Papers, Box 667–670.

42 Paludan, *"A People's Contest,"* 182–183. The difficulties of supporting a family were aggravated by a congressional tax bill passed on August 5, 1861, that included progressive property and income taxes but that hit lower income families hardest with a regressive excise tax that drove up the price of all consumer goods. Ibid., 117–122.

43 Bangor, Maine, woman to AWM, December 14, 1862, NEWAA Papers.

44 Circular, January 13, 1863, USSC Papers, Box 669.

45 Mrs. L. Seymour, Jamestown, N.Y., to LLS, January 30, 1863, USSC Papers, Box 669.

46 Cornelia Huntington, East Hampton, N.Y., to LLS, January 31, 1863, USSC Papers, Box 669. I have omitted "[sic]" from these passages, as it is distracting. When it adds to clarity, I have added the remainder of words that the original author abbreviated. In these cases, I have bracketed my additions.

47 Hattie Bennett to LLS, January 23, 1863, USSC Papers, Box 668.

48 L. B. Fitch, Paulet, Vt., to LLS, May 18, 1863, USSC Papers, Box 669.

49 A. J. Groves, New Hartford, N.Y., to LLS, January 31, 1863, USSC Papers, Box 669.

50 Mrs. A. M. O'Daniels, Bloomfield, N.Y.(?), to LLS, February 3, 1863, USSC Papers, Box 669.

51 B. B. Williams, East Varick, N.Y., to LLS, February 2, 1863, USSC Papers, Box 669.

52 Therese Seabrook, Keyport, N.J., February 8, 1863, USSC Papers, Box 669.

53 Mrs. L. S. Clement, Canadea, to LLS, January 26, 1864, USSC Papers, Box 669. See, for instance, "10 miles from the railroad," Caroline Jerome, "Broadalbin" [sic], Fulton County, N.Y., January 27, 1863; "20 miles from any transportation line," Mrs. E. A. Follette, North Pitcher, N.Y., February 7, 1863; "about thirty miles south of Rochester," Mary Brooks, Covington, N.Y., May 6, 1863; where the "roads are drifted very badly in Winter," Mrs. E. J. Follen, Chatham Valley, January 31, 1863, USSC Papers, Box 669. Melissa Miller from Caroline, New York, wrote, "We are so far removed from each other that we cannot meet in the winter season; but when the spring opens upon us I think we shall endeavor to send in our mite." Melissa Miller, Caroline, Tompkins County, N.Y., to LLS, February 20, 1863, USSC Papers, Box 669.

54 Correspondent from Ava, Oneida County, N.Y., to LLS, January 26, 1863, USSC Papers, Box 669; Mrs. A. Warren, New Marlboro, to LLS, February 5, 1863, USSC Papers, Box 669.

55 E. C. Curtis, Colchester, Conn., to LLS, May 14, 1863, USSC Papers, Box 669.

56 Emily Knight, South Hadley Falls, to LLS, February 3, 1863, USSC Papers, Box 669.

57 Mrs. A. McDougall, Dryden, N.Y., to LLS, January 29, 1863; A. J. Groves, New Hartford, to LLS, January 31, 1863; Julia Seward, Florida, Orange County, N.J., to LLS, March 4, 1863. All in USSC Papers, Box 669.

58 Mrs. William Grave, Florence, N.Y., to LLS, February 2, 1863, USSC Papers, Box 669.

59 B. B. Williams, East Varick, N.Y., to LLS, February 2, 1863, USSC Papers, Box 669.

60 Mrs. Mary Carlisle, Newport, N.Y., to LLS, January 29, 1863. See also Mrs. Alanson Tuttle, Depeyster, St. Lawrence County, N.Y., to LLS, January 29, 1863, and Miss Lucretia Brainerd, East Haddam, Conn., to LLS, February 26, 1863. All in USSC Papers, Box 669.

61 Miss E. J. Folen, Chatham Valley, Pa., January 31, 1863, USSC Papers, Box 669.

62 Mrs. Libby Pratt, Danby [sic], Vt., to LLS, January 27, 1863, USSC Papers, Box 669.

63 E. B. Towner, North Hartford, March 23, 1863, USSC Papers, Box 669.

64 The United States Christian Commission (USCC) was a rival organization that was launched in 1863 that promised to look after the spiritual needs of the soldiers. Because it also collected and distributed supplies, it was in constant competition with the USSC. Attie documents the Christian Commission's meteoric rise to power in 1863 and the threat this overtly religious organization posed to the USSC for the remainder of the war. Attie suggests that women supported the Christian Commission to punish the Sanitary Commission for mismanaging their supplies and for aligning itself too closely with science, rationalism, and anti-orthodox Unitarianism. Attie, "A Swindling Concern," 208–222, 213–220.

Although correspondence between branch women and local relief agents often referred to mixed allegiances, the evidence does not seem to indicate that provincial aid societies withdrew their support for the Sanitary Commission in favor of an allegiance to the Christian Commission. In fact, women at the local level often gave to both, and at the branch level there was some, albeit limited, willingness to cooperate.

Elizabeth Leonard notes that the case was different for Annie Wittenmyer, Corresponding Secretary of the Keokuk, Iowa, Ladies' Soldiers' Aid Society. Wittenmyer organized and ran a highly effective relief operation in Iowa that remained fiercely independent of the USSC throughout the war. Ongoing attempts by the state chapter of the USSC to take over Wittenmyer's organization and to discredit her efforts convinced her to ally with the United States Christian Commission in an 1864 project that created and established special diet kitchens in military hospitals. On Wittenmyer's battles with the Iowa Sanitary Commission, see Leonard, *Yankee Women*, 51–82. On Wittenmyer's diet kitchen project with the Christian Commission, see 87–103.

65 Jennie Vosburg, Ames, N.Y., to LLS, January 30, 1863, USSC Papers, Box 669.

66 Miss Lucretia Brainerd, East Haddam, Conn., to LLS, February 26, 1863, USSC Papers, Box 669.

67 Lucretia Spring, East Hartford, Conn., to LLS, February 5, 1863, USSC Papers, Box 669.

68 Mrs. Mary Carlisle, Newport, to LLS, January 29, 1863, USSC Papers, Box 669.

69 Ryan, *Cradle of the Middle Class*, 198–210.

70 Mary L. Barstow to LLS, January 29, 1863, USSC Papers, Box 669.

71 In her January 1863 survey, for instance, LLS asked the women if they'd heard any reports "prejudicial to the Commission." More than half of the 243 respondents mentioned that they'd heard these rumors.

72 Mrs. William Grave, Florence, to LLS, February 22, 1863, USSC Papers, Box 669.

73 Ophelia C. Wait, Belleville, Jefferson County, N.Y., to LLS, January 30, 1863, USSC Papers, Box 669. Mrs. E. F. Smith, Avoca, February 23, 1863, USSC Papers, Box 669. Some local women in contact with the regional branches expressed concern about the commission's connections to Unitarianism. Because of the influence of USSC President Henry Whitney Bellows, the commission was supported by a network of Unitarian ministers throughout the North and West. In Philadelphia, Clara J. Moore, Corresponding Secretary of the Women's Pennsylvania Branch, faced serious criticisms from the Christian Commission and met with resistance from women at affiliate societies who worried that the commission's link to the Unitarian church would hurt the cause. (Charles Stillé, Philadelphia, to LLS, April 15, 1863, LLS Papers. Unidentified newspaper clipping, Philadelphia, 19 June 1864, NEWAA Papers. Maria C. Grier, a veteran of the USSC transport campaign, was president of the Pennsylvania Branch that began operating early in 1863. Brockett and Vaughan, *Woman's Work in the Civil War,* 595–606.)

　　In Boston, a correspondent criticized an article May published about the commission as indicative of the organization's "heathenish liberalism." Because she worked for the commission, her correspondent explained, she was indifferent to the opinions of "those who look through thoroughly 'evangelical' glasses." (M. S. Buck to AWM, December 19, 1864, NEWAA Papers.) To May, these prejudices were similar to the views of women in Vermont and Pennsylvania who considered the commission a "'Boston Notion'" and Bellows "one of Boston's high priests." (Unidentified newspaper clipping, Philadelphia, 19 June 1864, NEWAA Papers; Alfred Bloor to AWM, May 14, 1863, USSC Papers, Box 954.) Outside of the major northeastern cities, people who were suspicious of Unitarianism often considered it an urban phenomenon, so it is often difficult to determine when resistance was religiously motivated and when it resulted from rural resentment. In fact, even in the burned-over district of upstate New York, branch women were able to build relationships with local women's affiliates that were not so much constrained by these prejudices as they were by the need to sustain local welfare networks.

74 Bloor to Frederick Knapp, February 26, 1864, LLS Papers.

75 LLS, Results of the Circular, April 1, 1863, USSC Papers, Box 667–670.

76 Miss Cornelia Huntington, East Hampton, January 31, 1863, USSC Papers, Box 669.

77 Mrs. William Grave, Florence, N.Y., to LLS, February 2, 1863, USSC Papers, Box 669. At the end of her letter, Mrs. Grave added the following post script that highlighted one difference between her and WCAR executives: "I hope you will ecuse (scratched out) Excuse me for i aint no gramarian."

78 Elsie K. Wheeler, Deposit, N.Y., to LLS, February 21, 1863, USSC Papers, Box 669.

79 Mrs. A. Warren, New Marlboro, N.Y., to LLS, n.d., USSC Papers, Box 669.

80 Mrs. E. A. Folett, North Pitcher, N.Y., February 7, 1863, USSC Papers, Box 669.

81 Lucretia Brainerd, East Haddam, Conn., to LLS, February 26, 1863, USSC Papers, Box 669.

82 Greenbie, *Lincoln's Daughters,* 68–69.

83 Sterling to HWB, November 8, 1862, USSC Papers, Box 954.

84 In a letter addressed to the commission in January 1865, the Woman's Central explained that "while the Commission has been obliged frequently to buy ready made flannel suits far inferior to ours in pattern and durability, at the cost of $3.50 per suit," the policy of fund-matching or doubling materials produced clothing of a higher quality and at a lower cost. Martha D. Lovett, Julia K. Fish, and Mary Roosevelt, WCAR Purchasing Committee, to USSC, January 9, 1865, USSC Papers, Box 954.

85 The letter from Sterling (n. 83), for instance, was a followup to a negative response she received from Bellows earlier in the year. See E. C. Sterling to HWB, April 7, 1862, USSC Papers, Box 954.

86 AWM to Bloor, September 20, 1862, USSC Papers, Box 954.

87 Apparently, in 1862 the commission tried to provide materials in a similar program but abandoned the effort after only a brief trial. Goodrich, *Tribute Book*, 88–90.

88 See Bloor to Dix, December 4, 1861, USSC Papers, Box 833.

89 In her forthcoming work "From Social Vision to Political Action: Chicago Women and Politics, 1871–1933," Maureen Flanagan argues that when Chicago women criticized men's spending of private money collected for fire relief, it amounted to a challenge of the men's authority to dispense funds held in "a public trust." Flanagan suggests that Chicago women involved in their own separate fire relief organizations asserted that "there might exist a public good distinct from the interests of wealthy businessmen" who were using fire relief to reconstruct the city to their own political and economic benefit. I thank Maureen for allowing me to see this manuscript.

90 LLS to HWB, January 22, 1863, USSC Papers, Box 667.

91 LLS to USSC, March 1864, USSC Papers, Box 954.

92 Early in 1865, the Purchasing Committee of the WCAR reported the success of the fund-matching program to the USSC. In May 1864, the WCAR counted only 32 active societies due to material shortages, etc. By January 1865, the WCAR had 250 societies that were regularly contributing uniforms. The Purchasing Committee had spent more than $18,292 in six months and was convinced that homemade uniforms were cheaper to produce (estimated at a $1.65 cost per flannel suit as compared to $3.50 per industrially made suit) and of a much better quality than anything that could be purchased from ready-made manufacturers. Martha D. Lovett, Julia K. Fish, and Mary W. Roosevelt, WCAR Purchasing Committee, to USSC, January 9, 1865, USSC Papers, Box 954.

93 J. Foster Jenkins to WCAR, April 2, 1864, USSC Papers, Box 954.

94 Lovett, Fish, and Roosevelt, WCAR Purchasing Committee, to USSC, January 9, 1865, USSC Papers, Box 954.

95 Brockett and Vaughan, *Woman's Work in the Civil War*, 80; Livermore, *Massachusetts Women*, 590–591. Both Wormeley and Gilson were veterans of the USSC's hospital transport campaign, in which they distinguished themselves as nurses.

96 Sterling to HWB, April 7, 1862, USSC Papers, Box 954.

97 Livermore, *Massachusetts Women*, 590. In Boston, Lowell paid the women employed at the Ladies' Industrial Aid Society twice as much (16 cents a shirt) as the government gave her for the finished products (8 cents a shirt). Anna C.

Lowell, *Report of the Ladies' Industrial Aid Association of Union Hall, from July 1861 to January 1862* (Boston: J. H. Eastburn's Press, 1862).

98 Livermore, *My Story of the War,* 586–600.

99 LLS to Julia Post, April 3, 1864, USSC Papers, Box 667. May probably shared Schuyler's sentiments about competing with the evangelical Christian Commission, for while she was preparing for the Boston Sanitary Fair, Alfred Bloor referred to people with "particular predilections to revivals (i.e. Methodists)" and wrote that he hoped "that these fairs all over the country may prove Sanitary revivals." Bloor to AWM, November 31, 1863, NEWAA Papers.

100 LLS to FLO, May 20, 1863, USSC Papers, Box 955; LLS to USSC, Results of the Survey, April 1, 1863, USSC Papers, Box 667–670.

101 LLS to Valentine Mott, October 1, 1863, USSC Papers, Box 955.

102 *New York Times,* 16 May 1864; *New York Tribune,* 13 May 1864.

103 *New York Tribune,* 13 May 1864.

104 LLS to Angelina Post, May 17, 1864, LLS Papers.

105 For instance, Schuyler was relieved that the "reporters have treated us better than I thought." LLS to Angelina Post, May 17, 1864, LLS Papers.

CHAPTER IV

1 While still working for the commission, Bloor complained often that he was overburdened and underappreciated. When Frederick Law Olmsted resigned his position as associate secretary and as Bloor's immediate supervisor, Bloor became openly critical of commission policies and voiced his discontent to his superiors. Bloor demanded more autonomy and a higher salary. Over the next few months, Bloor's confrontations with his superiors worsened, leading to his dismissal in October 1864. Even after his ties with the commission were severed, Bloor continued to lock horns with his former colleagues over many issues. Alfred J. Bloor, War Diary, Alfred J. Bloor Papers, NYHS; *Papers of Frederick Law Olmsted,* vol. 4, 90–92; *Diary of George Templeton Strong,* vol. 3, 492–493.

2 Alfred J. Bloor, Women's Work in the War, "A Letter to Senator Sumner," September 18, 1866, Bloor Papers, NYHS, 2.

3 Ibid., 5.

4 Ginzberg, *Women and the Work of Benevolence.*

5 Stillé, *History of the United States Sanitary Commission,* 74, 56, 151. In 1871, J. S. Newberry published *The United States Sanitary Commission in the Valley of the Mississippi during the War of the Rebellion, 1861–1866* (Cleveland: Fairbanks, Benedict, & Co., 1871), a volume that focused more on the commission's work in the western states but that was in many ways much more inclusive. Newberry made it a point to include separate accounts of the many ladies aid societies that made the work possible.

6 Stillé, *History of the United States Sanitary Commission,* 56, 151.

7 Bellows quoted in Frederickson, *Inner Civil War,* 106.

8 Stillé, *History of the United States Sanitary Commission,* 41.

9 Frederick Knapp, "Plain Answers to Plain Questions," USSC *Bulletin* 10 (March 15, 1864): 289.

10 Modern accounts continue to accept aspects of the commission's carefully constructed self-portrait.

   Maxwell's *Lincoln's Fifth Wheel,* although it at least mentions Blackwell and Dix, preserves the commission's postwar image. In *Doctors in Blue,* Adams goes even further than Maxwell. Adams dismisses the "legend" that many field nurses were women and criticizes those women who were nurses, because "being untrained, they behaved like women rather than nurses." Adams, 163.

11 Wormeley, *The United States Sanitary Commission,* 2. Wormeley chose not to have her name appear on this early history of the USSC and she adopted the same language and metaphors used by male commission officials.

12 In fact, the USSC received heavy criticism for paying its agents from the United States Christian Commission and other organizations competing for the public's support. "Paid v. Unpaid Agents," USSC *Bulletin* 30 (January 15, 1865): 941.

13 Frederick Milnes Edge, *A Woman's Example and A Nation's Work: A Tribute to Florence Nightingale* (London: William Ridgeway, 1864), 48. This work deals broadly with women's work during the war; parts of it deal explicitly with the USSC. Edge quotes Bellows and other commissioners extensively and seems to have discussed *Woman's Example* with Bellows.

14 At a more practical level, preserving this traditional image helped stave off criticism that the organization received from detractors who claimed that commission personnel were wasteful and self-serving and that the commission's top-heavy payroll indicated that the organization was a radical departure from older forms of war relief. Rejean Attie estimates that salaries for commission officers ranged from $1,500 to $4,000 a year, substantial yearly salaries for the period. Attie, "A Swindling Concern," 218.

15 Working with women on the hospital transport campaign in the Virginia peninsula convinced Frederick Law Olmsted, for instance, that the North might better make use of women's potential in other venues. On one occasion, Olmsted drew up a plan for encouraging enlistments by putting women to work in retail positions to free male clerks to join the war effort. FLO to Christine Griffin, July 12, 1862, USSC Papers, Box 655.

16 Though Schuyler explains that this decision was made based on the fulfillment of the original goal of the registration committee, other evidence suggests that had Blackwell, Dix, and the WCAR had more success with selecting and training nurses, perhaps the nursing work might have continued. LLS records the decision as it was made in November 1862 in the following manner: "As the military hospitals are supplied from many sources, and as this Committee have already forwarded more than the number of nurses that they undertook to supply the Government with at the time of the organization of the WCAR, they have deemed it proper to close their register." LLS to Dr. Valentine Mott, October 1, 1863, USSC Papers, Box 955.

17 Mary Livermore, *My Story of the War;* Hoge, *The Boys in Blue;* Brockett and Vaughan, *Woman's Work in the Civil War,* 560–561; M. Skinner to FLO, December 11, 1862 (re: Livermore and Hoge's salaries), USSC Papers, Box 953; Livermore and Hoge to FLO, April 19, 1863 (re: salaries), USSC Papers, Box 953.

18 Maxwell, *Lincoln's Fifth Wheel,* 128–163.

19 LLS to Dr. Valentine Mott, October 1, 1863, USSC Papers, Box 955, 7.

20 Ibid., 6.

21 "I do not think that this feature of our work should be over-looked," Schuyler added. Ibid., 7.

22 In meetings that often dragged on into the early morning hours, Bellows, Strong, and their colleagues drafted elaborate resolutions pleading with the government to exercise greater discipline over the soldiers, to enforce temperance, to promote morale, and to begin to establish sanitation standards in army camps. USSC Minutes, USSC Papers, Box 971.

23 In letters to Angelina (Angie) Post, during one or the other's absence from the city, Schuyler would recount her busy days and then close with an indication of the late hour and an estimation of how much work she expected to complete before retiring. See, for instance, LLS to A. Post, February 22, 1865, LLS Papers, NYHS.

24 Winifred Hathaway, "Louisa Lee Schuyler—Her Personality," in *Louisa Lee Schuyler*, 19.

25 LLS to Angie Post, June 8, 1864, LLS Papers, NYHS, 2.

26 Unedited Strong Diary, January 28, 1863, New York Historical Society Micro-film. This number corresponds to Schuyler's estimates for 1863. LLS to FLO, December 1863, USSC Papers, Box 667. Of course, Strong ended his description with his characteristic patronizing tone: "She is certainly a most intelligent ener-getic diligent young damsel . . . though not pretty at all."

27 Ellen Collins to Bloor, July 21, 1863, USSC Papers, Box 955.

28 Cheney, *Memoirs*, 17.

29 May Diary, February 27, 1862, MGP, Folder 29.

30 Cheney, *Memoirs*, 15. Similar remarks were made about May in a memorial in *The Woman's Journal* (8 December 1888).

31 AWM to Mrs. Edward Lewis, November 13, 1862, NEWAA Papers.

32 Ibid.

33 LLS to Valentine Mott, "Report of the Washington Council Meeting," Decem-ber 1, 1862, USSC Papers, Box 954.

34 As we shall see below, Hoge and Livermore tailored the associate manager plan to fit what they believed were the peculiarities of their particular constituency. Hoge, *The Boys in Blue*, 81–82.

35 FLO to AWM, Washington, November 24, 1862, NEWAA Papers.

36 "The Duties of an Associate Manager," n.d., USSC Papers, Box 1068.

37 Abby Hopper Gibbons describes an instance in which she asked Hammond for a placement at Point Lookout on the Virginia peninsula and the Surgeon General was rude and resistant. Sarah Gibbons Emerson, ed., *Life of Abby Hopper Gib-bons*, vol. 1 (New York: G. P. Putnam's Sons, 1897), 343–347. Throughout July 1862, Gibbons made frequent reference to Hammond's mistreatment of women nurses and his insulting preference for Catholic Sisters of Charity. Gibbons ex-plained, "He is at war with Protestant nurses." Emerson, *Life*, vol. 2, 389.

   Katharine Prescott Wormeley was very surprised to be approached by Ham-mond to take charge of women nurses at the newly created field hospital at Portsmouth Grove, Rhode Island. But when Hammond supported women nurses, he wanted their duties limited solely to domestic chores such as cooking, cleaning, and laundering, as in this case. Bacon and Howland, *Letters of a Fam-ily*, 478–481.

38 For a full account of what Ross calls Hammond's "undeclared war" on women

nurses (and on male contract nurses), see Ross, "'Women are needed here,'" 107–122. As for the commission's failure to stick to their original commitment to women nurses, a curious article was published in the *American Medical Times* on September 13, 1862, by a commission advocate reiterating the commission's ongoing commitment to women nurses. The author went so far as to "assert that no hospital, civil or military, can be well managed that has not a corps of skilled female nurses." The article ignored resistance to women nurses in the army and in the Surgeon General's office and instead blamed Dix for not appointing more women nurses. "Female Nurses in Hospitals," *American Medical Times* (13 September 1862): 149–150.

39 Notes from this meeting appear to be in Louisa Lee Schuyler's hand. It is difficult to say with certainty, however, because they were obviously meant only for her own use and are uncharacteristically messy, with a great deal of doodling and evidence of distraction. "Notes from November 23, 1862, Women's Council Meeting," USSC Papers, Box 954.

40 Hammond explained that if any women at all were to be allowed into the hospitals, he preferred that they be Sisters of Charity, particularly those from convents in New Orleans and St. Louis who had already been of some service in the Virginia peninsula. Hammond believed that Catholic sisters were more easily disciplined and hence more useful for military purposes. For a full account of the contest between Protestant women nurses and Catholic nursing sisterhoods, see Ross, "'Women are needed here,'" 150–185.

41 Gibbons was also a friend of the Schuyler and Woolsey families. For biographical information on Grier and Gibbons, see Brockett and Vaughan, *Woman's Work in the Civil War*, 596–599, and Emerson, *Life*.

42 Sophronia Bucklin, one of Dix's loyal nurses, was so annoyed with surgeons' mistreatment and arbitrary dismissal of nurses that she recommended that surgeons be held accountable for their actions in writing. Ross, "'Women are needed here,'" 118.

43 LLS, "Notes from November 23, 1862," USSC Papers, Box 954.

44 Gibbons particularly took issue with Hammond's claim that Protestant women were undisciplined and that Catholic sisters were better because they were more accustomed to discipline. This is an interesting protestation from Gibbons because she was notoriously outspoken about racism in the army and, on one occasion, received an indecorous discharge from the surgeon in charge at Point Lookout for demanding that a black man be treated as an equal in her hospital. Though she later claimed ignorance of military protocol and was reinstated, she continued to use her position in a military hospital to express her ideas on racial equality and to challenge her military superiors. Emerson, *Life*, vol. I, 349–354.

45 LLS to Dr. Valentine Mott, December 1, 1862, USSC Papers, Box 954, 6.

46 Jane Hoge tells of a visit she and Mary Livermore made to President Lincoln during their Washington visit. Although Bloor and Olmsted set up the meeting at the women's request and accompanied them to the meeting, Hoge recalled that the women themselves offered Lincoln advice on how to fight desertion effectively and improve morale. Hoge, *The Boys in Blue*, 83–84.

47 Although Livermore and Hoge are exceptional in this case, May sought no further nursing assignments after the hospital transport campaign of 1862, and Schuyler did not work as a nurse during the war. Schuyler may have attended

hospitals in New York City, but in her reorganization proposal, she admitted that "[w]e are *not* [her emphasis] in the habit of going into the hospitals, & I think I might say with truth, that we know less about the management and interior of these hospitals in our own vicinity, than we do of those in Washington, Alexandria, and Maryland." LLS to Dr. Valentine Mott, October 1, 1863, USSC Papers, Box 955, 6.

48 Ann Douglas Wood discusses the conflict between women nurses and army and medical authorities in depth. Wood suggests that the war offered women who had been driven from the medical profession in the early nineteenth century by men claiming a monopoly on scientific knowledge the opportunity to re-enter medicine by playing on contemporary skepticism about medical professionals. Wood, "The War Within a War."

49 Hoge, *The Boys in Blue*, 51–72.

50 Ibid., 81–82.

51 Ibid., 59.

52 Mark Skinner to FLO, December 11, 1862, USSC Papers, Box 953.

53 Ibid. See also Mary Livermore to FLO, April 19, 1863, USSC Papers, Box 953.

54 Livermore to Olmsted, April 19, 1863, USSC Papers, Box 953.

55 Diane Cobb Cashman, *Headstrong: The Biography of Amy Morris Bradley, 1823–1904: A Life of Noblest Usefulness* (Wilmington, N.C.: Broadfoot Publishing Company, 1990).

56 Ibid., 130.

57 Ibid., 155.

58 Conceivably Bradley was reacting to being publicly singled out of the various women nurses on the commission transports, for she was sensitive to what she believed was special treatment granted to some women nurses and not to others. Bradley referred to Ellen Ruggles Strong, Eliza Bellows, and some others as "the aristocracy of the Commission," in a letter to her sister because the women avoided making the ocean trips back North and the inevitable seasickness that came with these voyages. Ibid., 129.

59 This USSC argument is made, for instance, in USSC *Bulletin* 30 (January 15, 1865): 941–945.

60 Woman's Central Association of Relief, "To the Women of New York," April 29, 1861, in "Origins," *Documents,* vol. I, #32, 7–8.

61 Blackwell to Georgy Woolsey, July 10, 1861, Bacon and Howland, *Letters of a Family,* 151–152.

62 Ross, "'Women are needed here,'" 89. This rate was $8 less a month than white male contract nurses received in 1861 and $3 less than black male contract nurses. Ross, 111.

It is worth noting the difference in commitment to women nurses expressed in the South, even taking into account wartime inflation. In September 1862, the Confederate Congress arranged for women to be paid as matrons and nurses in military hospitals at the following rates:

     matrons: $40 a month
     assistant matrons: $35 a month
     ward matrons: $30
     nurses: $25

The law explicitly stated that nurses should be hired, "with a preference in all cases to females where their services may best serve the purpose." Faust, *Mothers of Invention*, 97. Though the Confederacy was willing to allow the exigencies of war to supersede domestic considerations, white slaveholding women found that working as nurses in wartime revealed their own inadequacies. In the end, black women and men shouldered most of the responsibility for caring for Confederate soldiers during the war. Faust, 112–113.

63 Regimental surgeons often made their own arrangements with women not under Dix's authority; these women came from a variety of class backgrounds.

64 Cashman, *Headstrong*, 130.

65 Mary Davenport, Brattleboro, Vt., to AWM, February 10, 1864; Davenport to AWM, February 22, 1864; AWM to Davenport, March 12, 1864; Davenport to AWM, March 16, 1864; all in NEWAA Papers. May modeled her contract with Davenport after the commission's agreement with Livermore and Hoge.

66 Livermore, *My Story of the War*, 170.

67 When their work piled up, though, branch women brought commission business home with them.

68 The Women's Pennsylvania Branch was officially organized in December 1862. Brockett and Vaughan, *Woman's Work in the Civil War*, 597.

69 LLS to FLO, December 22, 1862, LLS's letter copy book, USSC Papers, Box 667.

70 LLS et al., Survey, January 13, 1863, USSC Papers, Box 669.

71 LLS, Report of the Corresponding Secretary of the Subcommittee on Supplies, April 1, 1863, USSC Papers, Box 669.

72 Mary M. Hamilton to LLS, January 1863, USSC Papers, Box 668.

73 Bloor to Rev. B. T. Phillips, February 10, 1863, USSC Papers, Box 669; LLS, Report, USSC Papers, Box 669, 8; NEWAA, Final Report, July 12, 1865, USSC Papers, Box 992, 4. In appointing lecturers, Schuyler was also very careful to defer to the authority of associate managers, who "know better than I do whether a lecturer is necessary." LLS to Frederick Knapp, December 28, 1863, USSC Papers, Box 955.

74 LLS to Frederick Knapp, December 28, 1863, USSC Papers, Box 955.

75 LLS, Report, April 1, 1863, USSC Papers, Box 669. Mrs. Charles B. Stuart noted that in Elmira, New York, the churches closed down every three months in order for the entire town to meet and hear of the workings of the commission. Mrs. Stuart to LLS, n.d., USSC Papers, Box 953.

76 LLS to HWB, September 28, 1863, USSC Papers, Box 667–670.

77 Ibid., 5. It is unclear who Schuyler is quoting here.

78 USSC *Bulletin* nos. 4, 5, 7, 10, and 13–19 contained *Notes on Nursing*, as Schuyler had specifically requested (LLS to HWB, September 28, 1863, USSC Papers, Box 667–670, 3). No. 4 and various later issues contained instructions about obtaining pensions, etc.; and nos. 13, 16, and 23 contained sewing patterns.

79 The series was called "Western Scenes." See, for instance, "Women of the harvest fields" and "Where there's a will, there's a way." Mary Livermore, USSC *Bulletin* 12 (April 15, 1864): 368 and 16 (June 15, 1864): 503. Others followed Livermore's lead. Bloor wrote an article about a group of poor Milwaukee women who were granted a government contract to make underwear for the soldiers. USSC *Bulletin* 29 (January 1, 1864): 909.

80 Ellen Collins to Dr. Parrish, October 1, 1864, USSC Papers, Box 954. Schuyler

announced the beginning of regular WCAR contributions in USSC *Bulletin* 27 (December 1, 1864): 850. In fact, most branches had arranged with local newspapers to have their notices, reports, and announcements published free of charge, but the WCAR was unable to make similar arrangements with newspapers in New York. After Collins approached Parrish with this request, the WCAR began a regular column in the *Bulletin*.

81 LLS to Bloor, September 26, 1864, USSC Papers, Box 954.

82 Ibid.

83 The publication was *Three Weeks at Gettysburg* by Georgeanna Woolsey.

84 In 1865, the *Bulletin* boasted a circulation of 15,000 copies. By comparison, *The Advocate*, the official publication of the American Female Moral Reform Society, circulated 16,500 copies in the 1830s. Smith-Rosenberg, *Disorderly Conduct*, 115. The *Union Signal*, the official publication of the Woman's Christian Temperance Union, had 14,000 subscribers in 1884 and nearly 100,000 in 1890, when it was "the largest women's paper in the world." Bordin, *Woman and Temperance*, 90.

85 LLS wrote to Bellows asking his help in convincing railroad companies to ship supplies for commission branches free of charge. LLS to HWB, January 22, 1863, USSC Papers, Box 667.

86 These fairs were enormously successful organizational feats. Branch women held dinners, auctions, and raffles and brought in participants from all walks of life. Commission executives frowned on sanitary fairs because they helped support the branches at the expense of the commission treasury. Commission men held their own fair in New York in December 1863 but with notably less success. George Templeton Strong, USSC *Bulletin* 4 (December 15, 1863): 145.

87 "The Women's Fair," in Hoge, *The Boys in Blue*, 332–368; Livermore, *My Story of the War*, 409–462.

88 USSC *Bulletin* 5 (January 1, 1864): 145.

89 "The Women's Fair," in Hoge, *The Boys in Blue*, 332–368; Livermore, *My Story of the War*, 409–462.

90 Annie L. Endicott to May, November 28, 1863, NEWAA Papers.

91 Schuyler did not believe in the use of sanitary fairs. She did not help commission men who planned their own fair in New York in February 1864. See Attie's account of the Metropolitan Fair in "'A Swindling Concern,'" 289–303.

92 Bloor to May, November 21, 1863, NEWAA Papers.

93 Here Bloor was referring specifically to his desire to reach out to Methodists. Bloor to May, November 31, [*sic*] 1863, NEWAA Papers.

94 Bloor's unilateral decision to encourage these ventures might in part account for the criticism commission colleagues had of his performance, leading to his dismissal one year later. For an account of Bloor's conflict and dismissal from the USSC, see *Papers of Frederick Law Olmsted*, vol. 4, 90–92.

95 The Metropolitan Fair is the one exception.

96 Although Hoge and Livermore claimed the rights to plan and stage the Pioneer Fair in October 1863, the fairs that followed often raised more money. The Boston Fair, held in December 1863, for instance, raised $145,000. May, NEWAA Final Report, USSC Papers, Box 992, 11.

97 USSC *Bulletin* 40 (August 1, 1865): 1251.

98 LLS to Frederick Knapp, December 28, 1863, USSC Papers, Box 955.

99 William Hadley to "Miss May," Portland, March 3, 1864, NEWAA Papers.

100 Hadley to A. May, March 3, 1864, NEWAA Papers.

101 AWM to Hadley, March 8, 1864, NEWAA Papers.

102 AWM to Knapp, March 10, 1864, USSC Papers, Box 954.

103 Knapp to Hadley, March 18, 1864, NEWAA Papers.

104 AWM to Dr. Jenkins, April 20, 1864, USSC Papers, Box 954; Knapp to Jenkins, April 23, 1864, USSC Papers, Box 954.

105 See, for example, Philadelphia newspaper article, June 19, 1864, NEWAA Papers. The article was forwarded to May by one of her affiliates and referred to the commission as a "Christless philosophy" and a "Boston notion." This kind of sentiment was common throughout May's region and she was constantly dealing with this rural fear of an undue Boston influence.

106 See, for instance, Bloor to "Miss Schuyler," May 29, 1863, USSC Papers, Box 668. Bloor responded positively to LLS's suggestion that they more clearly "define the tri-partite relations," presumably between the commission, branches, and branch affiliates.

107 USSC *Bulletin* 24 (October 15, 1864): 739.

108 USSC *Bulletin* 26 (November 15, 1864): 820.

109 LLS to Parrish, December 6, 1864, USSC Papers, Box 667–670, 4.

110 USSC *Bulletin* 27 (December 1, 1864): 850–851.

111 LLS to Angie Post, December 6, 1864, LLS Papers, NYHS.

112 LLS to Dr. Parrish, December 6, 1864, USSC Papers, Box 667–670, 1. Schuyler also explained that WCAR *Bulletin* contributions were officially approved by the committee of correspondence and, afterward, "cannot therefore be altered by anyone else (subject only to the control of our own Board)."

113 Ibid.

114 Bellows, USSC *Bulletin* 40 (August 1, 1865): 1250.

CHAPTER V

1 Paul Hass, "A Volunteer Nurse in the Civil War: The Diary of Harriet Douglas Whetten," *Wisconsin Magazine of History* 49 (Spring 1965): 211.

2 Moore, *Women of the War*, 185.

3 Ibid.

4 Ibid., 192–193.

5 James McPherson, *Battle Cry of Freedom: The Civil War Era* (New York: Oxford University Press, 1988), 454–488.

6 Frederick Law Olmsted, *Hospital Transports: A Memoir of the Embarkation of the Sick and Wounded from the Peninsula of Virginia in the Summer of 1862* (Boston: Ticknor and Fields, 1863), 37; Wormeley, *United States Sanitary Commission*, 64.

7 Elizabeth Blackmar and Roy Rosenzweig, *The Park and the People: A History of Central Park* (New York: Henry Holt, 1994).

8 A transport woman was convinced that casualties and illnesses would be decreased significantly if they had access to "a good bath, seven days' rest, and twenty-one good meals." All that soldiers needed to stay healthy could be provided by a good "housekeeper," she felt. Olmsted, *Hospital Transports*, 62.

9 Southern white women were serving in army hospitals in Richmond at the same time. McPherson, *Battle Cry*, 478–480. For the most recent study of southern white women as nurses, see Faust, *Mothers of Invention*.

10 Olmsted, quoting a "transport lady," *Hospital Transports*, 50.

11 Alfred Bloor to Ellen Collins (WCAR Committee of Supplies), December 1861, USSC Papers, Box 833; Alfred Bloor to WCAR, August 2, 1861, USSC Papers, Box 839; Women's Central Association of Relief to the Army, *The Nurse's Manual: A Manual of Directions, Prepared for the Use of the Nurses in the Army of Hospitals, by a Committee of Hospital Physicians of the City of New York* (New York: Baker & Godwin, Printers, 1861). In May 1861 Bloor asked the women's branch for extra copies of *A Manual of Directions* to distribute to the troops. Charley Woolsey's letter to the *Evening Post*, 31 May 1862, *Family Letters*, 399.

12 Alfred Bloor to Ellen Collins (WCAR Committee of Supplies), December 1861, USSC Papers, Box 833; Alfred Bloor to WCAR, August 2, 1861, USSC Papers, Box 839.

13 Edge, *A Woman's Example*, 6.

14 Olmsted, *Hospital Transports*, 80.

15 Edward Jarvis, "Sanitary Condition of the Army," *Atlantic Monthly* 10 (October 1862): 486.

16 USSC *Bulletin* 39 (July 1, 1865): 1229.

17 See Schuyler's lament about New York women. LLS to Valentine Mott, October 1, 1863, USSC Papers, Box 955, 3–4. See discussion of Schuyler's attempt to organize a boycott among the urban elite in chapter 3; LLS to Angelina Post, May 17, 1864, LLS Papers, NYHS.

18 Whetten to Kate, June 1, 1862, in Paul Hass, "A Volunteer Nurse in the Civil War: The Letters of Harriet Douglas Whetten," *Wisconsin Magazine of History* 48 (Winter 1964–1965): 141.

19 Early on Wormeley remarked, "I often feel the pleasantness of our footing among all these persons,—official, military, naval, and medical. They clearly respect our work, and rightly appreciate it; . . . and when work is over, they do not feel towards us as 'women with a mission,' but as ladies, to be with whom is a grateful relaxation." Katharine Prescott Wormeley, *The Other Side of the War with the Army of the Potomac* (Boston: Ticknor and Fields, 1889), 128. Transport women privately chastised individual women whose behavior among commission men fell outside certain polite boundaries. See, for instance, Hass, "Diary of Harriet Douglas Whetten," 208, 218.

20 Eliza Woolsey Howland to Joe Howland, April 28, 1862, Bacon and Howland, *Letters of a Family*, 312.

21 The commission fought on ongoing battle to keep control of the ships assigned to them, for the army regularly confiscated them without warning to use them to transport troops, etc. The ships that were consistently used by the USSC hospital transport campaign were the *Spaulding, Elm City, Knickerbocker, Daniel Webster I, Daniel Webster II, Elizabeth*, and *Wilson Small*. Other ships passed in and out of commission hands.

22 This may not be the definitive list of middle-class women who served on the hospital transports. I define permanent members as those who I can document as having served on the ships for at least one month. A much larger number of

women worked on transports for one or more weeks before returning home. Many of those who worked for brief periods of time had already distinguished themselves in the women-run branches of the commission and in other relief venues. Abigail Williams May, for instance, spent several weeks on the ships. Life aboard the transports proved to be too much for Mary M. Hamilton, cousin of Louisa Lee Schuyler; she had only just arrived on the peninsula when she reported being too ill to continue. Mrs. John Harris of the Ladies' Aid Society of Philadelphia spent some time on various ships before returning to her responsibilities in Philadelphia. Transport work gave some young women the experience that helped them move into administrative positions elsewhere. Maria M. C. Hall, of Washington, D.C., worked on the *Daniel Webster II* before she became Nurse Superintendent at Navy Academy Hospital in Annapolis. Charlotte Bradford, of Duxbury, Massachusetts, left the transports to run the USSC Soldier's Home in Washington, D.C. For others, service in the Virginia peninsula was not followed by active service elsewhere in the war. Mary Gardner, of New York, spent six weeks on the ships, but I have only found her very brief account of her experience. Eliza Bellows worked on the boats for several weeks and then apparently retired from service.

This information was gleaned from a number of sources, including NEWAA Papers; Mary M. Hamilton to FLO, May 29, 1863, #1183, USSC Papers, Box 741. Hamilton is also mentioned in Bacon and Howland, *Letters of a Family*, May 27, 1862, 381; Mary Gardner to Rev. F. N. Knapp, "Minutes from Memory alone (and therefore imperfect) of my six weeks service in the Sanitary Commission," May 5, 1863, USSC Papers, #942, Box 741; Eliza Bellows to "Dear Friends," May 9, 1862, from aboard the *Wilson Small*, BP, MHS. Information on Hall, Bradford, and Harris came from Brockett and Vaughan, *Woman's Work in the Civil War*. Some information on Bradley came from Cashman, *Headstrong*. See also Ross, "'Women are needed,'" 125.

23 USSC *Bulletin* 39 (July 1, 1865): 1229.

24 Eliza Bellows to Russell Bellows (RB), May 17, 1862, BP, MHS.

25 Eliza Bellows to RB, April 21, 1861, BP, MHS, 2–3. Eliza and Henry Bellows usually wrote joint letters to their children. One of them (usually Eliza) would begin writing and then yield the pen to the other. Thankfully, the handwritings are distinctive, so it is always pretty clear who is writing, though one signed for both.

26 Wormeley, *Other Side of the War*, 17.

27 Whetten joined the team with Eliza Bellows and Ellen Strong, traveling in their party on May 6, 1862. Ibid.

28 Whetten to friend, May 11, 1862, Hass, "Letters of Harriet Douglas Whetten," 139. Whetten's use of the term "nurses" refers to male army contract nurses who were mostly convalescent soldiers (see chapter 4). At times the terminology is confusing, though, because Whetten and others referred to themselves as nurses as well, though they were always careful to delineate themselves from women and men who were doing similar work.

29 All the women record names of women who seem to have come and gone. When Ellie Strong, wife of George Templeton Strong, returned to the peninsula after a short trip home, six out of twenty nurses that were scheduled to return with her failed to report. I have not attempted to get a count of the women who left

after only a brief time. Unedited Strong Diary, June 15, 1862, New York Historical Society Microfilm.

30 Brockett and Vaughan, *Woman's Work in the Civil War,* 151, 152.

31 Moore, *Women of the War,* 185; Brockett and Vaughan, *Woman's Work in the Civil War,* 153.

32 Eliza Bellows to "Dear Friends," May 9, 1862, BP, MHS.

33 Georgy to Mother, May 1, 1862, Bacon and Howland, *Letters of a Family,* 321.

34 Wormeley, *Other Side of the War,* 102, 95.

35 McPherson argues that illness played a significant role in the Union's decision to pull out as "scores of new cases of malaria, dysentery, and typhoid were reported every day." He estimates that "nearly a fourth of the unwounded men were sick" by July. McPherson, *Battle Cry of Freedom,* 488.

36 In fact, many became ill from their work in the swampy malarial environment of the delta and at least one woman, Isabella Fogg of Calais, Maine, was permanently disabled as a result of an injury she sustained when she fell through a hatchway on one of the boats.

37 Wormeley, *Other Side of the War,* 27.

38 Wormeley, for instance, complained about the hired help and the freed slaves who were expected to do much of the heavy work. Wormeley and the others had difficulties managing the people who were presumably their subordinates; they often preferred to simply do the work themselves instead of fretting over how others were doing it. See Wormeley, *Other Side of the War,* 85.

39 Katharine Prescott Wormeley (KPW) to Mother, May 14, 1862, Wormeley, *Other Side of the War,* 32. KPW to Friend, May 21, 1862, Ibid., 62. Here Wormeley is referring to Olmsted's description of the women's responsibilities.

40 Recipes for all of these are in Woman's Central Association of Relief, *The Nurse's Manual.* Though it offered them a chance to visit family and friends, all of the women dreaded making the ocean voyage home, because the hard work was made even harder by the inevitable seasickness. Whetten remembered her first trip up to New York, when the entire crew was stricken, leaving her "ghastly sea-sick" and alone "in the pantry, trying with my weak hands to cut bread and butter and wash tin cups in cold greasy water, my gown torn in half in a dozen places by being thrown against barrels and boxes when the ship heaved." Whetten to "My dearest Hexie," May 30, 1862, Hass, "Letters of Harriet Douglas Whetten," 140.

41 Here the experience of transport women is very similar to Reid Mitchell's description of the psychological distance that grew between soldiers and civilians in *Civil War Soldiers* (New York: Penguin, 1988).

42 Wormeley, *Other Side of the War,* 81.

43 Ibid., 78. See also 70, 80, 115–116, 118–119; Hass, "Letters of Harriet Douglas Whetten," 147; and Bacon and Howland, *Letters of a Family,* 341.

44 Dorothea Dix's regulations for the commission's hospital transport campaign forbade women to wear ruffles, ribbons, "fur belows [sic]," and hoops. Anne L. Austin, *The Woolsey Sisters of New York: A Family's Involvement in the Civil War and a New Profession, 1860–1900* (Philadelphia: American Philosophical Society, 1971), 40.

45 Wormeley, *Other Side of the War,* 165; Austin, *Woolsey Sisters,* 65.

46 Wormeley, *Other Side of the War,* 118, 104. See also women's criticisms of gov-

ernment: Olmsted, *Hospital Transports,* 101, 114, 383–384; and Bacon and How-land, *Letters of a Family,* 321, 410, 418.

47 Transport women usually shared one room. Charley Woolsey, Letter to New York Evening Post, May 31, 1862, Bacon and Howland, *Letters of a Family,* 398.

48 Wormeley, *Other Side of the War,* 84.

49 FLO to Jenkins, May 18, 1862, USSC Papers, Box 741.

50 Georgy noted that she left "a polite message for the 'Colonel perdu,'—which had to stand him in place of his lost dinner." Bacon and Howland, *Letters of a Family,* 356–358.

51 Wormeley, *Other Side of the War,* 157.

52 Ibid., 69.

53 Ibid., 103; Hass, "Letters of Harriet Douglas Whetten," 142.

54 Wormeley, *Other Side of the War,* 193–194.

55 Mother to "Girls" (Eliza and Georgy), June 2, 1862, Bacon and Howland, *Letters of a Family,* 388. There are many examples of this disobedience: Georgy to Mother, 383; Whetten to "My dearest Kate," June 1, 1862, in Hass, "Letters of Harriet Douglas Whetten," 142. Some of this rubbed off on the Woolsey sisters at home. Jane was particularly critical of military authority. Jane to Georgy and Eliza, Bacon and Howland, *Letters of a Family,* 388, 405. Sarah to Georgy and Eliza, 418.

56 Whetten to "My dearest Kate," May 8, 1862, in Hass, "Letters of Harriet Douglas Whetten," 137.

57 Wormeley, *Other Side of the War,* 157–158.

58 Ibid., 148.

59 Ibid., 104.

60 Ibid., 76.

61 Through their exposure to abolitionist literature, liberal theology, and domestic fiction, Elizabeth Clark has argued, northern women like those who served on the transports were encouraged to seek "an intuitive empathic identification" with slaves and others who suffered and experienced pain. Clark calls the ante-bellum sensibility that encouraged readers of domestic fiction to sympathize with the suffering of others the "habit of sympathy." Conventional sentimental-ity encouraged women and men to sympathize, empathize, even, with another individual's (usually a slave's) pain. Elizabeth Clark, "The Sacred Rights of the Weak: Pain, Sympathy, and the Culture of Individual Rights in Antebellum America," *Journal of American History* 82 (September 1995): 463–493.

62 Wormeley, *Other Side of the War,* 114.

63 Ibid., 77–78.

64 Brockett and Vaughan, *Woman's Work in the Civil War,* 155; McPherson, *Battle Cry of Freedom,* 488.

65 Cashman, *Headstrong,* 119.

66 Wormeley, *Other Side of the War,* 77.

67 Ibid., 110. "Good-by!" Wormeley ended a letter to a friend, "I hope you may be happy this summer,—it would be something to be able to think happiness as existing somewhere." Wormeley, 115.

68 Ibid., 102.

69 Fredrickson, *Inner Civil War,* 89–97.

70 Martin Pernick, *A Calculus of Suffering: Pain, Professionalism, and Anesthesia in Nineteenth-Century America* (New York: Columbia University Press, 1985), 46–50. See Olmsted's remark about the military's opinion that a certain amount of suffering "is inevitable in war." Olmsted, *Hospital Transports*, 93.
71 Ginzberg, *Women and the Work of Benevolence*, 148.
72 Whetten, *Other Side of the War*, 144.
73 Bacon and Howland, *Letters of a Family*, 348.
74 Wormeley, *Other Side of the War*, 145.
75 Bacon and Howland, *Letters of a Family*, 382.
76 Pernick, *A Calculus of Suffering*, 46.
77 Wormeley, *Other Side of the War*, 63.
78 Olmsted's aide Edward Mitchell quoted in Bacon and Howland, *Letters of a Family*, 423.
79 Wormeley, *Other Side of the War*, 84, 126.
80 Unedited Strong Diary, May 13, 1862, New York Historical Society Microfilm.
81 Nevins and Thomas, *Diary of George Templeton Strong*, vol. 4, June 26, 1862, 233–234.
82 Ibid., vol. 4, July 11, 1862, 239.
83 HWB to Eliza Bellows, May 13, 1862, BP, MHS.
84 Censer, *Papers of Frederick Law Olmsted*, vol. 4, 394–395.
85 Wormeley, *Other Side of the War*, 202–207.
86 Ibid., 205.
87 David Blight, "A Union Soldier's Experience," in *Major Problems in the Civil War and Reconstruction*, ed. Michael Perman (Boston: Houghton Mifflin, 1998), 144.
88 Cashman, *Headstrong*, 132; Hass, "Diary of Harriet Douglas Whetten," 218–220.
89 See Blight's study of Charles Harvey Brewster. Blight, "Union Soldier."
90 Balestier served with Woolsey, Howland, Wormeley, and Whetten. Mr. Balestier to FLO, June 8, 1862, USSC Papers, Box 742.

CHAPTER VI

1 *The New York Times*, 3 January 1864, 1.
2 *The New York Times*, 11 November 1864, 4.
3 *The New York Times*, 6 February 1864, 5.
4 *The New York Times*, 3 May 1865, 4.
5 *The New York Times*, 7 May 1865, 4. Here the author was perhaps referring to Napoleon III's violation of the Monroe Doctrine by crowning Maximilian of Austria emperor of Mexico.
6 *The New York Times*, 6 May 1865; 3 May 1865.
7 Though Lee surrendered to Grant on April 9, fighting continued in some theaters well into the summer.
8 In *When Johnny Comes Marching Home*, Dixon Wecter discusses growing prejudices against hiring Civil War veterans and many other difficulties soldiers faced adjusting in the postwar years. (Cambridge, Mass.: Houghton Mifflin, 1944), 182–193.

9 Mary Livermore, *The Story of My Life, or the Sunshine and Shadow of Seventy Years* (Hartford, Conn.: A. D. Worthington & Co., 1898), 488.

10 Wecter, *When Johnny Comes Marching*, 226–236.

11 Joseph Parrish to John S. Blatchford, June 28, 1965, USSC Papers, Box 954.

12 *The New York Times*, 11 November 1864, 4.

13 Bellows went to California to look after the congregation of friend Thomas Starr King, who had died suddenly. While he was there, Bellows and his daughter and son did a lot of sight-seeing, and Bellows also looked in on commission operations in California.

14 Maxwell, *Lincoln's Fifth Wheel*, 264–265.

15 Nevins and Thomas, *Diary of George Templeton Strong*, vol. III, September 13, 1864, 486. In November he remarked, "Sanitary Commission is in trouble. I fear we must throw overboard either Knapp, or Jenkins and Collins to save the ship from foundering." Ibid., vol. III, November 20, 1864, 518–519. The internal fighting continued well into 1865. Ibid., vol. III, April 20, 1865, 590. To make matters worse for the USSC, in August 1864, Surgeon General William Hammond's heavy-handedness got him in trouble with the military hierarchy, and he was court-martialed and relieved of duty. As a result of the troubles with Hammond, the USSC's relationship with Secretary of War Stanton was strained. Maxwell, *Lincoln's Fifth Wheel*, 235–244.

16 HWB to RB, November 2, 1864, BP, MHS. Bellows also remarked on the internecine commission quarrels: "I found considerable want of *balance* in our *personnel*, and in our Board, not strange considering the balances wheel was in California." On November 22, 1864, he wrote Russell once again of these problems: "Jealousies have sprung up among our chief officers, Jenkins and Knapp and Collins, in my absence, which have created much (illegible?) and given me serious anxiety. The New York and Washington offices are not on smooth and confiding terms." HWB to RB, November 22, 1864, BP, MHS.

17 HWB to RB, February 12, 1865, BP, MHS. See Kring's discussion of the plans for a Unitarian meeting. Kring, *Henry Whitney Bellows*, 287–304.

18 HWB to RB, November 22, 1864, BP, MHS. In February, Bellows reported that "Dr. Jenkins has gone to live in Washington and really makes himself the centre of the hard work so that I am able to turn my attention toward denominational matters." HWB to RB, February 12, 1865, BP, MHS.

19 "Resolutions," *Documents*, vol. I, #21.

20 Frederick Knapp, "Third Report, concerning Aid and Comfort given by the Sanitary Commission to Sick Soldiers passing through Washington," March 21, 1862, *Documents*, vol. I, #39. Knapp reported that soldiers succumbed to the temptations of the city and spent "their time and money in the drinking saloons." In this case, he found three convalescent soldiers in a cheap lodging house; one had already died and the other two were nearly dead.

21 As secretary of the Special Relief Service of the USSC, Knapp initiated commission efforts like feeding stations, where soldiers released from their regiments could get a hot meal, and the Soldier's Home in Washington that acted as a temporary shelter for sick and disabled soldiers. See Maxwell, *Lincoln's Fifth Wheel*, 253 and passim. See also Knapp's reports of the Special Relief Service. Knapp, "Aid and Comfort given by the Sanitary Commission to Sick Soldiers passing through Washington, 1st and 2d. Reports," September 23, 1861, and Oc-

tober 21, 1861, *Documents,* vol. I, #35; "Fourth Report concerning Aid and Comfort given by the Sanitary Commission to Sick Soldiers passing through Washington—With Supplement," February 1, 1863, *Documents,* vol. I, #59a; "Fifth Report concerning the Aid and Comfort given by the Sanitary Commission to Sick and Invalid Soldiers," December 15, 1862–October 1, 1863, *Documents,* vol. II, #77; "Report concerning the Aid and Comfort given by the Sanitary Commission to Sick and Invalid Soldiers," June 30, 1865, *Documents,* vol. II, #94; "Report concerning Provision required for the Relief and Support of Disabled Soldiers and Sailors and their Dependents," December 15, 1865, *Documents,* vol. II, #95.

22 Attie details Knapp's campaign for sanitariums very insightfully. Attie, "A Swindling Concern," 340–357.

23 "Provision for Disabled Soldiers—Letter to S. G. Perkins," August 15, 1862, *Documents,* vol. I, #49.

24 John Ordronaux, "Proposed Scheme for the Relief of Disabled Soldiers," February 14, 1863, *Documents,* #58.

25 Bellows cheerfully added, however, that the problem had been taken care of quickly and efficiently by "the healthy mind of the American people all over the country." HWB, "Provision Required for the Relief and Support of Disabled Soldiers and Sailors and their Dependents," December 15, 1865, *Documents,* #95.

26 *Diary of George Templeton Strong,* vol. III, May 4, 1864, 439. Dr. Cornelius Rea Agnew brought the proposal before the USSC—apparently he headed a committee that was charged with looking into Knapp's recommendation.

27 Ibid.

28 Bellows was somewhat skeptical about creating institutions for invalid soldiers from the beginning. In 1862, he explained, "I should regard any general scheme for herding the invalids of the war into State or National Institutions, as a most dangerous blow to domestic order, to the sacredness of home affections and responsibilities, as well as a weakening of what may be termed the law of local sympathy." October 13, 1862, *Documents,* #49. This comment contrasts with Bellows's commitment to nationalizing (and rationalizing) the country's benevolence. In July 1865, Bellows announced the commission's intent to open "one or more asylums of this character," while he recommended that "the spontaneous, public, unofficial character of the ministry rendered to the sick and wounded through the war" ought really to take over the responsibility of caring for disabled veterans. "That government is best which governs least," he added. Here again this preference for laissez-faire government is uncharacteristic of Bellows, who saw the commission as a means of doing away with the spontaneity of local benevolence and extending the power of the national government. HWB, USSC *Bulletin* 39 (July 1, 1865): 1219.

29 Maxwell, *Lincoln's Fifth Wheel,* 267–268.

30 Ibid., 234–247, 263–264.

31 AWM, NEWAA Final Report, USSC Papers, Box 992, 11.

32 Ellen Collins, LLS, Angelina Post, Caroline Lane, and Catherine Nash to "Madam," October 25, 1864, USSC Papers, Box 667–670.

33 LLS to Angie Post, December 17, 1864, WCAR Papers.

34 Angie Post to Mrs. Wead, December 28, 1864, Wead Papers, Sophia Smith Collection, Smith College, Northampton, Mass., 2.

35 LLS, "Articles of Re-organization," October 20, 1863, USSC Papers, Box 955, #3143, 5. Attie explains that Christine Griffin reported on behalf of the Special Relief Committee in February that women were visiting soldiers and soldiers' families in New York City tenements. See Attie, "A Swindling Concern," 339, for Christine Griffin, Report of Special Relief, February 1864, Box 955. Unfortunately, I could not find this or any other reference in the NYPL collection.

36 Livermore, *My Story of the War,* 586–600.

37 Ibid., 594.

38 McClintock, "Civil War Pensions." As McClintock explains, family pension benefits were dispensed according to patronage, an arbitrary estimation of a widow's moral standing, and other sorts of nonhumanitarian concerns.

39 FLO to Oliver Wolcott Gibbs, November 5, 1862, in *Historical Sketch of the Union League Club of New York, Its Origin, Organization, and Work, 1863–1879* (New York: Henry Whitney Bellows, 1879), 12.

40 Bernstein, *New York City Draft Riots,* 57.

41 See, for instance, Bernstein's discussion of the Union League Club's raising of the Twentieth U.S. Colored Regiment and the presentation of colors to the same on March 5, 1864. Ibid., 65–70.

42 USSC pledges $5,000 to WCAR fund-matching in J. Foster Jenkins to WCAR, April 2, 1864, USSC Papers, Box 954. Schuyler offers a comprehensive criticism of the *Bulletin* and offers her advice for its improvement in LLS to Bloor, July 23, 1864, USSC Papers, Box 954. Parrish discusses trip to the battlefield in Parrish to LLS, October 27, 1864, USSC Papers, Box 667–670. The WCAR announces the meeting in LLS, Circular announcing council meeting, November 16, 1864, USSC Papers, Box 667–670.

43 May recorded in her diary, "August 10–September 7th. At Florence, Mass. Dr. Munde's Water cure." May Diary, MGP, Folder #29.

44 Parenthesis in the original. LLS to Post, June 8, 1864, WCAR Papers.

45 Angie Post to "Nannie," June 21, 1864, BP, MHS.

46 LLS to Post, June 29, 1864, BP, MHS.

47 Mrs. Charles B. Stuart to WCAR, December 1864 or January 1865, USSC Papers, Box 953.

48 Schuyler describes a daydream about the end of the war in a *Bulletin* article dated April 4, 1865. USSC *Bulletin* 37 (May 1, 1865): 1160.

49 HWB and J. S. Blatchford, "Circular Addressed to the Branches and Aid Societies Tributary to the U.S. Sanitary Commission," May 15, 1865, *Documents,* vol. II, #90.

50 Bellows later published this response in the *Bulletin.* HWB to AWM, May 26, 1863, USSC *Bulletin* 39 (July 1, 1865): 1217–1221.

51 LLS to Parrish, June 28, 1865, USSC Papers, Box 668. Schuyler is probably referring to the National Freedmen's Relief Association, a private organization that began in 1864.

52 Parrish to LLS, July 8, 1865, USSC Papers, Box 668.

53 LLS to Parrish, July 13, 1865, USSC Papers, Box 668.

54 HWB, et al., "Circular Addressed to the Branches and Aid Societies Tributary to the U.S. Sanitary Commission," July 4, 1865, *Documents,* vol. II, #93. Though the circular is dated July 4, it appears there was some delay in its distribution.

55 LLS to Parrish, July 13, 1865; Parrish to LLS, July 15, 1865, USSC Papers, Box 668.

56 Parrish to Blatchford, July 11, 1865, USSC Papers, Box 954. Parrish also re- ported that Massachusetts had already made comprehensive plans for finding employment for veterans (a Bureau of Employment was opened in the office of the Surgeon General of the State on January 1, 1865), training and educating soldiers whose disabilities prevented them from going back to their former posi- tions (veterans were reimbursed for college courses such as bookkeeping), and institutionalizing veterans who were totally disabled (the state opened a 600-bed structure on "Rainsford's [*sic*] Island").

57 As Theda Skocpol has argued, pensions in the postwar years were distributed in return for political patronage. Skocpol, *Protecting Soldiers and Mothers: The Political Origins of Social Policy in the United States* (Cambridge: Harvard Uni- versity Press, 1992), 65–130.

58 Parrish to Blatchford, June 28, 1865, USSC Papers, Box 954.

59 Ibid. The NEWAA had $5,900 left in its treasury. One wonders if this money ever wound up in USSC hands.

60 See Don Fehrenbacher, ed., *History and American Society: Essays of David Pot- ter* (New York: Oxford University Press, 1973).

61 Parrish to Blatchford, June 28, 1865, USSC Papers, Box 954.

62 LLS to Post, June 7, 1865, WCAR Papers.

63 LLS to Post, July 11, 1865, WCAR Papers.

64 LLS to Post, August 2, 1865, WCAR Papers.

65 LLS to Post, November 8, 1865, WCAR Papers.

66 The WCAR processed fifty-seven boxes of supplies on July 3. LLS to Post, July 11, 1865, WCAR Papers.

67 LLS to Post, July 11, 1865, WCAR Papers. LLS discusses the construction and presentation of these resolutions in LLS to Post, July 11, 1865, WCAR Papers.

68 "Resolutions" in Schuyler's hand, July 7, 1865, USSC Papers, Box 954. The reso- lutions are reprinted in the final issue of the USSC *Bulletin* 40 (August 1, 1865): 1256–1257.

69 Ibid.

70 LLS to Post, October 1, 1865, LLS to Post, November 8–9, 1865, WCAR Papers.

71 LLS to Mrs. Wead, September 8, 1865, Wead Papers, Sophia Smith Collection.

72 LLS to Angie, July 11, 1865, WCAR Papers.

73 LLS, Collins, et al., "Fourth Annual and Final Report of the Woman's Central Association of Relief for the Army and Navy of the United States," USSC *Bulle- tin* 40 (August 1, 1865): 1255. The report is dated July 4, but Schuyler was still working on it after July 4. The August issue of the *Bulletin* was not released until September.

74 Ibid.

75 AWM, "New England Women's Auxiliary Association, Final Report," July 12, 1865, USSC Papers, Box 992.

76 Mary Livermore, *Massachusetts in the Army and Navy during the War of 1861– 1865* (Boston: Wright and Potter, 1865), 588–590.

77 AWM, "New England Women's Auxiliary Association, Final Report," July 12, 1865, USSC Papers, Box 992, 11, 14.

78 AWM, "New England Women's Auxiliary Association," USSC *Bulletin* 40 (Au- gust 1, 1865): 1259. May enumerates these plans more specifically in the

NEWAA Final Report, in which she writes that "[t]he freedmen, the refugees, are our inheritance." "New England Women's Auxiliary Association, Final Report," July 12, 1865, USSC Papers, Box 992, 14.

79 Cheney, *Memoirs*, 21–22.

80 May Diary, MGP. Caroline Healey Dall began the American Social Science Association (ASSA) in 1865. William Leach describes this ambitious organization as "a concentrated effort by the reform-minded sector of the American middle class to come to grips with the pauperism and crime, the mental and physical disorder, the disorientation of family life, the instability and expansion of city and village populations, and the class conflict that resulted from the industrialization and urbanization of American society and the 'unrestricted' and 'unadministered' growth of the last two and a half centuries.'" Among other things, the ASSA encouraged women to become members and was always careful to have women represented on its executive board. Leach, *True Love*, 299.

81 May Diary, MGP. A letter from Abby Howland Woolsey, a veteran nurse of the USSC's hospital transport campaign, suggests that something remained of the old organization of the Woman's Central. In December 1867, she wrote a former commission officer inquiring about money the USSC still had in its treasury: "May I also take the liberty of asking you in what way the two hundred and fifty thousand dollars left in the hands of the C[ommission], at the close of the war is made available for soldiers now? We have often applications for relief from soldiers and their families, and must look to your organization, at least for information, if not something more substantial." Abby Howland Woolsey to J. Blatchford, December 20, 1867, #1867, USSC Papers, Box 649.

82 Collins made some effort to contact the associate managers, as evidenced by her September 18 letter to Mrs. Wead, in which she announced her intention to "renew the organization of the Women's Central Relief Association and continue its work for the support of the N.Y. National Freedman's Relief Association." Collins to Wead, September 18, 1865, Wead Papers, Sophia Smith Collection.

At the July 7 meeting, it was suggested that Schuyler write a final history of the WCAR. Privately she responded to the suggestion in the following manner: "It is all nonsense. I am not capable of doing anything of the kind—and I don't mean to." She was relieved when a committee was appointed to look into the matter. LLS to Post, July 11, 1865, WCAR Papers. Unfortunately, I can find no indication that such a history was ever written.

83 E. S. Roberts, Corresponding Secretary, "Soldiers' Aid Society—New Haven," USSC *Bulletin* 40 (August 1, 1865): 1258.

CHAPTER VII

1 By 1880, more than 4 million Americans lived in cities larger than 250,000. Immigration picked up again after the war—10 million people entered the United States between 1860 and 1890. Bruce Levine et al., *Who Built America? Working People and the Nation's Economy, Politics, Culture, and Society*, Volume 1: *From Conquest and Colonization through Reconstruction and the Great Uprising of 1877* (New York: Pantheon Books, 1989), 529–531.

2 Bellows to Stillé, November 15, 1865, BP, MHS.

3 See, for instance, Pascoe, *Relations of Rescue*, and Buhle, *Women and American Socialism*. Pascoe looks at women's missionary organizations, and Buhle considers the connections between groups such as the WCTU and socialist organizations.

4 Francis Greenwood Peabody, *Reminiscences of Present-Day Saints* (Boston: Houghton Mifflin, 1927), 264–265.

5 Schuyler, *Forty-Three Years Ago*, 6.

6 Ibid.; Cross, "The Philanthropic Contribution of Louisa Lee Schuyler," 295.

7 Joan Waugh, *Unsentimental Reformer: The Life of Josephine Shaw Lowell* (Cambridge, Mass.: Harvard University Press, 1997), 114.

8 Ibid., 115; Walter Trattner, "Louisa Lee Schuyler and the Founding of the State Charities Aid Association," *New York Historical Society Quarterly* 51 (1967): 243. Once the children of the poor were no longer housed in almshouses, the State Charities Aid Association (SCAA) initiated a program to place them in private homes instead of in the special children's institutions, which Schuyler and her colleagues believed were little more than workhouses. With this initiative, the SCAA became a tireless critic of the institutionalization of children and advocate for child welfare. Peter Romanofsky, "Saving the Lives of the City's Foundlings: The Joint Committee and New York City Child Care Methods, 1860–1907," *New York Historical Society Quarterly* 61 (1977): 51.

9 Peabody, *Reminiscences of Present-Day Saints*, 266.

10 Among the women veterans who played a critical role in opening the school were Abby Howland Woolsey, Mrs. William Preston Griffin, and Mrs. D'Orémieulx. Ellen Collins had worked closely with Schuyler as Chair of the WCAR's Supplies Committee and also served on the SCAA's special committee for creating the Nurse Training School. Elizabeth Christopher Hobson, "Founding the Bellevue Training School for Nurses," in Abby Howland Woolsey, *A Century of Nursing*, (New York: G. P. Putnam and Sons, 1876); reprint, National League of Nursing Education, 1950), 135–172.

11 Hobson, "Founding," 161–166.

12 In 1911, this institution became the City of New York Bellevue Hospital Training School for Midwives. This last is a very interesting development, indeed, for more than nurses, midwives operated outside the purview of the male medical establishment. Hobson, "Founding," 165–166.

13 Ibid., 162–166.

14 Hobson refers to "our friends" who met with the Medical Board at the Bellevue Hospital after the SCAA meeting proposing that the nurses take over the maternity wards. Ibid., 163. Hobson gives a more complete list of these friends on p. 150.

15 LLS to Dr. Cornelius Rea Agnew (former member of the USSC's executive board), March 22, 1881, LLS Papers, BL.

16 Schuyler's public advocacy did not stop with her SCAA work. For ten years, she lobbied the New York state legislature to pass legislation making the state responsible for the care of the insane and for the creation of a state committee to investigate and prevent blindness in children. Homer Folks, "Louisa Lee Schuyler—Her Work," in *Louisa Lee Schuyler*, 7–9, 10–11. Cross, "Philosophical Contributions," 297–298.

17 Cheney, *Memoirs*, 24. In a tribute to May published in *Woman's Journal*, the

author noted that May was vice-president of the New England Women's Club and vice-president of the Association for the Advancement of Women. "In Memoriam," *The Woman's Journal* (December 8, 1888).

18 Upon her death in 1888, the State Board of Education voted to have the school building at Framingham Normal School renamed May Hall in honor of her work with the state's teachers and students. Her portrait hangs on the first floor of that building today, which is part of Framingham State College.

19 Abigail Williams May, *Dress: A Paper Read Before the Association for the Advancement of Women* [1878] (Boston: Lockwood, Brooks and Company, 1879), 22.

20 Dall quoted in Leach, *True Love*, 283.

21 S. Agnes Donham, History of the Women's Educational and Industrial Union, typescript, Boston, 1955, Women's Educational and Industrial Union Papers (WEIU Papers), SL, B-8, v. 1, 1. Sarah Deutsch discusses the WEIU at length in her article "Learning to Talk More Like a Man: Boston Women's Class-Bridging Organizations, 1870–1940," *American Historical Review* (April 1992): 379–404.

22 Quote from description of the WEIU Papers, SL.

23 Three nurse training schools were opened in 1873: Bellevue in New York was the first, followed by New Haven Hospital in Connecticut, and Massachusetts General Hospital in Boston. Sandra Beth Lewensen, *Taking Charge: Nursing, Suffrage, and Feminism in America, 1873–1920* (New York: National League of Nursing, 1996), 17.

24 Zakrezewska received the charter for the school in 1862, but the opening of the school was delayed because of the war. Ibid.

25 Harriet Clisby Lecture, Langham Place, London, May 25, 1894, WEIU Papers.

26 Deutsch, "Learning to Talk," 390.

27 Ibid.

28 Livermore, *My Story of the War*, 604–610.

29 Ibid., 483.

30 Buhle, *Women and American Socialism*, 62; Leach, *True Love*, 186. Even so, May had difficulties scheduling Livermore for a lecture at the New England Women's Club because of Livermore's busy schedule. Livermore to AWM, November 11, 1877; Livermore to AWM, April 13, 1880, MGP.

31 Livermore, *Story of My Life*, 479.

32 Ibid., 480.

33 Bordin, *Woman and Temperance*, 59.

34 Livermore, *Story of My Life*, 602. See also Leach, *True Love*, 205–206.

35 Bordin, *Woman and Temperance*.

36 Ibid., 3.

37 Ibid., 158.

38 Ibid., 97–114.

39 Indeed, the connection between the WCTU and American socialism is suggested in WCTU discussions about women being paid for housework, for instance. Bordin, *Woman and Temperance*, 114, 108; Buhle, *Women and American Socialism*, 51–80.

40 Buhle, *Women and American Socialism*, 79.

41 Baker, "Domestication of Politics," 641.

42 Sklar argues that men's political culture was at a stalemate because middle-class

Notes to Pages 167–175

business interests kept taxes low and machine politicians were not meeting the needs of their constituents. Sklar, "Historical Foundations," 60.

43 Kelley and her National Consumers' League were the catalysts behind the 1908 *Muller v. Oregon* decision limiting to ten the number of hours women could work each day. For an excellent overview of the case and the debate that the decision inspired, see Nancy Wolloch, *Muller v. Oregon: A Brief History with Documents* (Boston: St. Martin's Press, 1996).

44 Kathryn Kish Sklar, "Hull House in the 1890s: A Community of Women Reformers," *Signs* 10 (Summer 1985): 658–677.

CONCLUSION

1 LLS, "Woman's Central Association of Relief: Organization, No. VI," February 4, 1865, USSC *Bulletin* (February 15, 1865): 1009.

2 Smith-Rosenberg, *Disorderly Conduct*, 120. The AFMRS was limited to greater New England, though, while USSC branches opened as far west as Chicago and as far south as Louisville.

3 LLS, "Woman's Central Association of Relief: Organization, No. VI," February 4, 1865, USSC *Bulletin* (February 15, 1865): 1010.

4 The AFMRS helped working-class women resist the devaluation of women's labor that came with the industrialization of the garment industry by lending them money to rent sewing machines, etc. Smith-Rosenberg, *Disorderly Conduct*, 122–123.

5 Freedman, "Separatism as Strategy," 12.

6 May quoted in Leach, *True Love*, 6.

7 See also May and Livermore's activities in the American Social Science Association. Leach, *True Love*, 205–206; Livermore, *Story of My Life*, 602.

8 See Sklar, "Historical Foundations," 45; Baker, "Domestication of Politics," 635–647; Epstein, *Politics of Domesticity*, 129–130; Bordin, *Woman and Temperance*, 105–108.

9 Fredrickson, *Inner Civil War*.

10 See, in particular, Richard Hofstadter's discussion of "the status revolution" in *The Age of Reform* (New York: Vintage Books, 1955), 131–172.

11 Fredrickson, *Inner Civil War*, 211–215.

12 For the WCTU's peace agenda, see Harriet Hyman Alonso, *Peace as a Women's Issue: A History of the U.S. Movement for World Peace and Women's Rights* (New York: Syracuse University Press, 1993), 48–55.

13 Hofstadter, *Age of Reform*, 143.

Bibliography

PRIMARY SOURCES

Unpublished Papers and Manuscript Collections
Henry Whitney Bellows Papers, Massachusetts Historical Society, Boston, Mass.
Henry Whitney Bellows Papers, Houghton Library, Harvard University, Cambridge, Mass.
Elizabeth Blackwell Papers, Butler Library, Columbia University, New York, N.Y.
Elizabeth Blackwell Papers, Schlesinger Library, Radcliffe College, Cambridge, Mass.
Alfred J. Bloor Papers, New York Historical Society, New York, N.Y.
Catherine Dall Papers, Massachusetts Historical Society, Boston, Mass.
Dorothea Dix Papers, Houghton Library, Harvard University, Cambridge, Mass.
Edward Jarvis, M.D., Papers, Countway Medical Library, Harvard Medical School, Boston, Mass.
Abigail Williams May Papers, May-Goddard Collection, Schlesinger Library, Radcliffe College, Cambridge, Mass.
New England Women's Auxiliary Association Papers, Massachusetts Historical Society, Boston, Mass.
Angelina Post Papers, New York Historical Association, New York, N.Y.
Louisa Lee Schuyler Papers, Sophia Smith Collection, Smith College Library, Northampton Library.
Louisa Lee Schuyler Papers, New York Historical Society, New York, N.Y.
Louisa Lee Schuyler Papers, Library of Congress, Washington, D.C.
George Templeton Strong, Unedited Diary, Microfilm Collection, New York Historical Society, New York, N.Y.
United States Sanitary Commission Papers, Astor, Lennox, and Tilden Foundation Collection, Rare Books and Manuscripts Division, New York Public Library, New York, N.Y.
Women's Educational and Industrial Union Papers, Schlesinger Library, Radcliffe College, Cambridge, Mass.

Woman's Central Association of Relief Papers, Museum of the City of New York.
Katharine Prescott Wormeley Papers, Newport Historical Society, Newport, R.I.

Official USSC Published Accounts

Edge, Frederick Milnes. *A Woman's Example and A Nation's Work: A Tribute to Florence Nightingale*. London: William Ridgeway, 1864.

Newberry, John S. *The United States Sanitary Commission in the Valley of the Mississippi during the War of the Rebellion, 1861–1866*. Cleveland: Fairbanks, Benedict, & Co., 1871.

Stillé, Charles. *History of the United States Sanitary Commission: Being the General Report of Its Work during the War of the Rebellion*. Philadelphia: J. B. Lippincott, 1866.

Wormeley, Katharine Prescott. *The United States Sanitary Commission: A Sketch of Its Purposes and Work*. Boston: Little, Brown and Company, 1863.

The Sanitary Commission of the United States Army: A Succinct Narrative of Its Works and Purposes. 1864. Reprint, New York: Arno Press and the New York Times, 1972.

Published Diaries, Letters, Autobiographies, Tributes, and Sermons

Alcott, Louisa May. *Hospital Sketches*. Boston: J. Redpath, 1863.

Bellows, Anna. *Recollections of Henry Whitney Bellows, a Paper Written for the New York League of Unitarian Women & Printed by the Branch Alliance of All Souls' Church*. New York: Branch Alliance of All Souls' Church, 1897.

Bellows, Henry Whitney. "Cities and Parks: With Special Reference to the New York Central Park." *Atlantic Monthly* (April 1861): 416–429.

———. *Historical Sketch of the Union League Club of New York, Its Origin, Organization, and Work, 1863–1879*. New York: Henry Whitney Bellows, 1879.

———. *Preparing for Old Age, A Sermon on Returning from the Funeral at Walpole, N.H. of Louisa Bellows Knapp*. Cambridge, Mass.: Press of J. Wilson and Son, 1872.

———. *Public Life in Washington: The Moral Aspects of the National Capital, An Address Read on Sunday, May 7, 1866*. New York: James Miller, 1866.

———. *A Sermon Occasioned by the Late Riot in New York, Preached in the Church of the Divine Unity, May 13, 1849*. New York: C. S. Francis & Co., 1849.

———. *Speech of the Rev. Dr. Bellows, President of the United States Sanitary Commission: Made at the Academy of Music, Philadelphia, Tuesday Evening, February 24, 1863*. Philadelphia: C. Sherman, Son and Co., 1863.

———. *The State and the Nation—Sacred to Christian Citizens, A Sermon, Preached at the All Souls' Church, New York, April 21, 1861*. New York: James Miller, 1861.

———. *The Suspense of Faith: An Address to the Alumni of the Divinity School of Harvard University, Cambridge, Mass., Given July 19, 1859*. New York: C. S. Francis, 1859.

———. *Unconditional Loyalty*. New York: A. D. F. Randolph, 1863.

———. *The United States Sanitary Commission*. Reprinted from Johnson's Universal Encyclopedia for Private Distribution. New York: Johnson's Universal Encyclopedia, 1877.

Bellows, Russell. "Henry Whitney Bellows, A Biographical Sketch with Portrait." In *The Bellows Genealogy, Or John Bellows*, ed. Thomas Bellows Peck. Keene, N.H.: Sentinel Printing Co., 1897.

Benton, Josiah. *What Women Did for the War, and What the War Did for Women. Memorial Day Address Delivered before the Soldiers Club at Wellesley, Mass., May 30, 1894*. Boston: n.p., 1894.

Blackwell, Elizabeth. *Pioneer Work for Women*. London: J. M. Dent and Sons, Ltd., 1914.

Bloor, Alfred J. *Letters from Army of the Potomac, Written during the Month of May 1864, to the Several of the Supply Correspondents*. Washington, D.C.: McGill and Witherow, 1864.

Brockett, Linus Pierpont. *The Philanthropic Results of the War in America*. New York: Wynkoop, Halenback and Thomas, 1864.

Brockett, Linus P., and Mary C. Vaughan. *Woman's Work in the Civil War: A Record of Heroism, Patriotism and Patience*. Philadelphia: Zeigler, McCurdy & Co., 1867.

Cheney, Ednah Dow. *Memoirs of Lucretia Crocker and Abby W. May*. Boston: Massachusetts School Suffrage Association, 1893.

Crane, Stephen. *The Red Badge of Courage*. 1894. Reprint, Toronto: Random House, 1954.

Documents of the United States Sanitary Commission. 2 vols. New York: n.p., 1866.

Emerson, Sarah, ed. *Life of Abby Hopper Gibbons*. 2 vols. New York: G. P. Putnam's Sons, 1897.

Folks, Homer. *Louisa Lee Schuyler, 1837–1908*. New York: National Committee for the Prevention of Blindness, 1927.

Goodrich, Frank B. *The Tribute Book: A Record of the Munificence, Self-Sacrifice and Patriotism of the American People during the War for the Union*. New York: Derby & Miller, 1865.

Hass, Paul, ed. "A Volunteer Nurse in the Civil War: The Letters of Harriet Douglas Whetten." *Wisconsin Magazine of History* 48 (Winter 1965): 131–151.

———. "A Volunteer Nurse in the Civil War: The Diary of Harriet Douglas Whetten." *Wisconsin Magazine of History* 49 (Spring 1965): 205–221.

Hobson, Elizabeth Christopher. "Founding the Bellevue Training School for Nurses." In Abby Howland Woolsey. *A Century of Nursing*. 1876. Reprint, National League of Nursing Education, 1950.

Hoge, Jane. *The Boys in Blue; Or Heroes of the "Rank and File."* New York: E. B. Treat & Co., 1867.

Jarvis, Edward. "Sanitary Condition of the Army." *Atlantic Monthly* (October 1862): 463–497.

Jarvis, Edward. *The Autobiography of Edward Jarvis*. Ed. Rosalba Davico. London: Wellcome Institute for the History of Medicine, 1992.

Livermore, Mary. *Massachusetts in the Army and Navy during the War of 1861–1865*. Ed. Thomas Wentworth Higginson. Boston: Wright and Potter, 1895: 596–603.

———. *My Story of the War: A Woman's Narrative of Four Years Personal Experience as Nurse in the Union Army, and in Relief Work at Home, in Hospitals, Camps, and at the Front, during the War of the Rebellion*. 1888. Reprint, New York: De Capo Press, 1995.

———. *The Story of My Life, or the Sunshine and Shadow of Seventy Years*. Hartford, Conn.: A. D. Worthington & Co., 1898.

Lowell, Anna C. *Report of the Ladies' Industrial Aid Association of Union Hall, from July 1861 to January 1862.* Boston: J. H. Eastburn's Press, 1862.

Loyal Publication Society. *A Few Words in Behalf of the Loyal Women of the United States, by One of Themselves.* New York: William C. Bryant and Co., 1863.

Lyon, William. *Frederick Newman Knapp: Sixth Minister of the First Parish in Brookline 1847–1915: A Sermon Preached in the First Parish Meeting House November 22, 1903 by William H. Lyon, D.D.* Brookline, Mass.: The Parish, 1904.

May, Abigail Williams. *Dress: A Paper Read Before the Association for the Advancement of Women.* 1879.

Moore, Frank. *Women of the War; Their Heroism and Self-Sacrifice.* Hartford, Conn.: S. S. Scranton & Co., 1866.

Nightingale, Florence. *Notes on Nursing: What It Is, and What It Is Not.* 1860. Reprint, New York: Churchill Livingstone, 1980.

Olmsted, Frederick Law. *Hospital Transports: A Memoir of the Embarkation of the Sick and Wounded from the Peninsula of Virginia in the Summer of 1862.* Boston: Ticknor and Fields, 1863.

————. *The Papers of Frederick Law Olmsted.* Volume II: *Slavery and the South, 1852–1857.* Ed. Charles Beveridge and Charles Capen McLaughlin. Baltimore: Johns Hopkins University Press, 1981.

————. *The Papers of Frederick Law Olmsted.* Volume III: *Creating Central Park, 1857–1861.* Ed. Charles Beveridge and David Schuyler. Baltimore: Johns Hopkins University Press, 1983.

————. *The Papers of Frederick Law Olmsted.* Volume IV: *Defending the Union, The Civil War and the U.S. Sanitary Commission.* Ed. Jane Turner Censer. Baltimore: Johns Hopkins University Press, 1986.

Ordronaux, John. *Report of the U.S. Sanitary Commission on a System for the Economic Relief of Disabled Soldiers.* New York: Sanford, Harroun and Company, 1864.

Peabody, Francis Greenwood. *Reminiscences of Present-Day Saints.* Boston: Houghton Mifflin, 1927.

Schuyler, Louisa Lee. *Forty-Three Years Ago or the Early Days of the State Charities Aid Association.* New York: United Charities Building, 1915.

Strong, George Templeton. *The Diary of George Templeton Strong.* Volume I: *Young Man in New York, 1835–1849* and Volume III: *The Civil War, 1860–1865.* Ed. Allan Nevins and Milton Halsey Thomas. New York: Octagon, 1974.

————. *The Diary of George Templeton Strong.* Abridged by Thomas Pressly. Seattle: University of Washington Press, 1988.

————. *The Diary of George Templeton Strong.* Volume IV: *Post-War Years, 1865–1875.* Ed. Allan Nevins and Milton Halsey Thomas. New York: Macmillan, 1952.

United States Sanitary Commission. *The United States Sanitary Commission Bulletin.* 2 vols. New York and Philadelphia, 1866.

Woman's Central Association of Relief. *The Nurse's Manual: A Manual of Directions, Prepared for the Use of the Nurses in the Army of Hospitals, by a Committee of Hospital Physicians of the City of New York.* New York: Baker & Godwin, Printers, 1861.

Woman's Central Association of Relief. *How Can We Best Help Our Camps and Hospitals?* New York: William C. Bryant and Co., 1863.

"Abigail Williams May." *The Woman's Journal,* 8 December 1888.

Woolsey, Abby Howland. *Hand-Book for Hospitals.* New York: G. P. Putnam's Sons, 1895.

Woolsey, Georgeanna. *Three Weeks at Gettysburg.* New York: A. D. F. Randolph, 1863.

Woolsey, Georgeanna, and Eliza Woolsey Howland. *Letters of a Family During the War for the Union, 1861–1865.* New York: Printed for Private Distribution, 1899.

Woolsey, Jane Stuart. *Hospital Days.* New York: Privately Published, 1870.

Wormeley, Katharine Prescott. *The Other Side of the War with the Army of the Potomac.* Boston: Ticknor and Fields, 1889.

SECONDARY SOURCES

Books

Adams, George Worthington. *Doctors in Blue: The Medical History of the Union Army in the Civil War.* New York: H. Schuman, 1952.

Alonso, Harriet Hyman. *Peace as a Women's Issue: A History of the U.S. Movement for World Peace and Women's Rights.* New York: Syracuse University Press, 1993.

Attie, Jeanie. *Patriotic Toil: Northern Women and the American Civil War.* Ithaca, N.Y.: Cornell University Press, 1998.

Austin, Anne. *The Woolsey Sisters of New York: A Family's Involvement in the Civil War and New Profession, 1860–1900.* Philadelphia: American Philosophical Society, 1971.

Bensel, Richard. *Yankee Leviathan: The Origins of Central State Authority.* New York: Cambridge University Press, 1990.

Bernstein, Iver. *The New York City Draft Riots: Their Significance for American Society and Politics in the Age of the Civil War.* New York: Oxford University Press, 1990.

Blackmar, Elizabeth, and Roy Rosenzweig. *The Park and the People: A History of Central Park.* New York: Henry Holt, 1994.

Bledstein, Burton. *The Culture of Professionalism: The Middle Class and the Development of Higher Education in America.* New York: Norton, 1976.

Bordin, Ruth. *Woman and Temperance: The Quest for Power and Liberty, 1873–1900.* New Brunswick, N.J.: Rutgers University Press, 1990.

Brown, Thomas J. *Dorothea Dix: New England Reformer.* Cambridge, Mass.: Harvard University Press, 1998.

Buhle, Mari Jo. *Women and American Socialism, 1870–1920.* Urbana: University of Illinois Press, 1981.

Cashman, Diane Cobb. *Headstrong: The Biography of Amy Morris Bradley, 1823–1904: A Life of Noblest Usefulness.* Wilmington, N.C.: Broadfoot Company, 1990.

Chadwick, John. *Henry Whitney Bellows, His Life and Character, A Sermon.* New York: 1882.

Clawson, Mary Ann. *Constructing Brotherhood: Class, Gender & Fraternalism.* Princeton, N.J.: Princeton University Press, 1989.

Clinton, Catherine. *The Other Civil War: American Women in the Nineteenth Century.* New York: Hill and Wang, 1984.

Clinton, Catherine, and Nina Silber, ed. *Divided Houses: Gender and the Civil War.* New York: Oxford University Press, 1992.

Cott, Nancy. *Bonds of Womanhood: Woman's Sphere in New England, 1780–1835.* New Haven: Yale University Press, 1977.

Dannett, Sylvia, ed. *Noble Women of the North.* New York: Thomas Yoseloff, 1959.

Dawley, Alan. *Class and Community: The Industrial Revolution in Lynn.* Cambridge, Mass.: Harvard University Press, 1982.

Douglas, Ann. *The Feminization of American Culture.* New York: Doubleday, 1988.

Douglas, Mary. *Natural Symbols: Explorations in Cosmology.* London: Barrie and Rockliff the Cresset, 1970.

DuBois, Ellen Carol. *Feminism and Suffrage: The Emergence of an Independent Women's Movement in America, 1848–1869.* Ithaca, N.Y.: Cornell University Press, 1978.

Epstein, Barbara. *The Politics of Domesticity: Women, Evangelism, and Temperance in Nineteenth-Century America.* Middletown, Conn.: Wesleyan University Press, 1981.

Evans, Sara. *Born for Liberty: A History of Women in America.* New York: Free Press, 1989.

Farrell, Betty. *Elite Families: Class and Power in Nineteenth-Century Boston.* Albany: State University of New York Press, 1993.

Faust, Drew Gilpen. *Mothers of Invention: Women of the Slaveholding South in the American Civil War.* New York: Vintage Books, 1996.

Fehrenbacher, Don, ed. *History and American Society: Essays of David Potter.* New York: Oxford University Press, 1973.

Foner, Eric. *Reconstruction: America's Unfinished Revolution, 1863–1877.* New York: Harper and Row, 1988.

——. *A Short History of Reconstruction, 1863–1877.* New York: Harper and Row, 1990.

Fredrickson, George. *The Inner Civil War: Northern Intellectuals and the Crisis of the Union.* New York: Harper and Row, 1968.

Ginzberg, Lori. *Women and the Work of Benevolence: Morality, Politics, and Class in the Nineteenth-Century United States.* New Haven: Yale University Press, 1990.

Gollaher, David. *Voice for the Mad: The Life of Dorothea Dix.* New York: The Free Press, 1995.

Green, James, and Hugh Carter Donahue. *Boston's Workers: A Labor History.* Boston: Boston Public Library, 1979.

Greenbie, Marjorie. *Lincoln's Daughters of Mercy.* New York: G. P. Putnam's Sons, 1944.

Grob, Gerald. *Edward Jarvis and the Medical World of Nineteenth-Century America.* Knoxville: University of Tennessee Press, 1978.

Haskell, Thomas. *The Emergence of Professional Social Science.* Chicago: University of Illinois Press, 1977.

Hill, Patricia. *The World Their Household: The American Woman's Foreign Mission Movement and Cultural Transformation, 1870–1920.* Ann Arbor: University of Michigan Press, 1991.

Hofstadter, Richard. *The Age of Reform.* New York: Vintage Books, 1955.

Jones, Jacqueline. *Labor of Love, Labor of Sorrow: Black Women, Work, and the Family, From Slavery to the Present.* New York: Vintage, 1986.

Kasson, John. *Rudeness and Civility: Manners in Nineteenth Century Urban America*. New York: Hill and Wang, 1990.

Kring, Walter Donald. *Henry Whitney Bellows*. Boston: Skinner House, 1979.

Leach, William. *True Love and Perfect Union: The Feminist Reform of Sex and Society*. Middletown, Conn.: Wesleyan University Press, 1989.

Lears, T. J. Jackson. *No Place of Grace: Antimodernism and the Transformation of American Culture, 1880–1920*. New York: Pantheon, 1981.

Lebsock, Suzanne. *The Free Women of Petersburg: Status and Culture in a Southern Town, 1784–1860*. New York: W. W. Norton, 1984.

Leonard, Elizabeth. *Yankee Women: Gender Battles in the Civil War*. New York: W. W. Norton, 1994.

Lerner, Gerda. *The Majority Finds Its Past: Placing Women in History*. New York: Oxford University Press, 1979.

Levine, Bruce, Stephen Brier, David Brundage, Edward Countryman, Dorothy Fennell, Marcus Rediker, and Joshua Brown. *Who Built America? Working People and the Nation's Economy, Politics, Culture, and Society*. Volume 1: *From Conquest and Colonization through Reconstruction and the Great Uprising of 1877*. New York: Pantheon Books, 1989.

Lewinsen, Sandra Beth. *Taking Charge: Nursing, Suffrage, and Feminism in America, 1873–1920*. New York: National League of Nursing, 1996.

Maher, Mary Denis. *To Bind Up the Wounds: Catholic Sister Nurses in the U.S. Civil War*. New York: Greenwood Press, 1989.

Marshall, Helen. *Dorothea Dix: Forgotten Samaritan*. New York: Russell and Russell, 1967.

Massey, Mary Elizabeth. *Bonnet Brigades*. New York: Knopf, 1966.

Maxwell, William Quentin. *Lincoln's Fifth Wheel: The Political History of the United States Sanitary Commission*. New York: Longmans, Green & Co., 1956.

McDowell, Agatha Young. *The Women and the Crisis: Women of the North in the Civil War*. New York: Oblensky, 1959.

McPherson, James. *Battle Cry of Freedom: The Civil War Era*. New York: Oxford University Press, 1988.

———. *What They Fought For, 1861–1865*. New York: Doubleday, 1995.

Mitchell, Reid. *Civil War Soldiers*. New York: Penguin, 1988.

Montgomery, David. *Beyond Equality: Labor and the Radical Republicans, 1862–1872*. New York: Alfred Knopf, 1967.

Morantz-Sanchez, Regina. *Sympathy and Science: Women Physicians in American Medicine*. New York: Oxford University Press, 1985.

Nevins, Alan. *The Ordeal of Union*. New York: Scribner's Sons, 1947.

Norton, Mary Beth. *Liberty's Daughters: The Revolutionary Experience of American Women, 1750–1800*. Boston: Little, Brown, 1980.

O'Connor, Thomas. *Bibles, Brahmins, and Bosses: A Short History of Boston*. Boston: Boston Public Library, 1991.

Oates, Stephen. *To Purge This Land in Blood: A Biography of John Brown*. New York: Harper and Row, 1970.

Osterud, Nancy Grey. *Bonds of Community: The Lives of Farm Women in Nineteenth-Century New York*. Ithaca: Cornell University Press, 1991.

Paludan, Phillip Shaw. *"A People's Contest": The Union and the Civil War*. New York: Harper and Row, 1988.

Parish, Peter J. *The American Civil War.* London: Eyre Methuen, 1975.

Pascoe, Peggy. *Relations of Rescue: The Search for Female Moral Authority in the American West, 1874–1939.* New York: Oxford University Press, 1990.

Pernick, Martin. *A Calculus of Suffering: Pain, Professionalism, and Anesthesia in Nineteenth-Century America.* New York: Columbia University Press, 1985.

Pessen, Edward. *Riches, Class, and Power Before the Civil War.* Lexington, Mass.: Heath, 1973.

Poovey, Mary. *Uneven Developments: The Ideological Work of Gender in Mid-Victorian England.* Chicago: University of Chicago Press, 1988.

Pryor, Elizabeth Brown. *Clara Barton: Professional Angel.* Philadelphia: University of Pennsylvania, 1987.

Rable, George. *Civil Wars: Women and the Crisis of Southern Nationalism.* Chicago: University of Illinois Press, 1989.

Rose, Anne. *Victorian America and the Civil War.* New York: Cambridge University Press, 1992.

Rosenberg, Charles. *The Cholera Years: The United States in 1832, 1849, and 1866.* Chicago: University of Chicago Press, 1987.

Rosenkratz, Barbara Gutmann. *Public Health and the State: Changing Views in Massachusetts, 1842–1936.* Cambridge: Harvard University Press, 1972.

Ryan, Mary. *Cradle of the Middle Class: The Family in Oneida County, New York, 1790–1865.* Cambridge: Cambridge University Press, 1981.

Silber, Nina. *The Romance of Reunion: Northerners and the South, 1865–1900.* Chapel Hill: University of North Carolina Press, 1993.

Silber, Nina, and Catherine Clinton, ed. *Divided Houses: Gender and the Civil War.* New York: Oxford University Press, 1992.

Simons, Judy. *Diaries and Journals of Literary Women from Fanny Burney to Virginia Woolf.* London: Macmillan, 1990.

Sklar, Kathryn Kish. *Catherine Beecher: A Study in American Domesticity.* New York: W. W. Norton, 1976.

Skocpol, Theda. *Protecting Soldiers and Mothers: The Political Origins of Social Policy in the United States.* Cambridge, Mass.: Harvard University Press, 1992.

Skowronek, Stephen. *Building a New American State: The Expansion of National Administrative Capacities, 1877–1920.* New York: Cambridge University Press, 1982.

Smith-Rosenberg, Carroll. *Disorderly Conduct: Visions of Gender in Victorian America.* New York: Oxford University Press, 1985.

Solomon, Barbara Miller. *Ancestors and Immigrants: A Changing New England Tradition.* Boston: Northeastern University Press, 1989.

Sontag, Susan. *Illness as Metaphor.* New York: Farrar, Straus, and Giroux, 1978.

Spann, Edward. *The New Metropolis: New York City, 1840–1857.* New York: Columbia University Press, 1981.

Sproat, John. *"The Best Men": Liberal Reformers in the Gilded Age.* London: Oxford University Press, 1968.

Stansell, Christine. *City of Women: Sex and Class in New York 1789–1860.* Chicago: University of Illinois Press, 1987.

Susman, Walter. *Culture as History: The Transformation of American Society in the Twentieth Century.* New York: Pantheon Books, 1984.

Trachtenberg, Alan. *The Incorporation of America: Culture and Society in the Gilded Age.* New York: Hill and Wang, 1982.

Vicinus, Martha. *Independent Women: Work and Community for Single Women, 1850–1920.* Chicago: University of Chicago Press, 1985.

Vicinus, Martha, and Bea Nergaard, ed. *Ever Yours, Florence Nightingale: Selected Letters.* Cambridge, Mass.: Harvard University Press, 1990.

Vinovskis, Maris A., ed. *Toward a Social History of the American Civil War.* New York: Cambridge University Press, 1990.

Waugh, Joan. *Unsentimental Reformer: The Life of Josephine Shaw Lowell.* Cambridge: Harvard University Press, 1997.

Wecter, Dixon. *When Johnny Comes Marching Home.* Cambridge: Houghton Mifflin, 1944.

Welter, Barbara. *Dimity Convictions: The American Woman in the Nineteenth Century.* Athens, Ohio: Ohio University Press, 1976.

Wiebe, Robert. *The Search for Order 1877–1920.* New York: Hill and Wang, 1967.

Wilson, Margaret Gibbons. *The American Woman in Transition: The Urban Influence, 1870–1920.* Westport, Conn.: Greenwood Press, 1979.

Wolloch, Nancy. *Muller v. Oregon: A Brief History with Documents.* Boston: St. Martin's Press, 1996.

Articles

Baker, Paula. "The Domestication of Politics: Women and American Political Society, 1780–1920." *American Historical Review* 89 (June 1984): 620–647.

Benson, Susan Porter. "Business Heads and Sympathizing Hearts: The Women of the Providence Employment Society, 1837–1858." *Journal of Social History* 12 (Winter 1978): 302–312.

Blight, David. "A Union Soldier's Experience." In *Major Problems in the Civil War and Reconstruction,* ed. Michael Perman. Boston: Houghton Mifflin, 1998.

Blustein, Bonnie Ellen. "'To Increase the Efficiency of the Medical Department': A New Approach to U.S. Civil War Medicine." *Civil War History* 33 (March 1987): 22–41.

Clark, Elizabeth. "The Sacred Rights of the Weak: Pain, Sympathy, and the Culture of Individual Rights in Antebellum America." *Journal of American History* 82 (September 1995): 463–493.

Cook, Blanche Wiesen. "Female Support Networks and Political Activism: Lillian Wald, Crystal Eastman, Emma Goldman." In *Women's America: Refocusing the Past,* ed. Linda Kerber and Jane Sherron De Hart, 306–325. 3d ed. New York: Oxford University Press, 1991.

Cott, Nancy. "Passionlessness: An Interpretation of Victorian Sexual Ideology, 1790–1850." *Signs* 4 (Winter 1978): 219–236.

Cross, Robert. "Louisa Lee Schuyler." In *Notable American Women,* ed. Edward T. James, Janet Wilson James, and Paul Boyer, 244–246. Vol. 2. Cambridge, Mass.: Belknap Press of Harvard University Press, 1971.

Cross, Robert D. "The Philanthropic Contribution of Louisa Lee Schuyler." *Social Service Review* 35 (September 1961): 290–301.

Deutsch, Sarah. "Learning to Talk More Like a Man: Boston Women's Class-Bridging

Organizations, 1870–1940." *American Historical Review* 97 (April 1992): 379–404.

Flanagan, Maureen. "Gender and Urban Political Reform: The City Club and the Woman's City Club of Chicago in the Progressive Era." *American Historical Review* 95 (October 1990): 1032–1050.

————. "The City Profitable, The City Livable: Environmental Policy, Gender, and Power in Chicago in the 1910s." *Journal of Urban History* 22 (January 1996): 163–190.

Freedman, Estelle. "Separatism as Strategy: Female Institution Building and American Feminism, 1870–1930." In *Women and Power in American History*, ed. Kathryn Kish Sklar and Thomas Dublin, 10–23. Vol. 2. Englewood Cliffs, N.J.: Prentice Hall, 1991.

Ingebritsen, Shirley Phillips. "Abigail Williams May." In *Notable American Women*, ed. Edward T. James, Janet Wilson James, and Paul Boyer, 513–515. Vol. 2. Cambridge, Mass.: Belknap Press of Harvard University Press, 1971.

Kelley, Robin. "'We Are Not What We Seem': Rethinking Black Working-Class Opposition in the Jim Crow South." *Journal of American History* (June 1993): 75–112.

Kerber, Linda. "Women and Individualism in American History." *Massachusetts Review* (Winter 1989): 589–609.

Marshall, Helen. "Dorothea Lynde Dix." In *Notable American Women*, ed. Edward T. James, Janet Wilson James, and Paul Boyer, 486–489. Vol. 1. Cambridge. Mass.: Belknap Press of Harvard University Press, 1971.

McClintock, Megan. "Civil War Pensions and the Reconstruction of Union Families." *The Journal of American History* 83 (September 1996): 456–480.

Monteiro, Lois. "On Separate Roads: Florence Nightingale and Elizabeth Blackwell." *Signs* 9 (Spring 1984): 520–533.

Morantz, Regina Markell. "Making Women Modern: Middle Class Women and Health Reform in Nineteenth-Century America." *Journal of Social History* 4 (June 1977): 490–507.

Romanofsky, Peter. "Saving the Lives of the City's Foundlings: The Joint Committee and New York City Child Care Methods, 1860–1907." *New York Historical Society Quarterly* 61 (January–April 1977): 49–68.

Rosenberg, Charles. "Sexuality, Class and Role in Nineteenth-Century America." *American Quarterly* 25 (May 1973): 131–153.

Rosenberg, Charles, and Carroll S. Rosenberg. "Pietism and the Origins of the American Public Health Movement: A Note on John H. Griscom and Robert M. Hartley." *Journal of the History of Medicine and Allied Sciences* 23 (January 1986): 16–35.

Rosenzweig, Roy. "Middle-Class Park and Working Class Play: The Struggle over Recreational Space in Worcester, Massachusetts, 1870–1910." In *The New England Working Class and the New Labor History*, ed. Herbert G. Gutman and Donald H. Bell, 214–230. Chicago: University of Chicago Press, 1987.

Rotundo, E. Anthony. "Body and Soul: Changing Ideas of American Middle-Class Manhood, 1770–1920." *Journal of Social History* 16 (Summer 1983): 23–38.

Schultz, Jane. "The Inhospitable Hospital: Gender and Professionalism in Civil War Medicine." *Signs* 17 (Winter 1992): 363–392.

Scott, Anne Firor. "On Seeing and Not Seeing: A Case of Historical Invisibility." *Journal of American History* 71 (June 1984): 7–21.

Scott, Joan. "Gender: A Useful Category of Historical Analysis." *American Historical Review* (December 1986): 1053–1075.

Sklar, Kathryn Kish. "Hull House in the 1890s: A Community of Women Reformers." *Signs* 10 (Summer 1985): 658–677.

———. "The Historical Foundations of Women's Power in the Creation of the American Welfare State, 1830–1930." In *Mothers of a New World*, ed. Seth Koven and Sonya Michel, 43–93. New York: Routledge, 1993.

———. "The Female World of Love and Ritual: Relations Between Women in Nineteenth-Century America." *Signs* 1 (1975): 1–30.

Theriot, Nancy. "Women Voices in Nineteenth-Century Medical Discourse: A Step Toward Deconstructing Science." *Signs* 19 (Autumn 1993): 1–31.

Thomson, Elizabeth H. "Elizabeth Blackwell." In *Notable American Women*, ed. Edward T. James, Janet Wilson James, and Paul Boyer, 161–165. Vol. 1. Cambridge, Mass.: Belknap Press of Harvard University Press, 1971.

Trattner, Walter. "Louisa Lee Schuyler and the Founding of the State Charities Aid Association." *New York Historical Society Quarterly* 51 (July 1967): 232–248.

Williams, Perry. "The Laws of Health: Women, Medicine, and Sanitary Reform, 1850–1890." In *Science and Sensibility: Gender and Scientific Enquiry, 1780–1945*, ed. Marina Benjamin, 60–88. Oxford, U.K.: Basil Blackwell, 1991.

Wood, Ann Douglas. "The War Within a War: Women Nurses in the Union Army." *Civil War History* 18 (September 1977): 197–212.

DISSERTATIONS

Attie, Rejean. "'A Swindling Concern': The USSC and the Northern Female Public, 1861–1865." Ph.D. diss., Columbia University, 1987.

Ross, Kristie. "'Women are needed here': Northern Protestant Women as Nurses during the Civil War, 1861–1865." Ph.D. diss., Columbia University, 1993.

Schultz, Jane. "Women at the Front: Gender and Genre in the Literature of the American Civil War." Ph.D. diss., University of Michigan, 1988.

Smith, Nina Bennett. "The Women Who Went to the War: The Union Army Nurse in the Civil War." Ph.D. diss., Northwestern University, 1981.

Index

CPSIA information can be obtained at www.ICGtesting.com
Printed in the USA
LVOW12s1751150913

352516LV00001B/255/A